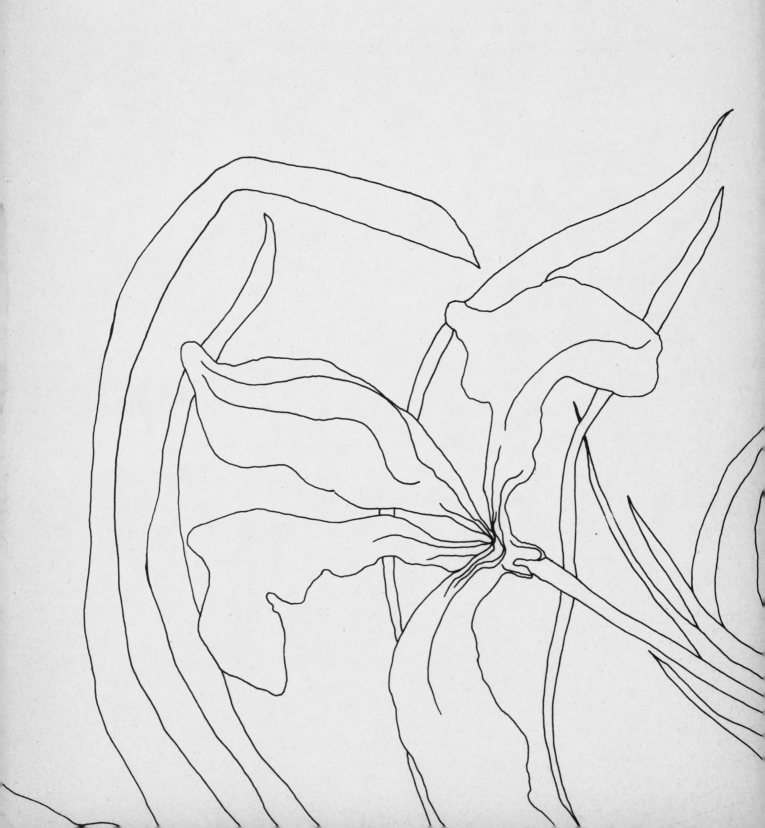

GETTING CLEAR

BODY WORK FOR WOMEN

ANNE KENT RUSH

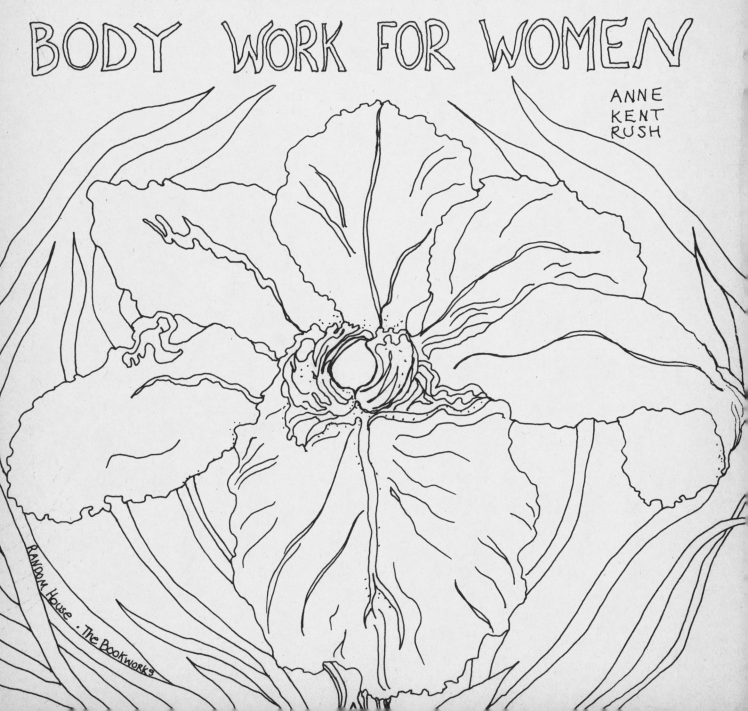

RANDOM House · The Bookworks

Copyright © 1973 by Anne Kent Rush
All rights reserved under International and Pan-American Copyright Conventions
First printing: March 1973, 1,500 copies in cloth
25,000 copies in paperback
Second printing: October 1973, 10,000 copies in paperback
Third printing: February 1974, 15,000 copies in paperback
Fourth printing: April 1974, 25,000 copies in paperback
Fifth printing: June 1975, 15,000 copies in paperback

Cover design, book design and illustrations by Anne Kent Rush
Typeset by Vera Allen Composition Service, Hayward, California
(special thanks to Vera, Dorothy and Betty)
Printed and bound under the direction of Peggy de Ugarte, Random House

The publishers wish to acknowledge the use of the following copyright materials:
Quote on page 290 from the *American Heritage
Dictionary of the English Language,*
Copyright © 1969, 1970, 1971 by American Heritage
Publishing Company, Inc. Reprinted by permission.

Exercise *Woman — Which Includes Man, of Course,*
Original and Revision Copyright © 1970, 1972 respectively by
Theodora Wells, M.B.A.

The book is co-published by   Random House Inc.
201 East 50th Street
New York, New York 10022

and   The Bookworks
1409 Fifth Street
Berkeley, California 94710

Distributed in the United States by Random House, and simultaneously
published in Canada by Random House of Canada Limited, Toronto

Library of Congress Cataloging in Publication Data

Rush, Anne Kent, 1947-
Getting clear.

1. Woman—Psychology.   2. Woman—Health and hygiene.
3. Women's Liberation Movement.   I. Title.
HQ1206.R787   301.41'2   72-12531
ISBN 0-394-48382-0
ISBN 0-394-70970-5 (pbk)

Manufactured in the United States of America

Contents

Contents

Contributors to this book

Magadalene Proskauer, Breath Awareness / 22 to 28

Cynthia Werthman Sheldon, Gestalt and Family Therapy / 57 to 63, 183 to 189

Lillian Pearson, Food Awareness / 77 to 89

Julia McKinney Barfoot, Berkeley Women's Health Collective / 89 to 101

Barbara Clemans, Movement and Belly Dancing / 104 to 111

Anica Vesel Mander, Consciousness Raising Groups / 119 to 126, 241 to 253

Roberta Ellner, Marriage Counselor and Masters & Johnson Sexual Counseling / 129 to 134

Theodora Wells, Management Training Consultant / 126 to 128

Stella Resnick, Gestalt Therapy / 166 to 175

Lynn Smith, Sex Researcher / 189 to 203

Carmen Lynch, Process and Family Therapy / 205 to 213

George Downing, Gestalt and Body Therapies / 226 to 228

Irving London, M.D., Sleep Research / 228 to 230

Marion Saltman, Adult Play Therapy / 254 to 268

Exercises

Exercises

Exercises

Starting With Myself

Starting With Myself

I started on my way to this book in 1966 one evening, in the library in college. Sitting in a chair feeling out of shape and tired, I began to let myself go into the way my body felt: flabby, numb, hungry, tired. I thought about how, as well as my mind, my body lived the life of a college student, yet I paid little attention to it. If I feel this way at 21, what will I feel like at 30, at 40? Answering that made me decide to do something to change, to include caring for my body as an integral part of my life. You could check in now and see how you feel, what kind of a life your body is living. Try to tune in to where your breathing is in your body, that is, where do you feel any movement in your muscles as a result of your breathing? You might feel movement in your chest, your throat, your abdomen, or even your back and pelvis.

Without shifting your position, notice how you are standing or sitting now; are you leaning more of your body weight to one side or the other? (If you pay attention to this over a period of time, you may find that you consistently lean more to your left or right so that the muscles all along that side of your body are under more physical stress and are probably much more tense than those of the other side.)

If you are holding this book, tune in to which muscles you are using to do so. Your fingers, your palms, your arms, shoulders, neck, jaw, face, chest, back? You may be using (tensing) all of these unconsciously even your legs and feet! Hold the book; feel its weight; experiment with supporting it with different muscles, gradually eliminating (releasing) unnecessary ones until you are holding the book with just the few vital muscles. Great dancers and atheletes know this secret. That is why you can watch them perform incredible and difficult movements which they seem to be doing "effortlessly" — that is "grace," tuning in to your body and using just the appropriate muscles for each act. This process is also less tiring because you are not exerting unnecessary effort, and you are not using muscles which counteract each other.

Now try an "aliveness" check. Starting at your head and moving down to your toes, tune in, body part by body part, to whether or not you can feel any sensations *inside.* Can you feel behind your eyes, inside your throat, inside your chest and abdomen; can you feel your spine or hip joints, inside your legs and feet? You will probably get a lot of feeling from certain places, such as your hands and stomach, but you may have difficulty picking up any internal messages from (being "aware" of) some other places — such as your feet, inside your calves, or your hips. Often there is a correlation between circulation in a body area and your own "awareness" of it. You can improve circulation in a body part by practicing this exercise and focusing your attention on "dead" areas. These are simple body awareness techniques from yoga exercises which I have found useful for decreasing tension during any activity.

Months after my resolution in the library, a friend of mine was taking yoga classes from a woman in Boston. I had noticed changes in her. She seemed to be feeling more energetic and certainly looked healthier. She invited me to go to class with her at this woman's home. In one afternoon of doing simple hatha yoga asanas I had a different feeling in my body than I'd had from any other kind of exercise. I felt whole. Even when we were only exercising one part, my movements seemed to take in and come from all parts of myself. Doing a spine stretch I could feel the muscle connections for that movement all through my body. The feeling was very pleasurable. These postures were clearly different from any kind of Western exercise I'd experienced.

Another effect new to me was the mental involvement. The state of mind of a person doing a yoga asana is considered an integral part of the exercise. There is supposed to be an attitude of non-competition. Each person is only concerned with doing what is comfortable for them. We were told to focus our attention on the center of our pelvis while doing abdominal breathing exercises and not to let our minds wander; this made the experience more intense and usually the movement was performed more easily and gracefully. Sometimes we were told to imagine ourselves doing a movement and what the muscles involved would feel like, before actually doing it. Afterward the movement was always easier, as though I had physically practiced it. In contrast to my usual feelings of exhaustion and strain from long exercise, I left after 2 hours feeling energized and refreshed.

4

I continued taking hatha yoga from this woman and learned many different asanas for different body parts. I did some in the morning and some each afternoon when I came home from my job doing commercial writing for a publisher. I usually came home feeling tense and tired, still thinking about my work. After yoga my body would feel relaxed and my head would be clear of the day's tension. I could face the evening fresh.

The ability to make myself feel good when I felt uncomfortable seemed like an incredible power to me. I wished I'd learned yoga earlier. I thought about the ways most people relax themselves, with pills, drugs, or food; about how dependent we are taught to think we are on outer cures and doctors; about how little we know our own bodies and the fear we're trained to have of ourselves; about how we're taught that someone else, an expert, can help us even with the simplest things more than we can from within. I wanted my friends to experience yoga and gain this power too. It should have been part of my most basic training as a child, I thought. Why don't we teach each child how to take care of herself this way, to know how to use the potential curative power of her own body?

My five year experience with yoga led me to investigate other body techniques aimed at more self-awareness and control over feeling states. When I came to Berkeley, California in 1969 I took a class in massage at the Free University here. That experience was a next step in learning new skills for making myself feel good and exploring my attitudes and emotions about my body. How wonderful I felt being massaged once a week! Giving the massage was pleasurable too. I began training in massage from an Esalen, San Francisco instructor, and later teaching classes to people who wanted to learn how to massage each other with the techniques particular to Esalen massage.

Through massage, I became interested in other forms of body work concerned with releasing deep muscular tension and dealing with the emotional attitudes connected with and causing tension. Currently my main work is a private practice in Polarity Therapy, an Oriental pressure point system (based on Chinese acupuncture) for releasing deep body tension. I also have trained with a Reichian therapist in Wilhelm Reich's breathing techniques which I combine with the Polarity. I have done some training at the Gestalt Institute of San Francisco learning Gestalt verbal techniques to use with the body work.

In this book I have included basic techniques from these systems and from many more. There are exercises from each of these forms of therapy which are easily and safely used by anyone and can be useful tools in daily life. I see the work I do and the work of the women psychologists I have interviewed as concerned with altering people's response patterns, with giving them techniques they can use from moment to moment to deal with conflicts or to heighten the intensity of any experience.

The philosophy behind all these therapies is different from the premise of most traditional kinds of therapy in which the attitude is that the "patient" is "sick," the therapist is the all-knowing "authority," and he "cures" the patient by imposing an outside world system on him or her. In contrast to this, the basic premise of Gestalt and most body therapies is that each individual has her own truth, and her "cure" is within herself, that the path to clarity and personal effectiveness is through self-awareness and integration of one's inner feeling with one's outer actions. The motivation for this integration is that when the two are disparate, tension is created emotionally and physically; effectiveness and mobility are blocked.

Another different and important attitude is that "therapy" is not something reserved for desperate and "sick" people — but rather that it can be for anyone functioning well who would like to function better. Therapy is viewed as a process of heightening one's consciousness and mobilizing one's personal powers. By learning tools for self-awareness, you can integrate the "therapeutic" process into your life so that you continue to develop and grow consciously. These are my attitudes and premises; they are reflected in this book. The book is written to be experienced and not just read. You can use it by picking sections and subjects interesting to you and trying out some of the exercises. Any of them done over a period of time will become more powerful; but even done once, each will have immediate results. Almost all of them can be done alone. There are also exercises for couples, families, and groups. You might want to keep a journal of any ways your feelings change because of the exercises. You might even try starting your own women's group and going through the book's experiences together, sharing your discoveries and learning from each other.

I am writing for women because I am a woman and can tell you what tools have been useful to me. I'm particularly interested in what it's like for me and my friends to be women today. There are so many gaps in our culture and upbringing when it comes to the reality of being female. Happily now women scientists and writers are filling in some of these gaps. I particularly recommend *The Nature and Evolution of Female Sexuality* by Mary Jane Sherfey, M.D. Other works I've found helpful are mentioned throughout the book. The women I have interviewed for this book have their own experience to share and the skills from their work.

The different body therapies, verbal therapies, and awareness techniques in use in the Bay Area in California are all lumped under the label "the Growth Movement." The term "Growth Movement" refers particularly to the attitude that "therapy" is a continuous process of levels of growth for everyone. There are *many* different techniques included under that roof, ranging from simple and relatively superficial techniques such as encounter, to extremely deep and intense processes such as Bioenergetics therapy which can result in major structural and personality changes. In between fall any activities which might be useful growth tools! "All of life is therapy," and the techniques are means of making the process more conscious, more satisfying. Women psychologists and lay therapists are in the process of altering male oriented techniques, of discovering and developing new and particularly female growth tools and a female psychology based on the authority and expertise of our shared experiences as women today.

Starting With Yourself

Starting With Yourself

This section contains physical and mental self-awareness experiments. Language gets in my way here because our Western words speak in terms of a body/mind dichotomy, but I experience no such division. What I feel and the work that I do are based on the premise that mind and body are one. When I use the word "body" in this book, I am always referring to the *whole person,* including mental functions.

Gradually new words will emerge to express some of the feeling states that happen when we allow our thoughts and sensations to integrate, and we experience ourselves as whole. (Some other cultures already include these categories in their vocabulary. The language of the Balinese, for example, is almost completely made up of such expressions, and they can't understand why foreigners cannot identify their feelings states.) We all have such experiences, but usually we do not pay much attention to them or they feel strange to us, and we don't communicate them to anyone else because our language and our culture say they don't exist. I've found that the generally accepted description of a human being is a flesh machine inhabited by a life spirit, or soul. To conceive of myself as divided into autonomous parts leads to a feeling that I am one part (my brain, my thoughts, or my "soul") and that my body is a separate stranger who speaks another language. If my self-perception is disjointed, my expressions will be that way too. There is no way to bridge the gaps in this system; there is no way for these unrelated parts to get to know each other. To think this way is to feel alienated even from the functionings of my own being! With this self-concept I don't exercise any of the power that I do have. I act in a way that has no relation to what's happening in my body; it seems as though I have no control.

The separated person's philosophy doesn't hold up on a physiological level. The brain has cranial nerve connections all over the body. I couldn't "think" any thoughts unless I had the rest of my body, my organs of perceptions to send messages up these nerves to the brain. My "thoughts" are really physical perceptions, by-products of physical processes, which occur from a stimulus to my body and become messages for action and feeling. Even memory is physical substance stored in the brain tissue and activated when certain synapse connections are made. Memory can physically decay in old age when the body chemistry changes and the circulation is not so good and the blood slows down or quits flowing between brain cells which formerly connected. We call this state senility.

I experience how my body state and mental state function together when I think of how my perception of the world is altered by my physical health. When I am sick the world seems to be set up so that everything is hard to do. When I feel happy, healthy and relaxed, the world seems congenial and easy. If I am feeling relaxed and then I tense all my muscles as hard as I can and pant fast in my chest even just for a minute, my relaxed state of mind is gone. Try it now for a few moments to see what happens to you. Next try deep slow breathing in your abdomen while imagining that your breath is massaging and loosening your tense muscles. You can change your mood simply by changing your breathing.

Begin to notice the bodies of the people around you and how they correspond to each person's mental attitudes. Begin to notice what clues you use to assess someone you see but haven't met, and you will find that you make a lot of your judgements on their body characteristics. An emotionally up-tight person will usually be up-tight (rigid) physically. A person who is wishy-washy and easy to push around will often have a body tone which is too loose, without strength. There will be differences in the tone of the tissue from body part to part indicating where a person is weak or strong, vital or undeveloped. In the middle of the continuum is the body which is supple *and* strong which gives a feeling of being open and energetic too. The exercises in this book are exercises for helping you get in touch with these different attitudes in your body and to give you ways of changing what you may want to.

"You are your body" is too limited a statement if translated in terms of the body as robot. It becomes an exciting statement when I realize that it speaks about wholeness, about a state of functioning where my feelings are manifested in my actions. Whatever I feel and express intellectually is also expressed in my body. It has been my experience that any mental tension will always create tension someplace in my body.

An important exercise in self-awareness is to begin paying attention to these parallel processes. Whenever you are feeling an intense emotion — anger, excitement, sadness, pleasure — tune in to how your body is responding to that emotion. When you are angry, do you tighten in your shoulder muscles? When you are afraid, do you tense your abdominal muscles and hold your breath? When you are sad, where do you feel it in your body? Where physically do you feel other emotions?

Because of the correspondence I experience between mental and physical attitudes, I have included verbal and body exercises for each issue in the book. Initially I may create a state within myself by either emotional or physical means, but eventually they always fuse; verbal therapy and body work are two ways of approaching the same issue. By approaching your self-concept from an attitude of wholeness you can increase your personal power. If you are frightened and tense and you would like to relax, you could learn a breathing exercise designed to release the muscles you are tightening and to slow down your metabolism. If you feel emotionally conflicted about something and you can't decide what you really want, you could learn a verbal Gestalt exercise which helps you get in touch with your deepest feelings about the conflict and with some of the parts of the issue which you may have been blocking from your awareness.

Because I can only experience people and my environment through myself, because my body is always the filter for incoming information, the way my body functions determines how I see the world. My relationship to myself is my relationship to others. If I am critical of myself I will criticize others. The more I like myself the more I like other people. Self-awareness is a critical factor in how we see the world. What we are aware of in ourselves, we can see in the world. When I first got my new car I noticed that about one-half the people in Berkeley had a new car of the same brand as mine! If I feel hung up about a certain body part of mine, I pay attention to that part on everyone I meet. If I've had certain feelings myself, I can pick them up and understand them in others.

One of the most liberating realizations for me has been that if I change, I can change what happens to me; this has led me to feel that my personal power is determined by the state of my awareness and energy. Power is not just whether I have a certain job or legal right. That does not necessarily give me power over the things that affect me deeply. There are intangibles which are as important power tools as material possessions. What affects me most and what I see affecting others most are inner feelings and resources.

The exercises in this book focus on tuning up your perceptions and giving you tools to mobilize your own energy, to get in touch with your deep feelings and begin integrating them with your outside actions.

My observation is that people are most unhappy when their actions and feelings don't jive. For us as women this is a particularly important process. For too long our culture has defined roles for women which do not reflect the reality of womanhood. I am interested in tools to help women today take the step from new ideas and feelings to action.

The exercises in this book may ask you to pay attention to your inner feelings at a time when you normally don't, or when you might think of them as unrelated to your outer action. If you do even a few of the exercises you will find yourself spending more time than you are accustomed to focusing on your body and your feelings. You may have questions like, "If I spend all this time paying attention to my body, how will I ever get anything done?" Give yourself space for something new to happen. If you allow yourself to live this way for a few days or a week, I think you will find that you actually get more done and that you are actually more efficient because you are more fully and intensely involved in whatever your present activity is. You can read this book better when you don't have a headache, when you're not distracted and when you are comfortable in your body position.

Though many of the discoveries will be pleasurable, you may also find yourself experiencing all sorts of new aches and tensions that make you ask, "Why am I doing this if becoming aware means to find pain?" Actually these aches and pains have been there all the time, but your muscle tension has blocked them from your awareness. One of the functions of tension is to stop feeling! ("If I hold my breath, I won't feel scared. If I grit my teeth this won't hurt so much.") Increasing your awareness and sensitivity means increasing your awareness of pain as well as pleasure.

Maintaining blocks to feeling takes energy away from your present activity. The first step in gaining access to more power in yourself is to become aware of how you use your body energy. When you tune in to the places where you are holding unnecessary tension you can learn to relax them and use that energy for something else.

I see the awareness process as peeling away layers, and between each layer of release and pleasure there is a layer of resistence and tension to be worked through first. Some of the exercises in this book will be neutral to you or uninteresting. Others will be a great deal of fun and very pleasurable; I assume these you will do again and again. It will be easy to learn from them. Others may seem irritating or shocking or frightening. I call these "Resistance Exercises." These exercises will be more difficult to learn from, but they may have special importance for you because they can put you in touch with the places in yourself where you feel afraid or threatened or insecure. You will feel resistant to doing them. When you come to one of your "Resistance Exercises," give it some special attention. Allow yourself to fantasize what it might be like to do the exercise. If you feel nervous and fearful, try to pinpoint exactly what it is that you are afraid will happen if you do it. ("If I do this, I will be punished. Or I will find out that I am a nasty person. Or if I do this, then my husband can too, and I don't want him to. Or I will feel sexual feelings at an inappropriate time. Or I may feel nothing.") This process is an important part of self-awareness. You need to become aware of what you avoid experiencing and why. This will enrich your understanding of yourself and others, and you may work through some of these fears to discover they are no longer threatening to you. If you go ahead and do the exercise, compare your experience with your fantasy. Also you can go back now and then to "Resistance Exercises" to check your feelings. You may be surprised to find that your attitudes and prejudices have changed!

If you try out some of these exercises you may have to take into account that if your friends are not sympathetic to what you're experimenting with, you may find yourself in an environment that does not encourage your growth. Getting together with one interested friend or forming a women's group to explore these exercises together can solve this need for support and communication. If you do the exercises alone you will have to give yourself special permission to be different and to honor your own feelings rather than those of people around you. You'll need to trust your own feelings and your own power. You are your own best healer.

Body Awareness Exercises For Yourself

The exercises in this section come from my work, and from the work of women psychologists and group leaders at the Gestalt Institute of San Francisco or Esalen Institute. The exercises are drawn from many different systems, but they are all directed at increasing your body awareness. Body awareness comes from movement, not just thinking; it is a continuous process of learning to re-integrate your feelings with your actions. When you are in touch with your body patterns and attitudes you have the choice to make changes.

I have included exercises I learned which have been particularly useful to me at different times in my life, and exercises I have made up to fit situations where there weren't any. Once you experiment with some of the techniques and become familiar with the philosophy of the systems, you can invent your own self-help exercises to fit an individual situation. I have modified many of the exercises to be particularly relevant to women.

The Outer Physical

How I feel about the way I look motivates a surprising amount of my behavior. Here are some questions you can ask to start becoming more aware of how your body attitudes influence your behavior. Take some time to think about them.

What about my body am I hiding? How do I hide it? What about my body am I proud of? How do I stress it? Where do my models for physical attractiveness come from? My mother? Men? A man? My own feelings? *Vogue*?

17

What parts of my body do I associate with pleasure? How do I stimulate them? What parts do I associate with pain? How do I deal with those parts? What parts don't I like? Why not? How much do I feel that people only like or dislike me for my body? Can I let myself look lousy sometimes and feel people will like me anyhow?

Do I feel that my appearance really expresses who I am? What qualities would I like my body to communicate?

After thinking about your body attitudes, get a full-length mirror in a room where you can close the door and be alone and quiet. Do this when you feel free to spend an uninterrupted hour with yourself. You may not take an hour, but you need to feel unhurried.

Take off all your clothes and jewelry and stand in front of the mirror. How do you feel in general right now? Are you pleased to see yourself? Are you comfortable being nude? Do you feel you have the right to touch and look at yourself?

Now be more detailed. Be very detailed; and take your time. Talk out loud and say what you are feeling. You are here to discover new things, and to make familiar attitudes overt.

Start at the top of your head and work down to your toes. Include your back side too. Touch each part as you go. Make statements about how you feel about your body parts and any connected feelings that seem important to you. For example:

"I like my hair okay. It is shiny and I like that. I like the color brown. It's too oily and I wish I didn't have to wash it every other day. I feel embarrassed that I have dandruff. I wish it were thicker. I like the feeling when someone strokes my hair. I like to have my scalp rubbed . . .

I am getting to like my breasts more, now that I don't mind that they are small. I can see that I used to judge them in terms of how men would react. They are a source of sexual pleasure to me. I like to wear blouses which emphasize my breasts. I feel self-conscious in front of some people because I don't wear a bra and that makes me hunch my shoulders and feel tense."

After you have talked through your whole body, you can talk about general feelings you have about your appearance.

When you feel finished, ask yourself, "What parts of my body have I left out? Why?" Did you include your body hair and your make-up?

Repeat this exercise after a period of time and see how your attitudes have changed.

The Inner Physical

This set of exercises can be done by yourself at your own pace or with a friend who reads the steps to you. You can also record the instructions on a tape recorder and play it back to follow.

Many people base their feelings about their body largely on outer appearance. The Inner Physical can help you get in touch with your inner space, and with an alternative way to sense your body — from the inside out.

Tuning In

Go to a room or place where you can be quiet and alone, at a time when you can spend a half hour or more without pressure. The light should be soft. Lie down on a rug or a pad, preferably on a level floor. Be lying on your back with your arms at your sides and your legs uncrossed. Let your legs relax and your feet fall out. Let your eyes be closed. Pay attention to how you are lying on the  floor and to any parts of your body which are not relaxed, which seem to be pulling up and not really resting on the carpet.

Focus your attention inside your body. Without changing your breathing, notice where you can feel it moving in your body; notice any small movement in your muscles which is happening as a result of your breathing. Do you feel any movement in the muscles of your neck and chest because of your breathing? Do you feel movement in your stomach, abdomen and sides? Can you feel any movement in your back as a result of your breathing?

Measuring With Your Breath

Another experiment — can you use your breath to explore the space inside your body? As you feel your breath inside your chest, can you get a sense of the width inside your rib cage? Let your breath relax and sink deeper in your body. Can you get a sense of the space inside your pelvis, or the distance between your two hip bones? Do you have a sense of the distance between your navel and your spine?

Do each of these experiments slowly at your own pace. If you are working with a reader, you can raise a hand to signal when you are through with each step and ready to go on. The next suggestions deal with another way of relaxing your muscles. You can do these separately or as a continuous exercise.

Squeeze and Relax

Bring your attention to the muscles of your scalp and forehead. Tune in to any feelings of tension there. Tighten the scalp and forehead muscles. Squeeze and hold the tension; and then release it, relaxing the area.

Repeat this cycle (awareness of an area; tension; and relaxation) with all parts of your body moving systematically down to your feet. Go slow. See if you can isolate the muscle movement so that only the part you are focusing on tenses or moves. Try to keep your focus on only one part at a time. Pay attention to which movements are smooth and which are jerky.

Tense, and then relax the muscles of your scalp and forehead.

Tense, and relax the muscles around your eyes.

Tense, and relax the muscles of your cheeks, mouth and chin. Your whole face.

Tense, and relax your neck.

Tense your shoulders — and relax.

Tighten your upper arms, and your lower arms — and relax.

Clench your hands and fingers — and relax.

Tighten your chest — and relax.

Tense the muscles around your ribs and diaphragm — and relax.

Contract the muscles of your upper back — and relax.

Tense your lower back — and relax.

Tighten your buttocks as much as you can — and relax.

Tense the muscles of your genitals — and relax.

Tighten the large muscles of your thighs — and relax.

Tense your knees — and relax.

Tense your calf muscles — and relax.

Tense your ankles and feet. Curl in your toes and tighten the whole area
of the foot.

Now relax.

When you reach your toes and have relaxed the muscles of your feet, tense all the muscles in your body and constrict yourself with all your effort. Intensify whatever position your body pulls into, and be aware if it seems to express some emotion. Now release the tension and relax your whole body.

Let every muscle relax. Imagine your breathing can relax your muscles more and more with each exhalation, as though the tension could flow out of your body with your breath. Let your whole body sink more and more into the carpet. Let the floor support your weight. Think of the floorboards under you which are holding your weight. And think of the structure which holds up that floor, which finally is connected with the earth below.

After you have gone through these steps you will be very relaxed. Don't jump up. An important part of this exercise happens after all the thinking is done. Let yourself lie on the floor as long as you want and try to allow yourself to relax more and more into the place you are feeling. When you finally do get up, move slowly.

You may have the feeling that you've been sleeping but conscious. If you can relax into it this is a very tension-releasing state to be in; and after even a few minutes there you will feel refreshed and calm as though you had slept deeply for a long time.

This Yoga exercise is good for anyone who has difficulty relaxing. You can also use it at night to put yourself to sleep. Some variations are:

- Do just Tuning In.

- Do Squeeze and Relax without the steps of tensing your muscles. Just think, "Relax the muscles of your scalp," etc. (think, Relax the muscles of your scalp," etc.)

- Do Squeeze and Relax less minutely when you only have a few minutes. The action of lying down, closing your eyes and focusing inside can be relaxing in itself, no matter how briefly you do it.

- You can go through the same technique for muscle relaxation in more public situations. Just close your eyes and focus inside.

- Some variation of this exercise is very helpful to do each day. It is gentle but it can dramatically increase your body awareness if done regularly.

It is important for your self-awareness to learn to sense inside yourself as well as outside. At different times in your life and during various emotions you will have different experiences of your inner space. You will also begin to feel more of what is happening inside you, so that your sense of your body at any time will include your inner as well as outer sensations. With practice, you can get in touch with sensations from different internal organs, and feel internal body temperatures and movements. Your evaluation of some outside body part may even change once you begin to feel it along with a connected inner sensation. Now that I feel my breath more in my abdomen and I experience that feeling as pleasurable and relaxing, I have a better feeling about that part of my outer body. I feel I have a more realistic sense of my body than its outer shape alone.

Centering, Breathing and Belly Power

If I had to choose one tool from all the body awareness techniques that I know, I would pick knowledge of breathing.

The breath, being the one body function which can be either controlled or automatic, is the bridge between the conscious and unconscious functions in our bodies, between our habitual responses and our deep feelings. When we know how to alter our breathing we can move back and forth between these two states and integrate the two so that powerful images normally locked away from our consciousness emerge while we are awake. A woman who teaches a breathing technique to help people integrate these two worlds into their natural breath rhythm is Magda Proskauer in San Francisco. I have been taking a class from her in Breath Awareness for about two years now and have included several of her breath exercises in this section.

Two other powerful body therapies, Reichian and Bioenergetics, are largely based on analyzing a person's breath pattern and clearing out any muscular tension blocks which prevent full movement of the breath; then re-patterning the person's breathing to allow maximum energy flow in the body. A simple Bio-energetics exercise which is safe and energizing for anyone to do has been included in this section. Some of the techniques included are from Hatha Yoga.

I want to talk about Magda Proskauer's work first because it focuses on getting your body back to its own natural breath rhythm. Most breathing exercises employ controlled breath patterns, rather than allowing the person to breathe in her individual way and at her own rhythm. A superimposed pattern of controlled breathing prevents me from rediscovering my natural rhythm. The deepest releases happen spontaneously. Magda's exercises help me relax into the place where my body begins to breathe when it wants to without an outside rhythm imposed on it. Once this happens I experience a sense of release; my body lets go and tension disappears.

Magda's exercises are gentle and slow and involve small body movements coordinated with the cycle of your breath. The usual position is lying on your back on the floor, eyes closed. In her Tuesday morning group classes, which she's been giving for about twenty years in her San Francisco home, there are about twelve persons. The class lasts an hour. The first forty-five minutes are spent doing the breathing exercises as Magda talks through the steps. The last part of the hour is open for anyone who has a comment to make on their response to the exercise or perhaps on an image they had. Sometimes someone will mention a dream they had during the week which concerned the part of the body they had worked on in Magda's class the previous week. Magda does very little interpretation of these images because she feels the images speak for themselves to the individual.

Over a period of time physical changes can be seen in the people who come regularly to her classes: tight high shoulders loosen and drop to their natural slope; faces gradually become less tense and more full and glowing; tight muscles everywhere in the body begin to let go and people gradually relax into their natural posture, become more comfortable, more open, more themselves. Magda also sees many private clients to work with them verbally, with their dreams, and with their breathing.

I talked to Magda about her work and aspects of it particularly useful to women:

Magda: I started as a physical therapist long ago. I went to the physical therapy school in the late 1920's at the University of Munich Medical School. The program there was a combination of studying medicine and physical therapy. At this time Freud and Jung had a strong new influence which made itself felt in all medical practice. So the whole aspect of psychosomatic medicine came up, and there were new schools in Germany where the psychologist or psychotherapist worked hand in hand with the physical therapist.

I became especially interested in people with breathing difficulties — asthma, tuberculosis, all kinds of pulmonary diseases. I always wondered about the strange results I got with people who did breathing exercises to be cured of these diseases. Sometimes people got cured very fast and then the asthma would come back, and sometimes one was permanently cured. And some people didn't respond at all! The results were very unpredictable.

Much later I got involved with spastic and polio cases, and I always used some breathing exercises. It would help them relax; and the breathing would help them get in touch with the areas of their bodies which they couldn't contact otherwise because they were paralyzed. In this way the breathing can be useful to anyone, to normally healthy people, in order to help them become conscious in parts of their body where they may have little awareness, to become more sensitive and to tune in there.

In 1933 when Hitler came, I went to Yugoslavia. There I started to practice with doctors. Later I came to this country and worked at the Columbia University Presbyterian Medical Center, New York City, with spastic, cerebral palsy and polio children. I went to school to study psychology and make my Ph.D., but I decided that was not my answer. Then I got involved in Jungian psychology, and my experience with Jungian psychology personally influenced my work most. That must have been about twenty-five years ago.

Now I work in San Francisco and I have a few people who come to me with special problems, such as asthma. But mainly I work with healthy people. So-called healthy people!

Me: Why would a person without a paralysis problem or asthma want to do this breath work? I think most people wouldn't know why it's important.

Magda: Through breathing we can reach the unconscious aspect of the personality. We breathe consciously, and we breathe automatically. The automatic body process is able to function without the mind. So from the day we are born, we breathe automatically, unconsciously; yet we can also take a deep breath at will. The breath is connected to the two kinds of nervous systems, the conscious one which works through the cortex of the brain, and the unconscious one, which works through the vegetative autonomic nervous system. In this way it seems the breath is a bridge between the conscious system and the unconscious system. Therefore, by observing the breath, you can observe a normally unconscious and unavailable function at work. *By observing your breath patterns you can see where you interfere with your natural rhythm.* The breath seems to be a microcosm of the personality, of our larger patterns. You can see where you interfere with your own nature by focusing on the breath as it is. When you focus on those places you can allow for spontaneous change to take place. You find your own rhythm. That's what we try to do in this work.

Me: I'd like to talk about some of the ways you think the breathing process can be useful when I'm not at rest. How could I do something right now to find out something about myself through my breathing?

Magda: Observe your breath and find where it is.

Me: It's in my chest.

Magda: It's higher than it is in the classes, isn't it? In action the breath is more in the chest, and in rest and quietness it is more in the abdomen. Since you are interviewing me, you have to be very conscious right now. You're active; and the action goes together with chest breathing.

Rest, meditation and sleep go together with abdominal breathing. Since at this moment you're alert, you automatically breathe more in your chest. If your breath would stay down in your abdomen, you would suddenly get bored with the interview!

Me: I know a lot of people who have recently come in contact with some kind of Oriental discipline and they have the feeling that they should always breathe in their abdomen.

Magda: There are many young people now who go around in a trance. They always want to be the Buddha! That's not appropriate all the time. You automatically breathe in your chest when you are active and disciplined and working. But we want to get access to the abdominal breathing which goes together with peace, with quietness, with letting it happen — so that we have a choice. You can't write that book breathing in your stomach! Nothing will happen.

Me: It'd take me ten years! ... How do you use your breath awareness techniques for yourself?

Magda: Many ways. When I'm standing in line for a long time, I do some breathing exercises. If my feet are tired, I imagine that I can send my breath into my feet. I imagine what that would feel like. It helps.

Or I think of a new way to breathe into my hands to use in my classes. Or if my shoulders are stiff, I lift a shoulder a little bit, and then let it sink down, and exhale as if I were sending the breath into my arm. This is a way to use the time to make room for myself. So that instead of being all stewed up, I am relaxed when I get out of line. The time of standing in line goes so fast!

Breathing teaches patience. You learn to be settled in with yourself and slow. These are the things which are left out of our education — how to slow down, and how to be good to ourselves. When you are too good to yourself you are always named egocentric! Sure there is a lot of narcissism around; that is different. To really act as though you have a right and a possibility to fulfill your own needs — that is being maternal and the mother to yourself. With this kind of behavior you can touch on the mother problem in yourself.

Vladimir and Magda

26

Me: I think that is really difficult for most women. They are everyone else's mother. They don't take care of themselves; and they don't think they can. They wait for someone else to, a man. I certainly know that place!

I want to talk about some more things that come up in your groups. Often while people are lying on the floor doing the exercises, they see images, or dream-like pictures, with their eyes closed.

Magda: When you open up your breath in your abdomen — which is where we breathe when we are asleep — and some of that gap between action conscious breathing and rest unconscious breathing is bridged, the unconscious opens up, and some people have visions. We are all different. Some people have a very rich visionary world; and some people don't have visions at all. Everybody dreams but the dreams don't always reach consciousness. Quite often, though, through this meditative attitude which we reach in our classes through breathing, the inner world of images opens up. Then we may talk about this in the class.

Me: How do you deal with those image associations in class?

Magda: What approach I take depends on what comes up. Freudian psychology touches more on what is called the shadow, or what is suppressed. If somebody's shadow comes up then we deal with it. Jungian psychology reaches more what you call the collective unconscious, the depths of the personality, archetypes. Jung was probably the first modern psychologist to realize man has a center. Sometimes the Jungian level of interpretation applies more than the shadow.

But I don't usually interpret very much. Do you realize that? It isn't necessary. The images, the symbols speak for themselves. You know what they feel like. They speak to you directly. I don't have to interpret them.

Me: I'm interested in the emphasis Jung puts on balancing the male and female parts within us. If I were a client coming to you saying, "I feel really cut off from my male part, my aggression. How could I do something through your work to help me get in touch with that part?"

Magda: Because you're a woman, I would rather say that through this work you will experience more your own femininity. Since you are a woman, this is you. The masculine aspect in a woman is the feeling that she can do with her life what she has to do — deciding herself and actually doing it. Such as writing this book. That would be what the Jungians call the creative animus.

The negative masculine side is this side which has ready-made laws. When people feel, I *should* do this, I *should* write this book! That's really the negative masculine side which makes laws about what you *should* do; while the creative aspect of the masculine side is to do what you are meant to do. In this work, for a woman, the way is to much more experience yourself as you are, as a woman, to open yourself to your femininity. Unless you are there as a woman, you cannot find your masculine side.

I would say to you, the body is mother nature, and when you are in your body and can feel yourself in your body, you can experience yourself as a woman. You experience your body as it is. The body is our utmost reality.

For the man, since he is a man, he experiences nature as a man. (We stress more the same sex in this world.) If a man is not really experiencing himself as a man then the creative aspect of his soul, which would be the feminine side, cannot enter. The same process as with a woman. First somebody has to be at home.

This is what we are doing when we have problems with our man because we are all "feminine." We lose our structure because we submit to the man, and project all the creativity into him, which is a very dangerous thing to do. You don't do that by "doing your own thing." Then you feel married to yourself.

Breathing Into Body Parts

There are different Proskauer exercises for each part of the body, but the same three-part breath is used in all of them. The cycle is geared to eventually trigger your own natural rhythm, so that your body's natural pace takes over.

Be in a quiet, softly-lit room with a carpet or a pad on the floor. Take off your shoes. Lie down on the floor on your back. Relax your arms at your sides and let your feet fall out. Let your eyes be closed.

Tune in to how you are lying on the floor. Notice any parts of your body which feel a bit tense or do not seem to be fully resting on the floor. Some likely places may be your lower back, your shoulders, and your legs. Now focus inside your body and notice where the breathing is in your body, and where you feel any movement in your muscles because of your breathing. Any place you feel tense, you can try imagining that you can breathe into that tight place, as though you could actually exhale through that body part. Imagine that the breath relaxes the sore muscle a little as it moves through the part. *Breathing into a body part* is something you can do anywhere, anytime you feel tense or nervous. Find the tight place and breathe into it. No one knows that you are doing it, and it is remarkably relaxing. The process can also change the whole quality of your movement if you do it in action, in time with the tensing and relaxing of your movement.

As you are lying on the floor now tune in to your abdominal muscles. If your clothing is tight at the waist, loosen it. Let the muscles of your stomach and abdomen relax and let your breath sink lower into your body. Place your hand palm-down at the lowest place on your body where you can feel your breathing. Let your hand rest on this place a little while until you begin to feel the rise and fall of your body under your palm from your breathing. Now let your hand and arm relax at your side again. If you see any pictures of yourself or other images during the breathing exercise, remember them and write them down or draw them in your journal.

Now relax your jaw and open your mouth a little so that you can exhale through your mouth. You don't need to breathe heavily. Just stay with relaxed natural breathing. Inhale through your nose; exhale through your mouth; and pause at the end of the exhalation, before you breathe in again.

This pause is the key to the effectiveness of the breathing. Many things are happening with your body during the pause which are important. One is that you are actually still exhaling though you may feel as though nothing is going on. Deepening the exhalation naturally is important for getting all the stale air out of your lungs so that there is more room for fresh air on the inhalation. Most of us don't exhale deeply enough. And often if you have the sensation that you can't take in enough air, that you'd like to inhale more deeply, it's because you haven't exhaled fully and there's no room in your lungs for new air. Lengthening your exhalation will help. This is usually the breathing difficulty in asthma.

You have stayed with that pause at the end of the exhalation for a long time now. Let yourself really explore the pause. How does it feel to you? Does it feel long? Are you nervous that your body won't breathe in again unless you make it? Think of your breathing when you are asleep. You  always breathe in again then and you don't have to tell yourself to breathe. Think of the breathing of animals when they are resting. Their breath is long and rolling. They don't think to tell themselves when to breathe next. You can learn to trust your breath. It will always come in again!

Allow that pause to be whatever length it wants. It may feel quite long. See if you can wait and stay with the pause until your body wants to breathe in again by itself. Inhale through your nose; exhale through your mouth; then pause and wait. Like standing on the beach, and waiting for another wave to come in. Try to find a place where you are neither forcing the pause nor making yourself breathe. Let yourself breathe this way for as long as you want.

This exercise in itself is deeply relaxing and opens up a peaceful, centered space. You can use this breath at night if you have difficulty going to sleep. Or anytime you feel tense and can take a few minutes off to yourself to relax and center yourself. It is a gentle but very powerful exercise. It brings you more into yourself.

Centering

Anytime you sense you are getting overrun by outside influences and losing your own feelings, put your attention inside your body. Relax your chest and stomach and abdominal muscles; let your breath sink low in your body; and breathe in your abdomen. Your stomach should puff out like a balloon as you inhale, and relax and sink in as you exhale. On a simple level, this is the meaning of centering. Going inside your body, going home. Focusing your attention, your energy, deep inside your pelvis at the center of your body, a bit below your navel, touching home-base.

Check in with yourself there even for just a moment or so, and when you bring your attention to outside events again, you will feel steadier and refreshed. Experiment with what it's like to keep your focus on your energy center in your abdomen at the same time that you are doing something else. Try it while walking across the room. Imagine the energy for your movement is coming from your center and moving down your legs and feet. Your balance and walk will feel entirely different from when you focus somewhere else.

The term *centering* comes from the spiritual body practices of the Orient. In all the powerful disciplines, from Yoga to the Samurai, one is taught centering as the core of the practice. The Yogi is taught that to focus on the energy centers inside himself and learn to release and channel them in his own body is the path to God; it is the path to physical and spiritual clarity. A Samurai is taught how to keep his focus on his own energy center, so that when fighting, no matter what is happening around him, he is rooted inside himself and can be precise and swift with his sword movements. Watch Toshiro Mifune closely sometime in a movie. Watch how his Samurai movements differ from those of the other characters. His training from a Western point of view might be divided into two parts: physical and spiritual. To an Easterner, there is no separation. The two elements always go together. When one is left out, the person's skill suffers.

30

There is in a sense no "end" to this practice; one could move through infinite layers of awareness. Centering through physical and mental practice is the route to opening up your inner energy powers and the route to emotional and physical balance.

I think it is important for women to begin to feel their bodies as powerful, not weak. With this change will come changes in your sense of emotional power in relationship to others. Many of the Oriental self-defense systems — such as Aikido, Kung Fu, Tai Chi Chuan and Karate

Julia McKinney Barfoot: Kung Fu

— if taught well, result in increased strength and agility without making you "muscle bound" as most Western "rough" sports do.

"Chakra" is the Indian name for an energy center which corresponds to a nerve plexus. Some Western psychologists such as Jung and Reich have dealt with this concept in their work. Reich talks about the abdominal-pelvic center, the Muladhara and Swadhisthana chakras, as the key to our deepest emotions and powers, the source of the energy in the rest of our body. Consider what tightening the stomach muscles does to that centering process.

Most women I know are taught to "hold their stomachs in" — and a concave curve is even better than flatness! In the language of centering and belly power, those women have a hole where their center is supposed to be. We are taught to constrict our bellies and to prevent movement in our pelvis ("Don't wiggle when you walk!").

Constriction in the muscles constricts the flow of blood in the area, and, therefore, cuts down on how much feeling we have in our pelvis, and inhibits the development of the tissue.

To center you need to free the abdominal muscles of tension and let breath and feeling move in your pelvis. You can use the Basic Proskauer Breath for this.

The abdomen is also the gate between the upper half of your body and the lower half, containing sexual feelings in the pelvis, and action and independence in the legs and feet ("standing on your own two feet"). As a woman, I am concerned that I have been brought up in this society to constrict my sexual feelings, my independence and my own power. I see that constriction too in the bodies of many of my friends.

Through relaxing the abdomen and letting the breath move down into the pelvis, you can begin to release the constriction in your body. You can allow for a new process to start. Pay attention to how you stand and how you hold your muscles in the pelvic area. Experiment with tensing your buttocks, genitals and abdomen as much as you can while you are standing (or in any position). Now release those muscles. This will help you get in touch with tension in your pelvis. Breathe into the area to relax it. Wear clothes loose at the waist in which you can breathe freely in your abdomen. Try to re-orient your cues for what is a "beautiful" woman's stomach from something which is rigid and constricted, to a belly which is relaxed, rounded and free to move, breathe and feel; from what is currently "fashionable" to what feels and functions most rewardingly to you from the inside.

Proskauer Breath Awareness

Several of Magda's breath exercises focus on experiencing the abdomen and hips from the inside to increase sensitivity in the pelvis. In her classes awareness exercises for the pelvic area come early in the cycle, and later we do exercises for other parts of the body. This pattern allows a person to open up feeling and awareness first in her "center," and then to branch out from this base to the other areas.

Breath in the Pelvis

Lie down, close your eyes, and take yourself through the steps for the Basic Proskauer Breath until you have been breathing awhile, pausing at the end of the exhalation.

Now slide one foot along the floor, bending the knee, so that your leg comes up to rest in a comfortable position. There will be a place where your leg feels

balanced and will stay in place without any effort from
your muscles to hold it up. Now bend the other leg
and position it the same way. Make note of how the
parts of your body are lying on the floor, especially
your lower back and hips.

Stay with the pause breathing and imagine you
can breathe into your pelvis, inhaling through your mouth and "exhaling" through
your right hip. What would it feel like inside your body if you could actually move
your breath there? See if you can get a sense just from the breathing of the bone
joint where your right leg comes into your pelvis.

Now add a small movement. Each time you inhale, tense the muscles of your
right buttock; and as you exhale release the tension. As you tighten your right
buttock, see if you can isolate those muscles so that you are not tensing any other
parts of your body at the same time. If you are, notice where that extra tension is.
As you exhale allow your right side to thoroughly relax and sink into the ground. Try
to let the movement be smooth rather than jerky, and to coordinate it with your
breathing. The movement need not be large. It can be very small. Contract the muscles
just enough that you can feel your right hip rise up slightly as you inhale and settle
down again as you exhale.

Rest a breath in between without moving at all. Now repeat the movement on
each alternate breath. Do this cycle about 15 times.

Now stop the movement; rest in the middle, but stay with the same breathing.
While you are resting take note of how your right hip feels. Do you feel any
difference between it and your left hip? Does either hip feel larger or smaller? Warmer
or colder? Lighter or heavier? Do you feel as though your pelvis is tilted to one side
or the other? Or is there no difference to you at all? Do they both feel the same?
Has there been any response in the rest of your right side?

If you want you can repeat this whole process for your left side by breathing
into the left hip and moving the muscles of the left buttock. The second side is
always a bit harder, because if you felt some sensations in one side as a result of the
breathing, you will expect the same to occur again. Almost always the effects in the
two sides are different.

After breathing into your left hip awhile with the movement, rest again and see
how that hip feels now in comparison to the other. Have there been any changes?
How does it feel compared to the way it felt before?

Now let your feet slide down so that both your legs are resting on the floor
again. Pay attention to how you are lying and to changes in your lower back or in
any places where you might have felt tension before.

Now sit up slowly, letting your eyes stay closed. Cover your eyes with your palms and look into your dark palms. After a moment, begin to move your hands slowly away from your face. Let them divide and let your vision include the rest of the room.

Some people, after doing this exercise on one side, report they feel the exercised side as "larger and more alive" and the "unbreathed" side as "cold, smaller and dead."

Consider what this means if we constrict our bellies and prevent the breath from moving into our pelvis. We have less awareness, sensitivity, relaxation and feeling in the area. Physiologically "breathing" into a body part creates some of those sensations of warmth because you can actually send more blood there that way. With increased circulation, the blood vessels expand (if you felt a little bigger on one side, you actually were!) and warmth and fresh oxygen rush in. This also accounts for a frequently reported "tingling" sensation in the area, such as when you leg wakes up after having been asleep. With better circulation the tissues and nerves function better, and you have more sensation and awareness in the pelvis. In a very real sense I am being taught to cut off feeling and life in my pelvis when I am taught to "pull my stomach in" or tighten my buttocks. When I tense my muscles anywhere, I am cutting down on the sensation in that area. When I relax the muscles and let the circulation move freely there again, I can feel more. I can receive more pleasure.

The Chest

Because of social pressure to define one's female sexuality by the appearance of the breasts, the chest is often another high tension area for women.

In the language of the body, the chest is the seat of the ego. When asked to non-verbally indicate "me" I automatically point to the center of my chest. Constriction in that area can relate to constriction in one's sense of self in the world. Women are treated in our society like lesser humans and second-class citizens; we need to start taking better care of ourselves. We don't need to wait for an outsider's approval. We need to start basing our feelings about our breasts on how we experience ourselves from the inside rather than on someone else's fantasies. To do so is to reclaim some of the power over our natural identity which we have given away.

Chest Exam

You can check for muscular tension on yourself. Work in the area of the muscles supporting the breasts rather than on the breasts themselves.

34

With your fingertips press on your pectoral muscles, the arc of muscle from your armpit to your breast. Is the muscle pliant and relaxed? Or is it tight and hard? Press firmly into the area between your collar bones and the top of your breasts. Feel with your fingertips for sore areas or lumps. These lumps come simply from tension and constriction.

How do you usually hold your chest? When you sit and stand do you collapse your chest and slump your back so that your chest seems concave? Judith Aston, who helped develop a fine posture alignment technique called Rolf-Aston Patterning in Stillness and Motion, pointed out a habit of mine of hunching at the center of my chest just before beginning to walk or move in any way. I feel a correlation between this posture and my tendency to "sink in my ego" — to tone down my power — before making contact with others.

Do you use a lot of effort to "stick out your chest" — creating rigidity in the muscles around the breasts, neck, and shoulders? Either extreme of pushing or sinking causes tension. Releasing that tension would allow the chest to relax into its natural place.

The Fountain Of The Ego

One of Magda Proskauer's breathing exercises which I call the Fountain of the Ego can bring a great deal of awareness into the chest.

Do the basic Proskauer breath until you feel relaxed and you feel your breath moving in your abdomen. The pelvis is the reservoir of the inner life; imagine it is a deep lake. Now let your breath open up in your chest. Tune in to the rising and falling of your chest with your breathing. Do you sense any movement in your ribs and sides from your breathing? With several fingertips touch the place on your chest which is "I" to you. Press in hard and then release the pressure. Do this several times. Do you feel how the cartilage gives to your touch? Rest your fingers there without pressure. Do you feel movement in that area from your breathing? Let your arm relax again at your side.

Now imagine that you can exhale through the spot you have just touched. What would it feel like if your breath could actually move out through that spot?

Your unconscious, your pelvis, is the pool of your inner life. Through your ego your inner feelings are translated and brought into the outside world. Imagine that the place in the center of your chest which you touched is a fountain for the deep water in the pool of your pelvis.

Inhale and simultaneously arch your chest up and your head back. Release your muscles on the exhalation and let your chest and head relax down into the carpet again. Rest a breath without movement. Repeat this cycle several times.

Now stop the movement, but continue "exhaling" through the middle of your chest.

Bring one arm out to the side so that it lies in approximately a straight line with your shoulder. On the inhalation stretch your arm away from your body toward your hand. On the exhalation let your arm relax back into your shoulder. Let the weight of the upper arm pull your arm back into its shoulder socket. Allow your arm to sink into the floor.

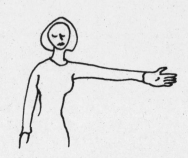

Do this movement coordinated with alternate breaths about ten times. Relax on the between breaths. Now bring your arm back to your side and let it be still.

How does your exercised arm feel? Compare this to how the arm you did not exercise feels. What is the difference? Can you get a sense of the ball and socket joint at your shoulder? Do you have a sense of space there? How does the "exercised" pectoral area feel? Do the effects reach from your shoulder and into the one side of your chest?

Repeat this process with your other arm. Compare the feeling in your two arms again. Then try it a few times moving both arms out at once, still exhaling through your chest. Do you have a sense of the connection across your chest between your two arms?

Making Up Your Own

The basic idea of breathing into a body part as you move it to release tension there can be used any place in your body. Invent your own exercises for areas where you feel tight, or for any areas where you would like more sensation, more feeling.

It is important to contract as you inhale and to relax as you exhale. The most tension release occurs on the exhalation as you "let go" with your muscles. It is natural to the breath pattern to sigh or exhale deeply when you relax.

You needn't consider any body part unreachable by the breath. Consider relaxing your eyeballs or your toes. One of Magda's most powerful exercises for me is one in which she has us breathe into our skulls and let our brains soften and loosen their attachments, slowly falling away from the sides of the skull, becoming jelly and slipping down the center of our spinal cords!

Aikido Exercises For Centering

Aikido is a Japanese practice of self-defense and centering. It is remarkable from other disciplines because of its subtlety, power and the degree to which the clarity of the individual student determines her skill at the art. Morihei Uyeshiba, a master of many Oriental forms of self-defense, developed Aikido late in his life living in the mountains, studying the movements of birds and animals and meditating on the nature of self-defense. The basic philosophy of Aikido is that to attack someone is to the break the laws of the universe. It is to generate negative energy which will eventually come back against oneself. Who "wins" a conflict should not be determined by who has bigger muscles or fancier weapons, but by who is more in tune with the universal spirit. Some women progress more quickly in Aikido than men because they are accustomed to using something other than muscle power in a struggle. The Japanese call this other power "Ki" or spirit. The Ki is dealt with as an actual molecular substance, an energy which "moves" and can be channeled and focused or "centered" in different parts of the body. It is the same as the "Chi" in Tai Chi Chuan. When the Ki is centered, a person is in a state of calm, balanced health, clarity and power. Much of Aikido training is spent developing sensitivity to the Ki within oneself and learning ways of heightening and focusing it. Uyeshiba, in his seventies in 1968, could take on the most advanced swordsman or Karate champion and defeat him because his skill lay in his own energy awareness rather than in his muscles. Many Sikido exercises will increase your centering power and train you to be very sensitive to the flow of your opponent's energy. If you are tuned in to his flow, you know where he will move before he does and you will make sure you are not there. Centering exercises are important to a warrior because no matter how good his weapon is, if he's very nervous and distraught he can't use it. To me Aikido exercises are important because my "opponent" is someone or some situation which throws me off balance, off center.

I use some basic Aikido centering exercises, which I learned from Robert Nadeau in San Francisco, for relaxation and focus. Some are for centering your energy in your *hara*, or belly center, and others are for experimenting with "centering" in another body part and feeling how differently you can function with that focus change. Centering is directly related to good health; you can also use centering exercises for self-healing.

The Steel Arm

This exercise is an experiment in comparing muscle strength and Ki. You need a partner. Choose someone of approximately your height and strength.

Stand opposite each other. Straighten your right arm and place your right hand on your partner's left shoulder. Your friend clasps her hands and rests them lightly on your elbow joint.

First tighten your right arm muscles as hard as you can. Your partner *gradually* increases pressure on your elbow joint and tries as hard as she can to bend your arm at the elbow.

Pay attention to how your body feels resisting with muscle power. Resist bending your elbow with all your strength.

Now quit using your muscle power and let your arm relax a moment. Place it back on your partner's shoulder and have your partner get in the same position again. This time try centering in your abdomen first. To do this focus your attention on the lower half of your body and imagine your strength comes from your belly. Imagine a lot of energy is moving out from your center, up through your body and out through your arm. Imagine your arm is a steel rod. It is hard and unbendable. It extends from your body across to your partner's shoulder and even beyond her shoulder in a straight line. Your arm is a steel rod and it is unbendable. When you have this feeling nod to your partner for her to begin applying pressure at your elbow. Keep your concentration and a calm breath. Do not tense your muscles against her pull. You do not need to — your arm is a steel rod. Stay with the image. Your partner should increase the pressure more and more and try to bend your arm.

Can you maintain your focus on the unbendable quality of your arm? Does it feel any different to you to meet her pressure with this kind of power than with muscle strength? Afterward ask your partner if *she* experienced a difference. If you did experience some differences between the two ways of meeting pressure, you can get a small taste of what the power of Ki is in your body.

The Mountain

Sit down comfortably cross-legged. Visualize a mountain and how it makes you feel. Now imagine that you are the mountain and that you feel as a mountain feels. What would you feel like if you had the qualities of a mountain: unmoving, massive and connected with the earth? Can you sit on the ground as a mountain rests without strain? There is comparatively little weight in the upper part of your body; the lower part of you is larger and heavier and anchors you to the ground.

Stay with these mountain feelings and slowly stand up. Let your weight be evenly distributed on both feet and sink toward the ground through your legs. Experiment with walking as a mountain, very drawn to the earth, steady and powerful. 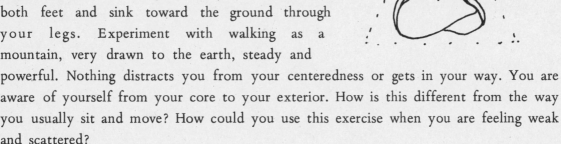 Nothing distracts you from your centeredness or gets in your way. You are aware of yourself from your core to your exterior. How is this different from the way you usually sit and move? How could you use this exercise when you are feeling weak and scattered?

The Light Bulb

Imagine a light bulb in your lower abdomen. Turn it on and feel the little bit of heat the light gives inside you. How would it feel if you could breathe into this light bulb and with each breath make it a little brighter and warmer?

Imagine that you can allow this light and warmth to radiate out from your center and flow to all parts of your body, making each part glow and grow warm as the light moves through.

What would it feel like if you could project some of this light from the bulb in your center out of your body through your abdomen and into the air in front of you in a steady stream? Let the beam take on whatever qualities you need. Let it flow in any direction inside or outside your body you wish. Do you want your energy now to be fast and concentrated, or slower and broader? Can you walk forward and let yourself move with this energy beam, so that you feel the energy flowing through you and you flowing with it?

The Brain In Your Abdomen

What would it be like if you had a second brain which rested in your abdomen, which could send messages out from your center? Imagine that this brain in your abdomen has been asleep and is now slowly waking up. It is becoming more aware of itself and aware of things around it. It is gradually awakening and wants to make a quiet sound as it stretches and opens up. What kind of sound would your

abdomen brain make? Can you make the sound and let it come from deep in your center? As the brain becomes more and more awake and functioning let the sound get louder. The brain is feeling more and more of its power. The sound is getting louder and louder. How do you feel when sound is coming from your abdomen?

Let the sound gradually quiet down again. What would it feel like if the messages for your actions came from your center? Let yourself stand a moment with your eyes closed and your focus on that abdominal brain. What kind of movement would your new brain like to tell your body to make? Try to let the message come not from your usual head center, but from your lower abdomen feelings. Let yourself come to motion in this new way with the energy for action originating in your center and flowing out to your different body parts for movement. Does this process feel different to you in any way from how you normally move? Experiment with simple actions like walking and imagine the energy for that movement coming from deep in your abdomen and spreading out into your legs and feet. The brain in your abdomen has different qualities from your head brain and with practice can open up new feelings and powers.

Stone Exercises

Dr. Randolph Stone is a man in his 80's who began as a chiropractor and traveled around the world investigating the medical practices of other cultures. From his study of Oriental medicine he put together an eclectic body treatment he called Polarity Therapy.

Polarity is based philsophically on Indian Yoga theories of the body and functionally on Chinese acupuncture. Polarity can be used to realign posture, release deep body and emotional tension, and treat particular body problems. The word polarity refers to the use of two acupuncture points simultaneously, based on a theory of balancing positive and negative electrical currents in the body. The practitioner stimulates acupuncture points on the client's body with her thumbs or fingers. Some chiropractic body manipulations are included in the treatment. If the area stimulated is quite relaxed and in good health, the sensation at the point is not painful and often creates waves of pleasurable feelings in the client's body which move to different points and relax the person even more. If there is some kind of tension around the acupuncture point and the tissue is contracted (hard or lumpy), pressure will be painful on that point but will gradually fade away and become neutral or pleasurable as the energy released from the acupuncture point spreads and the client relaxes. After a Polarity treatment the client usually feels refreshed, relaxed and more alive. Over a period of time, along with body and postural changes, come parallel emotional changes. Your body becomes more sensitive, alive and balanced.

There are Polarity exercises you can do on your own which are designed to keep the Ki energy, the source of life and health, flowing freely in your body.

The Stone Squat

Stand firmly with your feet placed wide apart. Bend your knees and squat as though you are sitting in an invisible chair with your back straight. Place your palms on your knees, and hunch your shoulders so that a good deal of your weight is now resting on your arms. Then begin rocking from side to side, bending one knee while straightening the other. Your weight should be on your bent leg.

Basic Polarity Meditation Posture

Spread your legs apart and stand firmly on your feet. Bend your knees and slowly lower yourself into a squat position with your arms in between your legs. Then clasp your hands together. Spread and push outward against your knees with your elbows.

Now relax your neck and head forward toward your hands. Close your eyes. Rest your head on your two thumbs, one thumb on either side of the bridge of the nose. Let your breath relax deep into your abdomen. You can rock a little back and forth (not from side to side) in this squat.

Centering Your Voice: Noise and the "Little Woman"

The Indian spiritual practice of chanting mantras is not done for the meaning of the words alone. Each syllable of a mantra is chosen because of its particular sound, and the vibrations of that sound affect a particular part of the Yogini's (female who does Yoga) body. The focused use of sound vibration is a subtle way to stimulate different body parts, and therefore, different energy centers, or chakras.

Most people habitually talk within a limited tone range. Their voice sound vibrations stay in one body area. Voices can be high and nasal, throaty, or deep as though coming from down in the belly. You can experiment now with feeling the voice vibrations in your own body. Make some different-pitched sounds from very high to very deep, sometimes with your mouth open and sometimes closed. Can you feel the vibrations inside? Now place your fingertips lightly on your skin as you make the sounds over the places where you feel your body vibrating from the tone. You will find that a very high-pitched nasal sound affects the area around your sinuses and forehead, while a lower one will cause vibration in your throat, and deeper sounds can affect other body parts.

Constriction of breathing is a critical factor in voice tone. How relaxed your throat, your pelvic area and your diaphragm are directly affects the breath and the resonance of the voice. Singers and actors know this well and do exercises to relax different body parts to open the voice.

I usually speak in a rather high soft voice. When I relax my throat and my abdomen I can let my voice move deeper in my body and become more powerful and resonant. One of the ideas that I was brought up with was that neither little girls nor ladies make loud noises. They are quiet and soft-spoken. Now that I am neither a nice little girl nor a lady I can enjoy making loud noises. I enjoy playing with the full range of sounds in my body. I enjoy letting my voice change with my emotions and not constricting it into a limited character role.

Get a tape recorder and try out different voices. Play it back to see how you feel about the sounds you make. Try listening to your voice during a conversation and tuning in to it as an index of your mood.

How do you use your voice? What does it's usual tone and rhythm express about you? How do you feel about making loud noises? Do you know grown women who still speak with little girl voices? Listen to the voices of female movie stars to notice what voice qualities are culturally encouraged.

The following Stone exercise is helpful for opening up your voice and torso breathing and for getting into your feelings about the kind of sounds you make.

42

Stand with your back to a table about hip height to you. Place your feet wide apart. Place your hands behind you, palms down over the edge of the table, fingers pointing toward the floor. Inhale. Now gradually lower your body into a squat position exhaling as you go down. Go slow and don't push yourself beyond the point of soreness. This will give your shoulder muscles quite a stretch. Now come up, inhaling as you do.

This time when you lower your body and exhale, growl as you move: let the growl get louder and louder.

Experiment with other deep sounds which seem to come from your lower abdomen. How would a sound from your abdomen be different than one from your throat? Make each sound three or four times at least, and allow yourself to go with your feelings.

Reclaiming Your Genitals

If you did the exercise called The Outer Physical, did you include your genitals as you explored your body? I left mine out the first time I did it, and I've found that many people do, particularly women.

If you omitted your genitals, include them now by saying out loud what you feel about that body part.

Do you enjoy your genitals? Do you feel your genitals as isolated or connected with other parts of your body? Do you have feeling and sensation in your genitals even when the area is not being touched? How do you think other people respond to your genitals? What role do you see your genitals playing in your life: biological function? social tool? for pleasure?

Looking

I've found that many women have never seen their own genitals. To go through life without looking at any other body part, such as a hand or a back, would be unthinkable. Yet many women don't feel they should look at their own genitals. They are ashamed. Someone else, a doctor or a lover, can look — but why should I? It's none of my business. What are your own feelings about looking at your genitals? Take some time now to consider where you learned these attitudes and how they affect you.

43

A helpful habit to get into is to look at your own genitals in the mirror regularly, and to pay attention to how this new self-knowledge affects your sense of yourself, of other women, and your interaction with men.

Try this now. You can use a hand mirror for close examination and a full-length mirror to get a sense of yourself as a visual physical whole. Look at your genitals as they are. Now fold back the outer labia and examine the appearance of the inner lips of the vagina and the clitoris. You have probably looked at diagrams in medical books of female genitals. 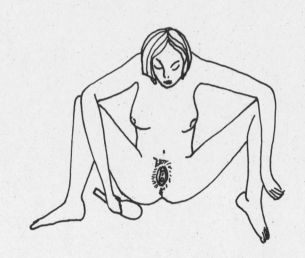 Find the parts now on yourself. How do you feel as you do this? Are you surprised at what you find?

Does the vagina respond simply to the rhythm of your breathing? Now contract the muscles of your anus and vagina and then release them. Do this several times and watch how the muscles move. If you want, stroke your genital area until you feel aroused. Then look at the resulting change in size and appearance.

Pay attention to your habitual response to other women's genitals when you are in situations where people are nude. In dressing rooms, doing massage, do you avoid looking at genitals? Allow yourself to include this body part in your looking. How does this make you feel? You will probably be surprised by the variety and individuality of people's genitals.

I saw a twenty minute film recently during a women's weekend seminar called *Near The Big Chakra* by Ann Severson which consisted of color close-ups of about forty vaginas of women of all ages. I responded with awe. I was struck by the great differences in vaginas. I also felt as though I were looking at an amazing natural phenomenon, such as an ice cave or a magnified sea creature. I was struck by the quality of being let deep inside the woman from looking at the open vagina — a woman is really letting someone in at a deep level when she accepts someone sexually. During the film other women in the audience responded differently, some with disgust, others with boredom. We each went out knowing ourselves and each other better.

44

Lie down on your back on a comfortable pad or rug or bed. Close your eyes and let your body relax. Give your tension over to the carpet. Relax your jaw and breathe through your mouth. Let your breath sink deep in your body. Tune in to what sense you now have of your genital area.

Imagine what it would feel like if you could let your breath move around inside your pelvis. Now try imagining you can exhale down through the center of your body and out your vagina. What would this feel like? Without forcing your breath, stay with this cycle for about ten breaths. Inhale through your mouth. "Exhale" through your vagina.

Now rest and tune in to any feelings you have in your body as a result of your breathing. How does your pelvic area, particularly your genitals, feel different from when you began the exercise? If you have more internal sensitivity in the pelvic region you might want to experiment with breathing into your genitals during other types of situations to explore how you feel about sensation in your pelvis at different times. This can also be very relaxing and pleasurable during sex.

If the difference in pelvic sensation before and after the exercise was marked for you consider how much feeling you are cutting off from the lower half of your body by tightening your abdomen and hip muscles and blocking your breath in your belly. What is your learned pleasure quota? What are your conditions for allowing awareness in your pelvis?

The Myth of the Passive Vagina

Your genital muscles need exercise just as any other muscles do. And just as in any other part of your body, exercising the genital muscles improves the tone, flexibility, and increases circulation to the muscle and to the surrounding tissue. With improved circulation the amount of sensation in the area increases.

Indian Yoginis — who believe that the genital area contains a key energy (the Kundalini) which must be stimulated and

brought alive so that it can spread up the spine and activate the higher energy nerve plexus centers — have been doing vaginal exercises for centuries. In their treatment for women with "sexual problems," Drs. Johnson and Masters give the women vaginal exercises to do daily to increase genital strength and feeling. The exercises are simple and can be done often and anywhere. No one will know!

Vaginal Push Ups

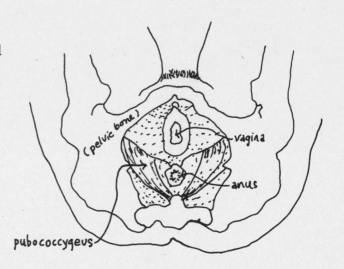

The muscles you are interested in contracting for this exercise are called the pubococcygeal muscles, or the pelvic floor. You can find them on the chart in this section. Feel them working by trying to stop your urine in mid-flow the next time you urinate. Do this several times and you will get a sense of how to contract these muscles. Then try it while not urinating. Contract and release the muscles alternately, slowly at about the speed and rhythm of the Blue Danube Waltz. Try to really contract the muscles and pull up so that you begin to get some sense of the connected muscles inside the pelvis.

This is an important set of muscles because it forms the "pelvic floor" which supports your organs when you stand. Flexibility in this area is very important during sex, pregnancy and childbirth.

The myth of the passive vagina is particular to our culture. In the erotic literature of the Far and Middle East, female genitals are described as aggressive and active. Fadehat el Djemal, a character in *The Perfumed Garden*, Shaykh Nefzawi's Arabian treatise on sex and love, has a vulva which "clasps" and "pinches" her lover's penis.

The more these pubococcygeal muscles are exercised, the more feeling and awareness develops in them, the more pleasure you will be able to feel.

Push Outs

Use the same muscles at the same slow place as in the exercise above. Alternate contracting and pushing out in the area, but this time emphasize the pushing out part of the cycle. Experiment with this during sex and in other situations too.

46

Begin to pay attention to your genital muscles while you are doing usual kinds of movements, such as walking, sitting, running, dancing and a variety of activities. Are you tightening your genital muscles in action and creating unnecessary pelvic tension? Can you walk and release your vagina? Can you stand still and rotate your pelvis without tightening your pelvic floor? Under what emotional conditions do you tense your genitals?

Deep Tension Release

One of the basic means of releasing deep muscular tension used in different forms of body therapy, such as Rolfing and Polarity, is to apply pressure on the tight muscle. When done gradually and not suddenly and only to the point of soreness, not pain, deep pressure massage on a muscle can begin to bring new awareness to the area and separate the connective tissue fibers which have become rigid from long constriction. When this happens the area becomes flexible again.

Pelvic Tension

You can use this massage on yourself to release pelvic muscle tension. Feel on either side of the center of your stomach for two long muscle groups which run from beside your pubic bone up to your ribs. There are several thin layers of muscles across the abdomen. The outermost one is called the external oblique. One section of this broad muscle area may become more developed than the rest and seem to stand out as separate on either side of your abdomen. Relaxation of these muscles causes a great deal of release throughout the pelvis.

Lie down on your back. Place several fingers  at the base of one of these muscle columns near the hip bone. Apply steady *gradual* pressure on the muscle so that your fingers press the skin in until you feel resistance. Stop where you are comfortable. Now begin stroking the muscle up toward your navel *at this deep pressure*. "Massage" this area several times. Now pick your fingertips up and massage a little higher on the muscle in small segments until you reach the ribs.

You will probably find that some areas along the muscle will be more sore or sensitive than others. Stay on these places longer. The soreness indicates more tension. You can relax it by gradual pressure. DO NOT GO BEYOND SORENESS INTO PAIN. Repeat this massage a little every day; the tension will lessen and the soreness will disappear.

The Vaginal Muscles

You can apply this same massage treatment to tense vaginal muscles. Lie down on your back with your knees up. Or sit on the toilet when you don't need to urinate. Insert one or two fingers inside your vagina and examine the muscular structure with your fingertips. There will be two prominent muscle columns which circle the inside of your vagina. Compare the inner muscles on the right and left. Is one side tighter than the other? Often the muscle on the right side is distinctly harder and tighter. Do some deep massage along the length of the tighter muscle fiber. If this process is repeated over a period of time, these muscles will begin to relax and become more flexible, more feeling.

Self-Massage

Touching is a critical means of learning and pleasure. Taboos on touching ourselves block some of our major ways of getting to know our bodies. If we accept them we become dependent on someone else for self-awareness and relaxation.

How do you feel about touching yourself? Are there parts of your body which are off-limits? Why? Does anyone else have the right to touch these off-limit places? Doctor, lover? Do your self-touching rules change with the situation? Start to notice what kinds of things feel "better" when someone else touches you and what feels "better" when you touch yourself.

The Secret Cold Cream Massage

Every day I rub creamy hand lotion into my skin all over my body. I do this for two reasons. One is that the lotion I use helps keep my skin soft. The other is that I like to touch myself all over each day because it makes me feel good and more in my body.

If you are shy about touching yourself, you can ease into it through a cold cream massage. You have an excuse. Your skin needs the lotion treatment.

Be sure to cover your whole body. You can rub lightly or deeply depending on what feels best to the particular muscle or body part you are touching. Get to know the different textures of your skin and your tissue. Try massaging with your eyes closed to get a sculptural sense of your shape. You know what feels best to your body. Do it to yourself.

Do the cold cream massage for a week and notice any changes in your body sense which may happen.

Breath Massage

One of the most effective self-massages is the technique from Magda Proskauer of "breathing" into a tight spot. Try it now on any place in your body where you feel constriction and you will immediately feel some results.

Foot Ball

One of my favorite self-massages is foot massage. All the nerves in the body connect eventually with the nerve endings in the feet so that a massage here can make your whole body feel better.

Get a ball in a dimestore such as a baseball or some ball that size which is relatively hard. Place it on the floor next to your right foot. Be barefoot and standing next to a table which is approximately hip high to you. With your palms on the table, lean your weight into the table and step on the ball with your right foot. (You can control how much pressure is on your sole by how much you lean onto the table.) Begin to roll your foot around on the ball. Try to eventually roll over all parts of the sole. Pay particular attention to any sore spots. Repeat this on your left foot. If you do the  football every day even for a brief time, much of the soreness will be worked out of your feet, and they will become more flexible and sensitive.

Bioenergetics and Grounding

Bioenergetics is a kind of therapy which uses both body and verbal techniques. Most of the theory and practice is based on Wilhelm Reich's work. Stanley Keleman in

Berkeley and Alexander Lowen in New York City are two prominent bioenergeticists working today.

Much attention is given to a concept called "grounding;" that is, a person's physical relationship to gravity. If a person does not have a balanced stance on the ground — if she tenses against letting her weight sink towards the earth, or distributes her weight in an unbalanced way on her feet — the rest of her body is thrown off balance too. There are emotional state correlations with grounding, as the phrases "having your feet on the ground," "taking a firm stand," and "being able to stand on your own two feet" imply. For women these aspects of the personality are significant. Few women are brought up to "stand on their own two feet." Most women are taught to be good helpers or assistants and to depend on men. According to bioenergetics theory, learning to stand on your own two feet increases your emotional independence as well as your physical balance.

The following bioenergetics position is a simple one designed to release some leg tension by causing vibration in the leg muscles and redirecting your energy and body weight more toward the earth.

Stand with your arms relaxed at your sides. Position your feet wide apart. Point your toes in toward each other, and bend your knees so that they move in toward each other too. You will feel a concentration of pressure from your body weight on the inside edges of your feet.

Hold this position awhile. Where is your breathing? Try to relax your adbominal muscles to allow your breath to sink deeper in your body as you stand. Notice any tension in other parts of your body, such as your shoulders or chest, and allow these areas to relax so that more of your weight can sink toward the floor. Are you tensing your genital muscles as you stand? If so, move your pelvis slightly forward and backward, or to the sides, to find the place where the genital muscles can relax and your pelvis is not held tight.

If you stay in this position several minutes, your legs may begin to shake. This vibration is caused by a rapid contraction and relaxation of your leg muscles. Try to allow it to happen. This reaction is desirable because it releases tensions in the muscles. Stop whenever you feel uncomfortable. Do this exercise often and you will notice more awareness and relaxation in your legs.

Walking With The Ground

Experiment with your relationship to gravity in motion. As you walk, try imagining that the earth is coming up to meet you; that each time as your foot steps down and is moving toward the ground, the ground is reaching up slightly toward the foot. Try to be aware of the texture and resiliency of the ground you walk on — the different relationships your foot has to grass, mud, hard earth, rugs, wood floors, concrete.

The Illustrious Guest

Plan ahead to have free an evening or several hours of time when you will be alone and not hurried. When the evening comes begin preparing at seven. An important guest is due in an hour, your long-awaited lover.

Draw a hot bath and relax in it. Treat yourself to a luxurious bath oil, or an after-bath scent. Give yourself a brief cold cream massage.

Arrange your room in your favorite way. Bring in some fresh flowers in a vase. Turn off some of the bright lights and replace them with softer candles. Be sure the bed is made just as you like it. Turn on some music. Do whatever you would do if your most exciting lover were to arrive any moment. What would you do to make yourself feel comfortable and relaxed? What would you do to your room in preparation? It is almost eight o'clock!

It is eight now. You are in your bedroom feeling fresh and ready. Your mysterious friend has arrived. The long-awaited lover is you!

Allow yourself to enjoy this illustrious guest and get to know her with all the attention you would give to another person. You know just how you want to be made love to. You know just how and where and when to touch yourself. Do it just the way you like. Talk to yourself. Experiment with new techniques. Give yourself all the time you want.

How did you feel when you realized you were to be your own illustrious guest? Did you want to continue with the experiment? If so, how did you feel? Did you get to know something new about your guest? How is this different from the way you usually treat yourself?

In a few days take some time to do the Outer Physical with yourself again. Notice any changes in your feelings about what you see.

Looking Back

In a few weeks, look over the rest of the body awareness exercises again. Which ones did you just read initially and not try? Notice any exercises which seem more interesting to you than they seemed the first time you read them. Which ones would you like to work with now that seemed uninteresting before? Have your feelings about yourself changed since you began reading and doing these exercises? If you have not tried any of the exercises, you still may find your attitudes about yourself are altered. Write them down in your journal. Try this throughout the rest of the book, looking over the sections periodically. Each time try only the exercises which interest or excite you.

Verbal Self-Awareness Techniques

Talking To Yourself

Some of the basic techniques of Gestalt Therapy have been helpful in my becoming aware of and changing my role concepts. By "role" I mean acting from a concept or image of how I think I should be rather than how I am. It's easy for me to see when someone else is playing a role — the good wife, the vamp, the prima donna, the intellectual — but harder to be aware of my own. Role playing in relationships with others can be a useful means of expressing different aspects of myself, or experimenting with new ways I want to be. The danger of playing roles is that often I forget that I'm acting. Without this self-consciousness I lose my power. I am no longer acting by choice. The exercises in this section are designed to increase your awareness of verbal roles and of how the roles affect your natural expression.

An exercise I use often is pillow talking. I like to do this exercise on the floor with two pillows. It can also be done sitting with two chairs.

Choose a time and room where you can be quiet and alone. Place two pillows on the floor (preferably large sturdy sofa pillows). Sit down on one pillow, facing the

other. Think of someone with whom you feel in conflict. Close your eyes and try to picture what this person looks like. Put her on the pillow opposite you. How would you feel if she were really sitting across from you? Let yourself go more into this feeling.

Now begin talking to her about how you feel towards her. Try to stay direct and with your feelings — for example: "I feel angry at you." "I feel cut off from you." "I feel sad." "I feel afraid." "I feel turned on." This is the tricky part of the exercise because it is easy to slip into intellectualizing and talking ideas, instead of staying with your feelings. If a Gestalt therapist were working with you she would be able to observe your process. When you started getting sidetracked or detached, she would point this out and bring your verbalization back to a direct feeling exchange. Working alone you'll need to watch out for sidetracking yourself. It takes some practice, but after awhile you will learn to sense the difference between what you feel like when you're being directly "feeling" and when you're being slightly removed and interpretive.

The basic format of the exercise is to speak your feelings from your pillow for awhile. Then get up and go sit on her pillow. Speak as though you are the other person and answer what you have just told her. Notice any ways you feel different playing the part of the person with whom you are in conflict. Notice if your voice changes. Then move back to your pillow and respond. Keep switching pillows and speaking from different personas until you feel satisfied with the exchange.

You can "talk to" a person with whom you have a current conflict, or you can talk to someone from long ago about whom you feel unresolved. During the conversation if you feel like doing something physical to the other person, do it to the pillow. Hug it or hit it. Pull it closer or push it away.

This exercise may sound superficial in writing, but it can be very powerful to do. If I am in conflict with someone but scared to confront them directly, pillow talking gives me the opportunity to express how I feel without risk. I can experiment with alternative ways of responding by playing different roles with the pillow. Often I discover that by changing my role, I can completely change the response of the other person and get rid of the conflict. After trying a new role out in private, I have more confidence to experiment with it with others.

There are also times when I don't want to confront the other person. I don't want to get closer to them, but I do want to release my own tensions connected with the conflict. I may not hit someone I'm angry with, but I sure feel better after I've released the tension in my arms and body by hitting a pillow, yelling at the pillow as though it were that person.

A frequent surprise in this exercise is to find yourself identifying with the person with whom you are in conflict! You may begin to understand their point of view more by playing their part. Or you may realize that their viewpoint also exists partly in you; *the reason you have the conflict with them often is that the issue is unresolved in yourself.*

Taking on the role of the other side of your conflict can put you in touch with parts of yourself you had formerly attributed only to your "enemy."

You can take the part of inanimate objects as well as people. Experiment with pillow talking to:

> your mother
> your current mate
> your boss
> your father
> your sister
> your house
> someone you are jealous of
> someone you feel afraid of
> someone you hate
> someone you love but are afraid to tell
> anyone you admire
> your femininity
> your sexuality

Feminine vs. Female

One role I catch myself slipping into often is the feminine role. To me this is a bullshit oppressive role for women because to most people being "feminine" means

54

being: sweet, good, polite, clean, pretty, small, skinny, soft-spoken, sentimental, illogical, tidy, indirect, dependent and subservient to authority, especially to male authority. The feminine role is closely tied to the role of the good girl. I had to ask myself, "What does being a good girl get me?" Most people don't really like or respect "the good girl." She's simply convenient and unthreatening. Does it get me what I think it does? Does it get me what I want? Is being feminine who I naturally am? Is being feminine the same as being female?

I began to realize a few years ago that the characteristics I was playing out in my feminine role didn't have any real power. I had only the illusion of power by trying to influence people indirectly. Somehow the men got all the successful adjectives: strong, independent, direct, big, in charge. I was training myself to play the role of helper, servant and second-in-command. I was being trained to see the relationships between myself and others, especially men, in terms of a hierarchy. I was participating in a power struggle and agreeing not to try.

It has been hard for me to let go fully of the approval I get for my feminine role. Too many people are put off by a direct, overtly powerful woman, even soft-spoken and powerful. When I give up my feminine role, I feel clear and communicative and more myself. Practicing some "bad girl" roles with pillows has been a crucial step in being able to let formerly censored parts of myself out with other people.

Try spending some time with yourself defining the kind of behavior which does or doesn't fit into your image of yourself as a woman. Do you feel it's "feminine" for you to get angry? To show your intelligence? To use your power directly? To be loud? To be sloppy? To be unfair? To compete with a man in his field? To ask for what you want? Then practice some of these taboo behaviors with your pillow. If you are always quiet, choose someone to "talk to" on the other pillow and say everything in a yell! Really exaggerate. Or put your quietness on the pillow and talk to it.

Loud: You are always so quiet and accomodating! Speak up! Make yourself heard! Don't be so afraid! Don't tone yourself down!

Quiet: But no one will like me if I'm loud and pushy. I may get my way but men won't be attracted to me. I'm not feminine when I'm loud and pushy. I'm threatening. I'm ugly. If I'm quiet people will want me around. I won't offend anyone.

... Keep going from here.

If you don't get angry very often, fantasize about what would happen if you did. Are you worried that another person will dislike you if you become angry? Are you worried that you'd criticize someone and be "wrong" in what you say? Are you afraid to make a mistake? Are you afraid to "lose control?"

Experiment with getting angry at a pillow. Let yourself come out with all the unreasonable things you may feel like saying but you usually censor because they're "unfair" or "unreasonable" or "unladylike." Explore your feelings of wanting to protect other people from certain "unreasonable" parts of yourself.

Tell the pillow, "I hate you." Repeat that sentence over and over. Experiment with beginning softly and then saying it gradually louder and louder. If anyone you know comes to mind as you do this, add their name to the sentence and experiment with what it feels like to say, "I hate you, Violet." "I hate you, mother." "I hate you, Zachary." Don't worry about whether you're being logical or fair. These are things you may not feel totally or may not want to say to the other person but which, if they exist in you, need to be expressed so that you can let go of harboring them. It takes effort to hold in these feelings. Once you let them out, even to a pillow, you will be freer to put your attention and energy in the present.

The concept of closing past unresolved conflicts is central to Gestalt Therapy. "Closing an unfinished gestalt" helps you live more in the here and now.

Cyndy Werthman Sheldon is a Gestalt and Family Therapist at the Gestalt Institute of San Francisco. She and I talked about her work and how she uses Gestalt.

Cyndy: Fritz Perls came from Europe to this country at a time in our society when people were very restricted in their behavior. He became aware of tension in their bodies (body armor) which was caused by their holding back behavior, feelings and experiences which they felt "should not" be expressed. The process of Gestalt introduced by Fritz is a way of

opening up and loosening a person's tight structure so that she can experience life more and more deeply. Two of the basic assumptions of Gestalt are: giving myself permission to feel anything; and taking responsibility for myself.

Me: Does Gestalt seem to work with all kinds of people?

Cyndy: Well, a lot of people think Gestalt is only useful in a group or workshop form, the way Fritz worked. There are many ways of using Gestalt. I like to alter the method to fit whomever I'm working with. That way Gestalt can be used with almost anybody. It seems that a lot of people now have broken out of their constricting behavior molds, so that the original Gestalt focus on letting go isn't, to me, the primary focus anymore. I feel many of the opening up methods have been misused, as an excuse to do whatever one impulsively feels like, without taking responsibility for oneself. That was, of course, not the original purpose!

Five years ago in my practice I was having many people act out their repressed feelings in the sessions. Now many of my clients come in and tell me all the "acting out" things they've done during the week, and I'm helping them integrate and structure.

Gestalt training was very good for me because I considered myself quite an uptight person until a few years ago. I needed permission to open up. However, once I opened up, I didn't feel I was well-grounded in myself, centered. I hadn't listened to my own inner places; instead I had adopted the "should be open" trip. I felt scattered and disassociated.

Me: So you'd say that Gestalt doesn't stress integration?

58

Cyndy: Well, I sure wasn't integrated! I'm not sure I want to blame that on Gestalt. The integration process is there in Gestalt, but I feel it's not stressed. The explosions and the breakthroughs are usually stressed. Training and working with Shirley Luthman of the Family Therapy Institute of Marin was really important to me in terms of getting in tune with my own internal structure and helping me integrate a lot of stuff I'd opened up in Gestalt.

Me: What kinds of clients do you work with?

Cyndy: I worked at a naval hospital for six years mostly with men. When I lived in Berkeley I worked with graduate students and people at transition points in their lives. Now I also work with families in Marin, a wealthy community, and with professional therapists. I also teach Gestalt and Family Therapy to psychiatrists, psychologists, social workers and lay therapists.

Me: I've been talking in my book about exercises to help resolve old conflicts. Do you want to talk about how that particularly relates to Gestalt?

Cyndy: Gestalt deals differently in some ways with a person's past than traditional therapy. Fritz saw his method as a growth model rather than a medical one; rather than looking at a person and deciding black and white whether she's sick or well and focusing on her symptoms, he looked at the person as a whole — whether or not she was congruent. When I say, "I hate you," does it show in my body

posture, voice, words, everything about me? (How many people do you know who smile when they tell you they don't like something?) Fritz's focus would be

59

on how to get a person aware of herself so she can get all the parts together and come out clear (congruent).

Me: Or if you feel ambivalent and not whole, at least be aware that you're mixed . . .

Cyndy: Right. Otherwise it's a "should" and a rule. A lot of people in the third world movement of therapy and around Esalen believe that the goal of therapy is to become open, warm and loving. I don't believe in that. The important thing is to have the choice.

There are times I don't feel open and I don't want to be. Or I don't want to be loving or show anger or be honest. All those things can be misused. But if I am not aware, I don't have a choice.

A lot of the process of therapy for me was learning how to be straight and direct with my feelings. I never knew how. I learned how; I learned some alternatives. I could be angry. I could be straight. I could be loving. I could show my fear. Then I had a choice. Up until then I could just make my messages known by playing devious games. Now, through awareness, I have a choice about *what* I want to express, *when* I want to express it, *how* and *if* I want to at all! That really is being responsible. That's the ultimate, to me, in my own personal development.

60

Me: How can the Gestalt technique of playing different roles help me become aware of my alternatives?

Cyndy: Most of us as kids have to play certain roles in our families in order to survive; the good girl; the disturbed one; or the Lucy Van Pelt. Most families are crazy enough that no one can be close. Everyone, therefore, has to adopt a role for protection. As we get older, the primary roles we play no longer help; we move towards closeness with another and our roles get in the way. We discover we don't know how to be intimate! Also, usually when we try letting go of our protective roles, we experience the fear we used to feel when we felt vulnerable as a kid. "If I really get close, daddy will ignore me, or my mommy will swallow me up!" Whatever. We're still protecting ourselves from a family situation that probably doesn't exist in the present.

Me: That goes back to finishing past business so you can come to the present fresh.

Cyndy: Yes. Letting go of roles means that a person is going to have to start nearly from scratch in some places to build a solid internal structure. To do this I have to allow myself to experience the fear, and to see that now I can handle this feeling as an adult. Once I know that, I don't "need" the protective roles (though I still may choose to use them sometimes). I don't "need" to play Lucy and keep people away. I'm more capable of closeness.

It's important to have the choice of when to let someone in and how close. I'm for playing roles in society. It's great. It's fun. But with someone you really want to get close to you have to be able to be open. Therefore, to finally answer your question — "talking" to pillows is a way of becoming more aware of your roles and of experimenting with letting out feelings that normally don't fit your image!

Rerun and Revise

Me: I remember an exercise you did with me that helped me a lot. You had me go back in my memory to a conflict incident and replay it as it happened. Then you had me replay it, but the second time imagine a new ending — to change my response to the incident. That gave me a chance to explore different alternatives to a key past incident. I remembered a time when my father was scolding me and I had felt very angry but kept quiet. When I reran the memory I fantasized myself letting my anger out, what his response would have been, and how I might have felt. It helped me see that I did have an alternative. I didn't have to clam up. I've used this technique since with other childhood memories. It gives me a sense of power over a period in my life when I felt I had none. It also gives me a perspective on my present attitudes. I can relate this to current situations where I hold my anger back when I really don't have to.

Role Awareness

Cyndy: Another exercise a person can do is to pay attention to when and where she plays what roles. How does the role seem useful? What would I lose by being direct? Could I experiment with another kind of behavior? You can try new roles with people you feel close to and don't mind taking risks with. Or with people you don't know at all and probably will never see again.

Me: Like sales clerks and taxi drivers.

Cyndy: If you're always nice to sales clerks, try being really bitchy and see what the difference is for you and what the response is. Or if you're always cold, try being really open. If you're always quiet, talk constantly.

Me: I've found that I depend on my eyes a lot for communication and that wearing dark glasses is a real struggle for me; I feel terribly out of touch. I think experimenting with different body habits is useful.

Cyndy: Yeah. Like if you smile all the time, try going through a whole day without smiling. Pay attention to when you would normally smile, what you use it for, and how it makes you feel not to do that.

Fantasy comes in here; I think it's very useful for people to fantasize different behavior patterns even if they don't want to act them out. I have a basic belief that inside of me is every conceivable feeling, place and experience. I may not be aware of it all yet, but it's in there. This attitude used to be scary; now it gives me permission to feel whatever I feel. It doesn't necessarily give me permission to act on my feelings, but it gives me a lot of freedom to fantasize. I can test out new behaviors and I can work through and resolve old conflicts.

Me: I want to talk about Gestalt exercises that deal with projection, exercises for getting in touch with where and how I transfer stuff about me onto other people.

62

Cyndy: Projection — that means if I say something about you, there's a good chance I'm really making a statement about myself. Test for this next time you make a statement about someone else by trying it on for yourself — "I know you're having an affair! Well, I'm having an affair." Try it next time you find yourself giving advice. Usually when I tell other people, they "should" do something, it applies to some degree to me.

Fritz used to say that Freud lived in the age of hysteria, and we live in the age of projection (paranoia). "If it weren't for the Communists — the Establishment, the Radicals, the unions, my parents — I'd be . . . ," etc., etc. It's a blame trip — "It's your fault." Projection is a way of my not taking responsibility for myself. All my energy is focused on the other person or group. A lot of Gestalt exercises focus on bringing projections to my awareness and then helping me take responsibility.

As long as I blame others I don't have to look at myself, or be aware of myself. I can just go on being a neurotic mixed-up blob filled with hostility for everyone else. Many people live like that. They give all their power away to those they blame, and feel power*less* as a result. "Being responsible for myself" sounds like a drag. That's because when people say that to me they usually mean being responsible to everyone else *but* myself. What I mean by being responsible to myself is getting into my own power — being alive!

Gestalting Your Dreams

Dreams can be deciphered on different levels: through Freudian analysis, Jungian interpretation, Gestalt role playing, or any other system of symbols that feels relevant to you. The Gestalt method of decoding dreams has been the most helpful to me on the level of my interaction with others. From the Gestalt point of view, everything that occurs in my dreams is a part of myself. When I have an unresolved conflict, my unconscious works at resolving it through dreaming — my body is constantly trying to close the gestalt.

Because each person's dream is unique to her, the Gestalt attitude is that you need to go below the layer of outside systems (which at best can only point to general themes) and find out what the dream means to you. To get at the personal power in a dream you must go past your daytime reasoning and into the emotional logic of your unconscious.

Your dream world is made up of issues from past and present conflicts. Each object in this world is a symbolic part of yourself which is segmented. "Working on" these segments through dreaming is an effort to connect the parts again harmoniously with your whole Gestalt. The basic format of Gestalting a dream is to play the role of each person and object in the dream, speaking as each would speak. Getting a dialogue going between these parts can result in them coming to an "understanding" and getting together again — or simply in bringing the deep issues in the dream to your conscious awareness.

If you want to Gestalt a dream pick one to work with whose "meaning" preferably isn't obvious to you, so that you haven't already decided what it "means" and can discover something new. At first choose a short dream, or isolate one part of a long dream which interests you. There will probably be a lot to work on in just one incident.

Sit on the floor or on a bed with two pillows. Close your eyes and tune in to how your body feels inside. Notice any parts which feel tense or particularly good. Where is your breathing?

Now go back and let yourself picture the dream in your mind. If in the dream you are in a room, "look around" at what the room is like. Are you standing or sitting? If you are outside notice your environment and what the weather is like. Really let yourself go into what you feel like in this place.

Now begin talking out loud, telling the story in the present tense. Telling your story this way will have more immediacy and impact for you than talking in the past tense. Start with statements about yourself and how you feel.

Me: I am standing at the edge of a big meadow. The meadow is filled with yellow grass and surrounded by huge pine trees. I feel excited and a little tense about entering the field. I am hesitating on the edge. I can feel the sun warm on my face and hands. I feel good but nervous and expectant."

If any part of what you say feels special or important to you as you talk, stay with that part awhile. Repeat the sentence that has the most emotional impact several times. "I feel nervous and expectant. I feel nervous and expectant." This will help you go more deeply into your feelings.

Now let yourself get into the action part of your dream. If there is another person with you, talk out loud about what she looks like and what you are doing in relation to her. If you are alone choose an object or a quality to talk to.

Me: I am noticing a particularly large and beautiful pine tree across the meadow from me and a little to my left. I feel in awe of how huge and old and beautiful it is.

Whatever your feelings are about the thing or person, tell them directly.

Me: Pine tree, I like you but I am a little afraid of your height. I envy you. I am looking at you and wishing I were as strong as you. You seem very stable and alive. You seem really in touch with the beautiful things that are happening in the meadow. You enjoy the sun and the breeze on you.

Now change pillows and sit on the one you've been talking to. Let yourself take on the mood of that thing or person. Begin talking out loud and answer what you have just said.

Pine: I am a huge and old pine. I have stood on the edge of this meadow for a thousand years and grown taller and taller. I used to be small and scrawny like you when I was young. I was nervous and expectant. I was easily blown by the wind. I was afraid I would break. I was afraid I would not last long enough to grow strong and tall. But I did. I wanted to and I just kept growing stronger. Now I stand here way up in the sky where the winds blow hard on my top branches and many things are happening along my middle branches and the sun shines on my bark. Far below my huge roots sink deep into the earth. I have dug my roots in so deep by now that I am not afraid of the hard winds blowing me. I enjoy them. I can just rest in my place and let things move me. I feel full and alive and at peace. I feel alive and at peace. I feel at peace.

Me: I think that's why I like you. I don't feel at peace now. I feel scared and anxious. I want to be alive and at peace and full like you. I want to feel strong. I want peace. I'm tired. I'm very tired of struggling and I want peace.

I made up this sample "dream" as I wrote. It is not a dream I had. It is a scene which I saw just now when I closed my eyes to think of an example to write. I didn't figure out the conversation beforehand. I wrote whatever came out as I "talked." The mood in that "dream" has a lot of feeling for me now. I can tell that it is related to something which happened to me today, to a conflict I have. I know, after having worked this way with my images, that any dream or image I have can be explored to uncover the feelings underneath being expressed through the image. Because I project my emotions and my world view into what I do and see, I can "talk" to anything or anybody in the dream to find out more about myself. I can use this technique outside of dreams also. I can "talk to" my car. Then act the role of my car or my cat or my clothes and answer to find out a lot about what these things mean to me.

These "conversations" may sound silly or superficial. However, doing them can be quite meaningful and powerful. It takes practice to stay with your feelings and to learn to recognize when something important is happening. I use this technique frequently to help me get more in touch with my conflicts at any time. Usually when a conflict lingers for me it is between what I think I *should* do and what I *want* to do. Many of my "shoulds" are so ingrained that I need to do an exercise like "talking" to help me get in touch with my deeper real feelings.

Something I have learned from this way of working is to trust my inner resources. I don't look outside of me for answers about my feelings. I feel better making decisions from this place. My interactions have a more real quality for me than they used to. I don't like feeling I am living out someone else's theory. When I do choose to act against my feelings I can stay aware of what I'm doing.

When you first start role playing your dreams, it may take awhile before the process has much emotional impact for you. You may feel silly talking like a pine tree! If you stick with it through this initial strangeness, gradually the mood of the dream will take over and the interaction will become meaningful. All of us are constantly feeling deep feelings inside and working on conflicts, but we choose only to focus on one level of what's happening within us. These Gestalt techniques are a way of changing levels when you want to.

Some more general attitudes to follow are:

Check in periodically to how you feel in your body during the session at moments when you go through a change in emotion, to see how you are reacting physically to the feelings.

The key to making the dialogue process valuable for insights into your deeper feelings is not to *think* before you speak — very hard to do! Try to respond immediately so you don't have any time to think about what you should say if you were that person. You will probably be surprised at how much of a mind of their own these parts you play have!

Try to move gradually from step to step to stay with the immediacy of your feelings and not jump ahead to something you think you're leading up to. You may be correct about what direction you're moving in, but if you jump there too quickly, you may miss some important foundation steps for the change.

Recognize that you are dealing with deep emotional feelings in yourself and often when you open up, you will feel vunerable and frightened; stay with those scared feelings awhile until you pass through them, and then the next feeling will flow naturally. Respect that you are doing something difficult and sensitive. Don't push.

Think of the process as an awareness tool, not "therapy to change yourself." You are simply exploring your own feelings and becoming more conscious.

Each time you finish talking a dream ask yourself what you censored, and notice what you avoided.

For a thorough and more detailed exploration of Gestalt, see Fritz Perls' books, including *Gestalt Therapy Verbatim* (Real People Press).

Dream Diary

Keeping a diary of your dreams in pictures and words is a good way of tuning in to what's going on for you at a deep emotional level. After several months, clear patterns emerge which you can see in your diary. When an important change occurs, you can look back over your dream diary and often see how you were dreaming about that change and related issues months before it surfaced in your actions. You can learn to recognize the steps along the way.

If you have trouble remembering your dreams, draw a simple picture in your book of the image you saw. Drawing or painting it helps bring this normally unconscious image into your waking consciousness.

Keep a notebook and pen beside your bed so you can write down the dream when you wake before you forget it.

Language, Size and Self-Image

When I was trying to think of a title for this book, I was struck by the fact that each time I used a word referring to a female person it lacked dignity or negated the power of the phrase. Add "women's" as an adjective to neutral nouns and you come out with a putdown.

Women's Work — house chores, of course. Men are out doing "man's work" where it counts. Women are home fretting and hoping they get their chores done before the master comes home.

Women's Pages — Men read the rest of the paper with news of business and the war. Women read two or three pages about what kind of party somebody had; Dear Abby tells her that if her husband plays around it's her fault for not keeping herself up.

Women's Magazines — Stuff about making quilts, meatloaf and Christmas tree ornaments.

Women's Books — a new category of books these days that contains tips to help ladies be less prim, walk more sexy and rebel against Daddy. A sort of blown up Dear Abby with four letter words. Women read "men's books" and are expected to get something out of them. Do men read "women's books?"

An enlightening awareness exercise can be to start paying attention to your own language and that of the people around you. Notice what words you choose to insult someone. Do you scold your child for being "a sissy" (that is, having girl-like qualities)? When you're really angry at someone, do you say "fuck you?" What does that imply about your attitude towards the sexual act? When you're disgusted do you mutter, "shit?" Do your bowel movements disgust you? When you're in a restaurant with another woman and the waiter asks, "What would you girls like?" — how do you feel? How would he feel if you asked him to "Get me some water, boy?" Do you think of your female friends as "girls?" How does it change your attitude towards them to start thinking of them as women?

Our roles and self image are strongly defined by the language we choose. Experiment with completing this sentence: "If I were a man, I would . . ." Fill in the blank several times in different ways. Pay attention to what qualities or activities you consider exclusively masculine. Now try filling in, "If I were a woman, I would . . ." How would you be different if you considered yourself a woman and not a little girl?

In Your Own Image

Now tune in to some of the ways you shaped your self-image. Sit down and write a list (starting from when you were very young) of all the decisions you can remember making about "how to be." I can remember several of those moments. For example, I remember the day I decided that getting angry and fighting was no good because either someone punished you or you hurt someone else's feelings. I decided that if people really loved each other they could work things out by talking reasonably and quietly. Now I can see how my interaction with others has been affected by that decision. I have used a great deal of energy holding in my anger. Making a "decision" list helped me become more aware of how many rules I have about how I act. Remembering how those rules got made gives me a chance to decide whether those old attitudes fit me in the present.

To get in touch with some of your family image patterns, try describing a parent or sibling's personality. Talk about their moods and especially about how each of them dealt with different kinds of emotions and situations.

"My brother is a distant person. He is very critical of others and of himself. He has a hard time relaxing with people but when he does he is charming and has a good sense of humor. When he's angry he doesn't let it out. He gets stern and smoulders. I feel that because of this his feelings don't change and he holds onto grudges."

Now keep the description the same but substitute "I" or your name for "mother" or "father." When you do this with your own name, does the description fit you?

The Little Woman

In ancient Tahiti the queens were encouraged to be fat. Being big was a sign of health and power. In our culture women are rewarded for being small (thin, skinny, svelte, petite). And without muscles. Weak. It is still a matter of social awkwardness if the woman in a couple is taller than the man. The symbolic hierarchy is upset.

The following exercise gives you a chance to experiment with feelings about your size. It is a powerful exercise and I use it often. Once when I was feeling particularly aware of a habit of constricting myself physically and emotionally, Cynthia Werthman Sheldon showed it to me. When I am into that place I feel crowded and defensive. I want to define my boundaries because someone else, by overstepping them, is threatening to me.

The basic idea of the exercise is to fantasize yourself growing and shrinking, like Alice with her mushrooms, and to notice how you feel being different sizes. Be sitting. Close your eyes. Go inside and tune in to how your body feels now. Do you get a general sense of pulling in or of expanding? Are there particular parts in your body which feel more constricted or more open than others? Where can you feel your breathing?

Now imagine you are getting slightly thinner and smaller. How does that feel? Imagine that someone you are close to is in the room. They are now larger than you.

Let yourself "shrink" even more until you are very tiny compared to that person. How do you feel in relation to them? Imagine that you are tiny and that the other person in the room is your father. How do you feel in relation to his bigness? Talk out loud and tell him how you feel. Be detailed.

"Dad, you are really big and I am very small. I don't like your being so big in relation to me. I feel scared of you. I don't feel powerful enough. I want to be big too so I can be equal to you and you can't push me around. You are high up and very far away from me. You make me sad and lonely. Maybe you could get smaller so we could talk together. Would you try to get smaller now to reach me? I would like to be close to you."

Now imagine that you have the power to expand yourself, so that you are proportionately growing broader and taller. Pay attention to your attitude toward your father as you get larger. At which size do you feel most comfortable with him? Is it when you are tiny; when you are nearly as large as he; when you two are equal in size; or when you are bigger than he? Keep expanding and growing.

Let yourself blow up like a balloon so that you are huge in the room and your father is proportionately very tiny. How do you feel now? Talk to him each time you change to a different size, and tell him how you feel about your relationship.

Do this same exercise imagining you are with your husband or mate. Pay attention to the size at which you feel most comfortable with them. Are you really this size in relation to them? Or do you alter your space to "get along?"

This is an exercise which can be very useful when you are with other people and feeling tense or insecure. The particular sensation I have when I feel tense is that I am pulling in to a core place inside my body and using my skin as a boundary shield between "myself" inside and the threat on the outside. When I become aware of what I'm doing, I relax my muscles, breathe deeper in my abdomen and imagine that I am growing slightly bigger.

Sometimes I go one step further. I imagine that I can project a kind of invisible aura from inside myself which becomes my protective boundary instead of my skin. The feeling is that I have an aura of energy all around my body and no one can come inside that aura unless I want them to. This allows me to protect my own space and also keep relaxed in my muscles; I don't need to use tight muscles as my shield.

Talking From Different Body Parts

This exercise is a Gestalt variation of the Outer Physical. Instead of saying how you feel *about* different parts of your body, let each body part speak for itself. You may be surprised to find that each part has a mind of its own.

The more you explore your body the more you will find that your whole body is a brain. There are different memories and attitudes stored in the nerves and tissues all over your body. If you have an accident and bruise your right leg, that leg "remembers" — the reaction to the trauma remains in your leg and the nerves keep sending out protection messages about that part, in the form of tension which becomes the "attitude" of that part. You will find yourself unconsciously being cautious about a previously injured body part long after the injury has healed. Your body "remembers" pleasure as well as pain, or any other emotion. This exercise gives you a way of finding out what each part of your body thinks.

Be sitting. Close your eyes. Go inside and tune in to how you are feeling. Without changing them, notice the positions of your right and left arms. Are they touching each other or apart? Does one feel more relaxed and loose than the other? How does each hand feel?

Now begin talking out loud as though you are your right hand talking to the left hand. Speak in the first person and call the left hand "Left Hand." Think of yourself as "Right Hand." Let the right hand describe itself to the left hand. Be detailed! Talk about whether or not you, Right Hand, feel strong or weak or numb or sensitive or nervous. Talk about how you feel in relation to Left Hand. How do you, Right Hand, see Left Hand? Is Left Hand still and weak or more alive? Do you like how Left Hand is? Do you wish Left Hand were different? If so, make a demand. "Left Hand, I want you to be more assertive. You're too still and quiet."

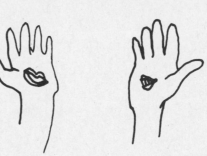

As you play these two roles let your hands interact physically too. Do they want to touch or gesture at each other?

Now be Left Hand. Answer Right Hand's comments and demands. "I admire you. I wish I could be more like you but I'm scared. I feel far away from you. When I reach out and gesture I feel as though someone is going to hit me."

Now switch to Right Hand and answer the Left. Keep switching back and forth until you get a sense of dialogue and until you feel satisfied with the exchange. Try to stay with your spontaneous feelings. Don't think about what you *think* your hands would say. Let them do the talking. They have a lot to tell you.

You can do this kind of role playing dialogue between any two body parts. Some interesting conversations might be between: you legs and the rest of your body; your eyes and your feet; your mouth and your stomach; your torso and your pelvis; your genitals and your brain.

There are two major body divisions which can be important to explore in this way; your right side and your left side; your upper and lower halves (that is, above and below your waist). The symbolism for these sections has many exceptions, but does emphasize some general associations which I have found relevant.

Symbolically the right side is concerned with aggression, with the outside world, with action and with reaching out. The left side seems to be concerned with the unconscious, with the inner life, with more passive, creative acts, and with receptivity. The upper and lower halves of the body have other patterns. Above the waist is conscious action, daytime, and the intellectual brain. Below the waist is the pelvic bowl of the unconscious — deep feelings, night and "irrational" emotions. Your body is separated at the waist into reason and passion, sky and earth, up and down. Or in some cultures, Heaven and Hell! This symbolism is prevalent in many diverse cultures. The ideal is to achieve balance between the parts; to overemphasize either half is to disrupt your harmony. Balanced in between Heaven and Hell is earth; to be "down to earth" is to be centered in your being, to be grounded, to balance the yin and the yang in yourself.

Good Medicine

We are taught that sickness is caused by germs which float through the air and invade our bodies from the outside; the cure comes from outside us too, in the form of medication, pills and operations, etc. This attitude toward disease leads me to ignore messages from within.

If I listen to my body messages I learn that many ailments such as headaches and stomachaches are manifestations of tension. Try viewing your ailment as a valuable body message. If your mechanicsm is to internalize frustration rather than express it, it's likely that you'll develop recurring ailments from the strain these habits put on your body. Colitis is caused by chronic tension in the lower abdomen. Ulcers, hemorrhoids and other diseases of the digestive tract are the result of tension too. I usually get the flu when I don't want to work (or do whatever I'm doing) but feel guilty about stopping without an excuse.

When you do get sick, do you usually get a cold, a headache, a stomachache, or a backache? Notice which area of your body usually "gets sick." Which part is your "target organ," the one that breaks down again and again? You probably have several.

Also pay attention to what service your particular ailment performs. When you get sick, do you stop everything and go to bed? Did you need to rest anyway? How do you feel about taking care of yourself? If you start listening to your body messages, you can learn to understand some sickness as a functional state you create in yourself.

Tension illnesses are caused and maintained by directing your feelings inward instead of out toward the person or situation to which you were initially responding. You need to get in touch with the situations to which you respond overtly and those in which you internalize your real feelings. We are taught that the way to make a feeling "go away" is to pull it inside. I've found that it is just the opposite. When I keep my feelings inside, they don't disappear no matter how I try to ignore them. They remain and keep pushing to come out. If I don't let them out directly, they come out indirectly or in an unrelated situation. Supressed anger often comes out as resentment. You may yell at your children when you're really mad at your boss.

There is a fine book out now called *The Well Body Book,* by Hal Bennett and Dr. Mike Samuels. The book deals in detail with ways of becoming more tuned in to and in control of your health. One of the basic ideas of the book is that we need to get rid of the expert model, to quit thinking of ourselves as "patients" going to the doctor "expert" to get the answer and cure. In that relationship we transfer our healing power to the doctor. When we want to "get well" we do. In reality we can cure ourselves often.

This attitude is particularly relevant to your sense of yourself. Health is a major area where you give away your power.

Relating to Your Doctor

Preventive medicine is virtually unknown in America. Have you ever been to a doctor who told you how to take care of your body? All the doctors I've dealt with have acted as though my body is too mysterious and too complicated for anyone but an M.D. to understand. In China you pay your doctor to teach you how to take care of yourself; when you are sick you don't pay him because he's not doing his job!

You can begin to reclaim your body from your doctor. Spend some time with yourself tuning in to how you feel about your body, your health, and your doctor. Do you enjoy going to your doctor? Is your doctor a man? Is he condescending to you? Is he too busy? Does he tell you what he's doing to you and why? Have you found that the treatments help you get better and stay healthy? How would you feel about going to a woman doctor? Do you know of any women doctors?

Next time you feel you need to go to your doctor for something, ask for a complete explanation of everything he does to you. Ask him about preventive steps you can take at home. If he prescribes a drug, have the nurse write down what it is composed of. If you go to buy a brand-name drug, ask your pharmacist about the non-brand name version. Almost every pharmacist carries two forms of each drug: brand name and generic. They are often the same except the brand name costs about three times more than the generic. The *New Handbook of Prescription Drugs* (Vintage, paper) tells in detail exactly what's in every drug. Take it to your doctor and when he prescribes a drug you can look it up in the handbook and ask him to prescribe the generic form instead. Or get a medical student to buy you a *Physicians Desk Reference* from a medical school bookstore and look it up. Every drug has side effects which your doctor doesn't mention. The PDR lists them. Make him tell you what they are before you accept the prescription. It is illegal for a pharmacist to tell you the comparative prices of the different drugs which fill your prescription — which means you are forced to take whatever your doctor prescribes — but a doctor has immediate telephone access to this information. Ask him to call your pharmacist and find the cheapest prescription for you.

It is time to begin listening to our own feelings, to let them be an authority on our own health.

Pain

We think of ourselves as more fragile than we really are. This attitude is particularly strong in situations involving pain. We go to great lengths to deaden uncomfortable feelings. Pain-killing drugs decrease sensitivity in the entire body, killing pleasure as well as pain. Oriental medical theories of sickness and health offer some practical alternatives; good health is thought to be caused by the state of relaxation and the balance of energy in the body. Many Oriental systems attribute pain to tension and constriction in the tissues and blockage of the life energy flow. Pain is un-health! Most Oriental body treatments train the client to go into her pain to release it rather than avoid it. It creates tension and takes energy to avoid feeling pain. In Polarity Therapy, Shiatsu, acupuncture and other Oriental pressure point therapies, the painful spot is stimulated. (In Western medicine, this same spot might be anesthetized.) The client is told to focus her attention on this sore area and relax it while it is being massaged.

You can use this technique in a simple but very effective way to release pain in your own body. Here's how.

Explore your body for any sore or painful areas. A good way to do this is to run your hand slowly over your body pressing gently as you go. If you have an injury which has had time to heal its bruises you can work on it, or on any place which feels tense or sore. The tightness and soreness stays because the tissue is still reacting to and contracting against the original injury. In the tissue the fear of being hurt remains.

Do not work directly on nerve centers, blood vessels or soft tissues such as the breasts. Don't work on lymph nodes. Unless you know anatomy well, stay on muscles and tendons. When you find a sore spot on a muscle, massage it with your fingertips. Press on the area firmly and move your fingertips with the grain of the muscle. Your pressure should be to the point of soreness but not pain. It is very important to apply pressure *gradually*. Begin lightly and increase your pressure as you become accustomed to being touched there. Jabbing or poking irritates the area more and the tissue will contract against the surprise. With practice you will get the feeling that your fingertips are having a dialogue with the tight spot. As you massage, imagine you can "send your breath" to the area, "exhaling" out through the sore spot. As the area grows accustomed to being touched again, the muscles relax and you can press in deeper. With practice you will learn to feel subtle changes in the tone of a muscle. You can feel it soften under your fingers.

Keep working this way through layers of tension. Press and massage the spot some each day and gradually the soreness will disappear. When we try to avoid pain, it either takes a long time to disappear, or it remains in our bodies. Deep massage is a way to free yourself of outdated physical fear and pain. After any surgery, accident or stress, trauma remains in the muscles. Remember this technique next time you bump your head, stub your toe, or have any small accident.

It is especially important to pay attention to the remaining tension after "female" operations — abortion, hysterectomy or childbirth. Tension remains in the muscles of your pelvis which could be "massaged" away. Use the deep massage method described above on the muscles of your hips, abdomen, thighs, perineum and vagina.

Food Awareness

I am including food in the medical section because what you eat is so directly connected to your health. Food is a powerful medicine. Food is a substance which you ingest and which becomes you. It becomes your tissue. Eating is a way you keep yourself alive; and what you eat determines to a great extent the state of your aliveness.

There are countless books on different theories of diet. One which I have found extremely useful is *Composition and Facts About Food* by Ford Heritage. (Write to him in Woodstown, New Jersey. The book is $5.50.) Here I want to deal with food as emotional medicine, and about women's special relationship to food.

Because of social pressure to be thin, most women eat poorly. I grew up feeling that the ideal state would be to not have to eat anything at all, because whatever I did eat seemed to make me "fat."

At the Pearson Institute in Berkeley, California, Lillian Pearson and Dr. Leonard Pearson have developed new ways of approaching a person's relationship to food. I tried out the Pearson's method and my attitude and eating patterns completely changed! A lot of tension is gone from my daily life.

The first step is to develop sensitive food awareness. The next step is to give yourself guilt-free permission to eat whatever you want, with no forbidden foods! When I can allow myself total freedom to eat, many of my cravings disappear. I don't have to "stock up" and overeat because I won't be quarantining those "forbidden" foods tomorrow. The energy I formerly used for struggling with food is free for other places in my life.

The Pearson's have had much success with their method for people who want to lose weight or deal with any other problem they have with food. Their food therapy focuses on the varied emotional connections their clients have with food. The traditional medical view has been to assume people with eating problems simply need to learn more self-control. The Pearsons believe that this emphasis on self-control is psychologically naive and rarely works in the long run. Controlling yourself usually means being in a state of perpetual warfare with yourself, with a tremendous amount of energy being drained. And it often means a weight chart that looks like a roller coaster. Studies done with children who are allowed to eat exactly as they wish show that after a short period of imbalances the children all choose a well-rounded, healthy diet with no resulting obesity. The Pearsons try to help people find their individualized and liberated style of eating, with no diets forever. They've found that this means re-educating people in how to view eating and food. And in some instances it also means having to delve into psychological dynamics. For instance, is there some advantage to you in remaining fat? Is there anything you fear about being thin?

The Pearsons have written a book which presents their work in detail: *The Psychologists' Eat Anything Diet* (Peter Wyden Press, cloth). You can write to them for information at: The Pearson Institute, 1600 LaLoma Avenue, Berkeley, California 94709.

Lillian Pearson and I did several food awareness exercises together, and talked about her work.

Lillian: I am a psychiatric social worker in private practice. I see women and men with problems that have nothing to do with food or eating, but I am getting more and more involved with the topic of women and food, how it's related to their bodies, and how women view themselves. Len and I formed the Pearson Institute just for dealing with eating problems and food awareness.

Me: I'd like to talk about dieting; that seems to be most people's response to their eating problems.

Lillian: Yes, many people diet. But dieting rarely works in the long run. The UC Medical Center reports that 98% of dieters regain their weight.

Me: It seems to me that women are often desperate about their weight and dieting.

Lillian: Most of our clients at the Institute are women. I have several theories about causes of women having a weight problem. One of them is that women are trained to the role of putting other's needs before their own, and if a woman is always giving to others, she has to eventually give to herself in some way or become emotionally depleted. Often the only channel left for giving to oneself is through food.

I think another reason that women have weight problems is that women view themselves as objects — they have to have a "perfect" figure, and that starts a whole cycle of dieting, deprivation, guilt, and then overeating.

We've had a number of obese women in our workshops who told us the only times in their lives they've lost weight easily and naturally has been during pregnancy, when they were allowed to eat 'crazy' and go with their cravings. We sometimes recommend to women that they eat as if they were pregnant!

Along these lines, another thing that happens with women is that they find themselves living boring lives. There's shopping and taking care of the children and being housekeeper. Or maybe having an unchallenging job, such as a clerk or secretary. What some women experience as wanting to munch and nibble throughout the day is boredom. It's a feeling that has to be delved into deeper. Usually I find that under the boredom is despair. How do you feel about living a boring life? How does it feel to have each day go by without meaning or excitement or aliveness? I think especially women end up living boring lives, and blaming themselves for not being happier. When a child complains of boredom we usually feel no sympathy and tell the child to "Go find something to do;" but the woman has plenty to do! It's the boredom of living a life for others — even those you love — that can lead to a very real and justifiable sense of despair because of the lack of fuller living for one's self.

In general, when people are on diets, they usually feel as though they're in a jail, and then when they go off the diet they feel as if they are on parole. The diet becomes like a prison that everyone has to break out of. Once out, they go on binges or they eat things that they may not even want because they think "I'll never do this again, just this one more time — on Monday, I'll go back on my diet, forever." They're on that diet cycle of losing and gaining. One of the consequences people tell us is that they've grown fat eating the foods they hate! They have to eat a lot, not only for pleasure but because they're out of jail.

Telling yourself you can't have something often makes you lose perspective on what you do want. The more you deprive yourself, the more dissatisfied with yourself you are and the more that causes binging, or overeating in some way, all of which puts the person out of tune with what they really want. They're reacting rather than eating.

Me: I often feel when I deny myself something that I go on binges to store up for the famine.

Lillian: Yes . . . but you can't store up sensation, which is why you have to come off the diet again fairly soon and keep repeating the cycle.

Me: How do you approach these feelings in workshops?

Lillian: We try to help people learn to differentiate their hunger feelings, and what different things will satisfy them. Hunger can be a lot of different things connected with a lot of different sensations in the body. We met someone in our workshop who, for instance, felt hunger between her shoulder blades. Most people feel hunger in their teeth or jaw or tongue or in their stomach. Usually when I feel hungry I experience a craving in my throat. We've often found that what a person craves can be a specific food or it can be a body sensation. This is where eating awareness exercises can be really helpful because they pinpoint for you what it is that would satisfy you and how you can pleasure yourself best.

What Do I Want?

Me: On my own I could ask myself when I feel hungry, "What do I want to do? Do I want to get this feeling in my throat to go away or do I really want a cream puff?"

Lillian: Do I want something soft and squishy? Or do I want something warm and sweet in my throat that will feel good? Or do I want maybe something bulky that will give me a full feeling in my stomach? Do I want something in my mouth that will give me a full mouth sensation? Maybe I want something that will exercise my jaws, to really bite into something. We've found that going into any psyching yourself out, historical stuff, like, "My mother weaned me too soon, and, therefore, I have cravings in my teeth," isn't very helpful! The important thing is "What do I want right now?"

Me: I think in our culture any time that you feel you need something from the outside, often it's translated as hunger; people aren't allowed to need.

Lillian: Or to pleasure themselves. This kind of conflict comes up for people under tension or a great deal of stress, in an emotional crisis, or studying for an exam. They need to relieve some of their tension, but they feel guilty about using food this way. If you realize this is legitimate, then you can focus on what would really efficiently satisfy you.

I know while working on my book, which I feel is like studying for an exam in college days, I found that I needed a very distinct spicy food. If it's bland it doesn't give me enough of a sensation. My favorite snack food, that I'm going down to the store for as soon as we stop talking, is raw zuchini tossed with herbal spicy French salad dressing. Mixed together — the salad dressing is really sharp and spicy and the raw zuchini is crunchy — it's a perfect thing that I love and leave out on the kitchen counter to pleasure and "reward" myself while I do difficult work.

Me: I decided that I was probably going to get heavier while doing this book because I get so little exercise. I'm not going to fight it because that would just mean more tension.

Lillian: Right. I'm sure I've gained a few pounds too, but they will go away once I'm out of this situation.

We don't believe in people weighing themselves, by the way. It's a bad trip to put yourself on. The scale can become a morning indictment. You can set the sentence for your whole day. It will upset you and condemn you.

What Do I Need?

The issue of how to satisfy your body needs and how you feel about having such needs is particularly relevant to women. Personal needs often get translated into a food hunger. If you feel a need, check it out. Ask yourself what possible kinds of things you could do that would make you feel good. Maybe it's a hot bath. Maybe you're tired and you think you'll get energy from eating chocolate. Maybe you'd really feel better if you lay down and took a nap. Or maybe you're angry and need to yell. Or sad and you need to cry. If you can go with the feeling and express it directly, that's fine.

It's important too not to guilt-trip yourself about always having to figure it out. Not everyone can cry all the time, and often you don't know what you're feeling. So if you can stay in touch and allow yourself to effectively and efficiently give yourself the sensation you want with food, that can often be a clue to what you're feeling, too.

I've noticed, for instance, that whenever Len is going for a chocolate milkshake he's under a lot of tension. He may not even know it, but he goes for a chocolate milkshake.

I have a funny habit of wanting to gargle with martinis. And I know that when I'm doing this my throat is constricting itself because I'm really under a lot of tension and I want to do something with my throat which feels squeezed in, as if I can't let enough air through. Sometimes if I notice I want to gargle that martini, I know that I'm probably feeling tense.

Humming And Beckoning

Me: What is the difference between what you call "humming" and "beckoning" foods?

Lillian: Len and I have categorized food into two kinds: ones which you want because of an inner craving, and ones which you want because the stimulation comes from the outside. Much eating is a craving for a sensation. It can also be a craving for a specific food. That can be tied into security feelings associated with food. It can also be tied into reward food. People may crave sweets for reward foods or comfort foods. Or they can be security foods such as holiday foods, turkey with stuffing, breads, ethnic foods.

We say that specific foods which you crave "hum to you;" it's like something that's coming from within, a tune that you can't get out of your head. And you can do a lot of eating *around* the food that's humming to you if you don't allow yourself to get it. For instance, we had one man who really craved pilaf, but because it's fried in butter and it's high-calorie and high in carbohydrates he never let himself eat it. He would eat a whole chicken and a lot of other food in an attempt to satisfy that very specific hunger. He discovered he didn't need much pilaf once he let himself get it. That was a food that hummed to him really loud.

"Beckoning" foods don't come from inside. You usually see them and then you want them. You're walking down a street and you see something in the bakery window. You can eat these foods and they will taste good, but they're not really satisfying a hunger or a craving. They're just there. Beckoning foods are foods that you can overeat, especially if you're ignoring what you really want, and going with what's beckoning instead of what's humming. You don't feel deprived if you pass them up. It may take an effort not to eat them when they're available, but afterwards you don't think about it.

I think it's important to keep track of the difference. The humming food is what you'll really be pleasured on, satisfied, and you'll feel deprived of if you don't eat it. It's food that comes from an inner need. With food that "hums" you usually know you crave it without seeing it.

Me: Seems as though it would be easy to start unconsciously "dieting" again by forbidding yourself the beckoning foods and saying "only humming foods are okay." That would put you back in the old framework.

Lillian: That's true, in a way. But you don't feel deprived if you do without the beckoning foods. The trick is to make distinctions, but not to make prohibitions.

The minute you classify any food as forbidden, then you also have deprivation and rebellion. "Nobody is going to tell me what to do, not even myself!"

The focus is not a negative one of cutting out something but a positive focus on "What do I really want and what will give me pleasure? How do I want to eat? And when? And with whom, if anyone?"

Eventually you get to the place where you're eating what you really want and need. And not eating what you don't want. Much of people's eating is a waste of sensation. Can you really taste much at a party when you're busy talking? Have you ever had people over for dinner and then eaten a second dinner after they left — because you can't remember having eaten?

Me: What are some ways I could develop my food awareness?

Lillian: It's complex. One way to start is to eat only *when* and *what* you really want. Don't eat just because it's "mealtime." Spend a moment before you eat tuning in to how your body feels and if you're really hungry. If you eat dinner to get to the dessert, forget the dinner and have the dessert first.

Food Fantasies

Let yourself go into fantasies about things you'd like to do with food other than eat it. Try out some of your fantasies.

An exercise we do in our workshops is to imagine you are alone for as long as you wish with all the foods you want to eat! Fantasize yourself doing anything you want there. Many people have sensual and sexual associations with food that they need to become more aware of. And then apply the awareness.

Get as much sensual satisfaction from the process of eating as possible. Eat with your fingers. Try chewing food for the sensation and then spitting it out. (We often swallow things we only want to chew.) Move your mouth any way you'd like as you chew. Play with your food. Chew with your front teeth only. Try using a straw. Let some foods, such as cheese, melt against the roof of your mouth.

I also like to go over cookbooks in terms of what kinds of sensations, what kind of textures, what kinds of taste qualities certain recipes will give me. It's a different way of reading a cookbook.

Me: What happens if you have a lot of things humming to you? Or if you're confused between what's humming and what's beckoning?

Lillian: If a lot of things seem to be humming all at once, ask yourself, "Will I feel cheated if I don't have this?" I was in a restaurant the other day and I couldn't decide which of three things I wanted to eat, so I asked myself that question for each thing. "Will I feel cheated afterward if I don't have the eggs, the club sandwich, or the avocado and crab salad?" I knew that I would definitely feel still hungry and cheated afterwards if I didn't have the eggs and hash brown potatoes. That's what I had and it was really fine. It was just perfect!

Me: Let's talk about some problems particular to women.

Lillian: I do think women are particularly burdened with this hang-up about having a "perfect figure." It's interesting to me that the term "figure" only applies to women. Men don't have figures. They have bodies. Women are taught to look upon themselves as objects. My 12-year old daughter's friends are already on diets and many of them are not heavy, but their parents are already telling them that their hips are too large and their stomachs stick out. They're already being expected to fit into a mold.

Me: That pressure to look alike really undermines your sense of identity.

Lillian: And self-acceptance! And women treat each other this way. Nowadays it seems that women talk to each other a great deal about dieting and losing weight. There are dozens and dozens of women's diet organizations where women relate to each other only in this way. It is often the most significant relationship that a woman is having with other women. I feel that this is sad because relating to other women on the basis of diets and weight is often relating with envy, competition, jealousy, smugness, and superiority. It depends on whether you're losing or gaining, whether you're fatter or thinner. It all too often interferes with women developing close relationships with one another.

Me: I should think these attitudes toward food and your body would also carry over into relationships with men.

Lillian: They do. Some women hate themselves for eating, reject their bodies because of imperfections, and drain their energy into trying to diet. It often does interfere with closeness and intimacy with men. And this can shape a woman's whole attitude about pleasuring herself as well. If you feel you can't pleasure yourself with food, this is such a basic function that it carries over into your whole attitude toward your body. You constrict your responsiveness. When you let go of your central food inhibitions and allow yourself to pleasure yourself with food, it can affect your entire style of living, your whole sense of what you "deserve."

There was a woman in her late twenties in our Chicago workshop who used to love nuts. But she'd put them in the trunk of her car so she wouldn't be tempted to eat them. She'd be driving on the expressway and every once in awhile she'd have to

or go out to dinner more often, or just go out for dessert. Sometimes an atmosphere is craved. Or, as I mentioned earlier, other body sensations.

You also may feel that nothing hums to you and you don't know what you want. If you don't know what you want to eat, the answer is probably, "Nothing right now." With freedom from guilt and slavish dieting comes freedom from the compulsion to overeat. I've also found that from the freedom to eat comes the freedom to not eat when you're not hungry, and that's an important freedom to have. You need to free yourself from guilt and stop battling yourself about diet, forever.

Me: What you're talking about is a completely different mentality from a "diet." You're talking about how to do something that will last for your whole life. I think people might get discouraged if initially they gain weight when they eat what they want to, unless they have a sense that ultimately it will work.

Lillian: Yes, there has to be trust. However, it's surprising that few people do gain weight. If a person does gain a lot of weight then they're doing something that has nothing to do with what we're talking about. They may be surrendering to food, tuning out. If you're aware of sensations and sensitive to your body and food tastes, then being over-full becomes unpleasant. It's a contradiction to say you're pleasuring yourself with food if you're stuffing and feeling too full. Most of the people we work

with need rethinking about how they relate to food. For those who find themselves surrendering to food, giving in almost, then I have to explore with them other things. They may have reasons for wanting to stay fat. All behavior has meaning and even though a person may hate being fat, there's sometimes a good reason for it, too. Or there can be psychological factors blocking that person, something they're not aware of, that keeps them in a diet rut. But for most people, and in general, pleasuring yourself with food doesn't mean surrendering to food. I'm talking about having a love affair with food — not raping it! It's important not to get these two mixed up.

In our workshops, and in our book, we describe a number of other exercises for becoming more sensitive and aware of food. These new ideas can be very hard work for some people because you have to center on yourself. You need to give time and energy to learning about yourself and how you relate to food. The first step is to give yourself permission to pleasure yourself, including pleasuring yourself with food.

Free Health Care for Women by Women: The Berkeley Women's Health Collective
by Julia McKinney Barfoot

I talked with Julia McKinney Barfoot of the Berkeley Women's Health Collective about the collective's efforts to pioneer a new kind of medical treatment for women. She wrote this article about her involvement with the clinic.

Julia

My collective experience has helped me learn to function well in large groups, to accept my body and my whole self as I naturally am, and to care for myself and other women knowledgeably. Because of the need for women working all night in a busy clinic to know self-defense, many of us started taking karate classes. In July, 1970, I began studying Kung Fu (Chinese Karate) which I still practice, and which has helped me learn the discipline and control necessary for a strong healthy body. Working and sharing with other women, watching us grow strong in body and mind, developing self-confidence in ourselves and our work has changed me.

This is my perspective of the collective after active involvement from its beginning. For the last six months, I have been inactive except for occasionally leading workshops, as I am now interested in doing community health work. It has been good to put together thoughts from these two years of learning. I want to thank all the women in the collective who made this possible and who gave me invaluable criticism in the writing.

Who We Are and Why We Came Together

Feeling great frustration about the lack of good, humane, health care for ourselves and other women, a group of about thirty Berkeley women came together in November, 1970, to organize a women's health collective. With only one exception, we were originally white, middle-class women ranging mainly in age from nineteen to thirty. This composition has stayed the same, even though at times the collective has

WOMEN'S CLINIC
IS ON WEDNESDAYS
from 1pm-11pm
at the Berkeley Free Clinic
2339 Durant (at Dana)

been as large as one hundred and twenty women. Today about fifty women are actively involved.

Basic to our philosophy and our coming together is the concept of health care as a right of all people (rather than as a priviledge) on a free or at least a pay-as-you-can basis. On the wall near our pharmacy is a poster reading "Drugs for Health — not Wealth." Our collective focus is on the demystification of medicine, the deprofessionalism of doctors, and the promotion of preventive medicine. We want not only to reclaim our bodies emotionally from "experts," but also to learn technically how to care for ourselves. We want to be treated individually with respect; to be told exactly what our illnesses are, what the treatment is, what medicine we are being given and what it is doing to us. We want to be related to as whole persons, psychologically as well as physically.

Health care is the second largest industry in this country in terms of profits. Drug companies (usually owned by doctors) fill the market with frequently untested, dangerous products creating a new category of illness called iatrogenic disease, or disease caused by reactions to drugs, for which 1,500,000 people are treated a year. Another example of drug company's irresponsibility is their promotion of vaginal sprays which are unnecessary and harmful, causing infections and skin irritation.

Another large industry we must deal with is the food industry. Eating well is of major importance in maintaining good health and strong bodies. Many people never make the connection between what we eat and how we feel.

All of us had had humiliating and unsatisfactory experiences with the medical profession. We realized that if our needs were going to be met, we would have to meet them ourselves. Self-reliance was our goal.

Collectivism

Other than the orientation to women and to medical care, we were intentionally undefined. We wanted what we became to develop from our group experience. We are constantly in process, constantly evolving. We felt collective problems (social ills) should be dealt with in a collective manner, by full participation of every person offering ideas, making criticisms, sharing information, responsibility and work. We worked on a system of job rotation. We were anti-hierarchical (there was not a president or even a chair-woman during the first six months), and we discouraged irresponsible, long-term "leadership" in order to create a supportive atmosphere for women who hadn't yet learned to speak in groups.

We learned about collective medicine from reading Joshua Horn's book *Away with All Pests,* which describes the Chinese collective medical system. We spoke with him personally at a collective potluck. The Chinese have trained paramedics (called "barefoot doctors"), have mass innoculations, and most significantly have completely eliminated venereal disease (now a United States epidemic). We modeled our training on the paramedic system — we trained ourselves by organizing classes and "apprenticing" ourselves to other trained people. Then we trained other women. There are a few medical schools, such as Denver and Stanford, where you can train as a physician's assistant, or paramedic, but so far there are only about one hundred trained paramedics in this country.

Approaching the Berkeley Free Clinic

Once deciding what we wanted to do, actualizing these things was quite another problem. We had no money, no location and limited skills. We were a health collective who wanted a women's health center ultimately, but immediately we needed space, equipment, and money to print literature.

We presented a proposal to the Berkeley Free Clinic (run on community donations) asking that women, as a large portion of the community not being represented at the clinic, be given a day and night once a week to run a women's clinic. Wednesday became our day.

Preparation for Opening

Getting ready was a major effort. We organized professional and non-professional friends and acquaintances to teach us pharmacy, laboratory work, treatment of women's problems (vaginal infections), VD treatment, nutrition, and physical diagnosis.

We wanted women doctors, but given the state of medicine (men are doctors; women are nurses), that was impossible. Two young male doctors agreed to work with us and teach us as learning experience for them and as a political project.

We wrote and printed "fact sheets" on the treatment of various problems and sent away for *The Birth Control Handbook,* (P.O. Box 1000, Station G, Montreal 130, where you can also order an excellent handbook on V.D.) and for the *Women and Our Bodies* course book published by the Boston Women's Health Collective, now called *Our Bodies and Ourselves,* available through Simon and Schuster Publishers. We developed a course based on *Women and Our Bodies* which eventually became a course at a nearby community college.

We also developed a form called a herstory (vs. *history*) form used for personal information, from one's childhood innoculations to current problems. A woman called a "herstory taker" goes over the information and helps to complete the form. She also accompanies the woman to see the doctor, assists him/her, makes sure she understands the diagnosis, and prescription, and arranges any future appointments. This was a change from routine medical procedure of seeing a different person at each phase to one providing continuity.

When we were criticized by some gay women for a heterosexual bias in our herstory questions, we became sensitive to the fact that not all women *choose* to relate sexually to men; some of us relate sensually and sexually to other women.

We met and worked together but also emphasized getting to know one another individually. We had social events and a weekend outing. We are a work collective but many women involved have also chosen to live together in a collective manner.

With only word of mouth and a few posters to advertise, we finally opened in late February, 1971. From the beginning, the demand has been greater than our facilities can meet; every week we have had to turn away twenty to twenty-five women. These women are either referred to a hospital or to another clinic, or are given "priority slips" for another clinic night. This situation continually reminds us of the limits of our work unless it is accompanied by larger social change. We have been trying to develop a patient advocacy program in which a woman on call would accompany a woman in need of medical treatment to the hospital or clinic and stay with her throughout her treatment to make sure her needs are met.

Initial Organization

After finding our initial groups too general, we broke down into short-term work projects which printed "fact sheets" and contacted doctors and nurses. Once a short-term task was completed, we would regroup and re-divide for the next project. There were also entire collective meetings each Thursday night to discuss business and decide policy. As we grew, a chairwoman and an agenda became necessary. We have alternated business meetings and political education meetings. To facilitate communication in our large group, we made "phone trees" with each woman's number and set up bulletin boards in the clinic and in strategic neighborhoods around town.

Being a collective with full participation and little or no structure has made functioning difficult but allows for vital new ways of working and relating to develop.

The Clinic in Operation

We started with a staff of about forty women on afternoon and evening shifts; a receptionist, two switchboard operators, an appointment screener to accept patients or refer them, herstory takers, medics, four doctors, a nurse, counselors, lab techs and pharmacy workers.

Abortion and birth control counseling are provided. If a woman decides on an abortion, a woman from the clinic will go with her through the whole process. We ask for feedback from the women we send to outside doctors so that we can maintain a good referral service.

Pregnancy counseling and nutrition counseling are also offered. The Pscychology Group leads drop-in rap groups, individual talk sessions and emergency pschological care; it has helped start women's consciousness raising groups in the community. We experimented on ourselves with techniques we might use at the clinic. Child care is provided by a men's group.

We have experimented with job rotation so that everyone has the opportunity to do all jobs and to share the interesting jobs along with the more tedious tasks. After-clinic meetings are an important aspect of the clinic, but our least successful attempt to make change. They are intended to be forums for dealing with any problems which occur during the clinic, but often people are too tired or too intimidated to participate fully.

The population we serve is mainly young, white women, transients, street people and students. A major reason that we wish to move from our present "campus" location and have our own center is to reach a wider variety of people.

Pelvic Exams

Initially we assisted doctors giving pelvic exams. Then we learned to do them ourselves. We set up classes on how to check for vaginal infections, take pap smears, send out cultures to labs for diagnosis, use a speculum, do a bi-manual, and do a breast exam along with the pelvic. We learned from doctors, taught each other, and then trained women from other clinics to do pelvic exams. Doctors were available for consultation. Our first woman doctor, who joined us that first spring, learned all she knows about GYN right along with us. She had only received fifteen minutes of GYN lecture during her entire medical school experience! Being able to help a sister change her pelvic exam from a tension, guilt and pain-filled humiliating experience to a sympathetic and educated coming together over common problems is one of the great satisfactions and major accomplishments of the collective.

Later some of us began doing pelvic exams at home on ourselves. We discovered that any woman can get to know what "normal" is for her vagina and cervix if she regularly checks herself. She can make note of any changes which might be infectious, or simply the changes which occur inside of her during her menstrual cycle.

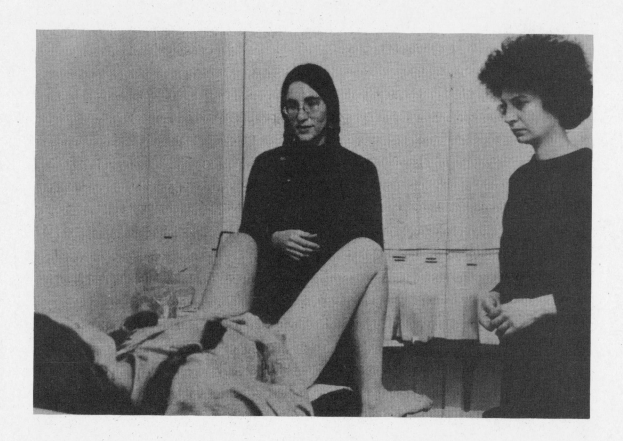

We feel that in addition to being a model for quality, sensitive, women's health care, we need to make demands on existing health facilities to provide this and to meet community needs. With the Medical Committee for Human Rights we started a project to force the only local community hospital to change its inhumane (Pay first — Treatment later) emergency room procedures. We set up a complaint table for patients and presented these complaints at hospital meetings. The result to date has been a change in the billing schedule; patients are now mailed a bill, rather than asked to pay when they are brought in.

Women's Health Center

In June, 1971, we presented a proposal for a woman's health center, including a proposal for a rape care center, to the Berkeley City Council. The Berkeley Free Clinic, the West Berkeley Family Planning Clinic, and the George Jackson Free Clinic also made proposals. Our first proposal was rejected on grounds of our lack of third world involvement. When we contacted black, brown and Asian women's organizations, we received lots of support. But they felt that they needed to put all their energy and commitment into their own community at that time.

There are two ways a clinic can legally exist: as a clinic or as a doctor's office. A woman lawyer donated her advice and the health center group worked all fall gathering information on becoming incorporated, non-profit, tax-exempt and zoned, on learning about bookkeeping, getting insurance, and fund-raising.

At the same time by December the collective was in a real crisis state. We couldn't keep the clinic staffed and we had to suspend the afternoon clinics. We also felt a tremendous contradiction about having a corporate entity within our loose collective structure.

The Health Center Function Group decided to write down what we'd learned and make a recommendation at a meeting about our collective priorities. We recommended that (1) instead of incorporating into a health center we establish a storefront for community women in an accessible, diversified neighborhood (2) we assume financial responsibility for our day at the Free Clinic, (3) we write down our experiences and knowledge in collective health care and pass it on in an expanded community educational and research program. These proposals are now being carried out.

The Storefront

Eventually after much struggle the City Council allocated $6,000.00 to our collective to run our day at the clinic and rent a storefront. The storefront was a much easier and less expensive project to accomplish than the one which required legal non-profit corporation status. It was a much-needed information center to be open more than once a week. In May, 1972, we rented a building where we now hold all meetings, do abortion counseling, show films, and most importantly, make referrals.

Orientation Meetings for New Women

We grew rapidly and the integration of new women into the collective has been a major concern. There have been many variations on orientation. Although we have had up to one hundred women in the collective, we have had trouble staffing the clinic because we are too lax in asking for a time commitment from new women. Many people join us, take our training and then split, without necessarily going to work at another clinic. We get some new energy and ideas from these people but they lack the long-range perspective needed to make knowledgeable decisions and get long-term projects done.

An unintended "elitism" is also created because "new women" feel a distance between themselves and "old women" in terms of knowledge, skill and familiarity.

Reorganization

New women continued to join, and it became clear that we were becoming a mass organization, although we really didn't want to admit it and didn't know how to deal with it. Maintaining the clinic became a huge effort. The chaos and confusion drained our energy for growing and functioning in a positive way. Fear of alienation from our sisters grew. Policy decisions were very difficult in such a large group. Formulating a cohesive political basis among everyone was impossible.

A group of women drew up a proposal for a new collective structure which was revised and adopted. We decided to divide into two collectives, one clinic oriented and one research and education oriented. Instead of project groups, we had function groups based on our interests and the work we were doing. Each collective had a steering committee (composed of representatives from the function groups) which would meet together. Eventually one steering committee evolved because many women worked in both groups. We found that most women did not want to be on the steering committee. Presently our structure is still evolving and we are now considering yet another kind of structure.

Changes

The clinic continued as before although more smoothly because we had formed groups for women with the same jobs to meet together and discuss common problems

and experiences. New community education groups were formed. The Nutrition group revised their handbook, *Feeding Ourselves,* now also available through New England Free Press.

The Herrick Hospital project continued, as did the Abortion and Psychology groups. There were several inter-collective education classes. Some research projects, such as on herbal remedies and applying yogurt to cure yeast infections were discussed, but these groups had trouble sustaining themselves because the members were spread thin working in other areas.

The community education function group developed women's workshops for high schools and college use, including a slide show demonstrating how pelvic and breast self-exams are done. We also did a workshop for Esalen Institute in the fall, 1972, and taught First Aid courses to the Asian Health Team which does community health work in Chinatown, San Francisco.

The Community Health Workers Function Group began a neighborhood health screening and referrals project. They are currently expanding their group to include more women interested in staffing the Health Collective Storefront and developing new community projects.

Funding

As you can see we have worked on little or no funds. Our City Council money may not be reallocated (it is always a fight!). We also receive Emergency Employment Act funding which is federal money administered through the City of Berkeley. Federal grants are available but require great work and a legal, "stable," long-range, corporate structure. Some money is available for birth control, VD treatments, and other women's health concerns (except abortion, of course). One of our problems has been the fact that we are a volunteer organization. Women have to find a means of support for themselves while giving their time and energy to the collective. It would be ideal if we could do this work and earn a living at the same time. We shall continue to pursue what we can. Contributions are greatly appreciated, although if you have the energy we would rather see other health collectives beginning!

Current Situation

The Collective is presently reorganizing itself around two collectives, a storefront staffed by community health workers and the clinic as before.

We started a course on pediatrics and now are offering a well-baby clinic in the afternoon with trained paramedical workers.

We are also involved in the current national debate of free clinic personnel regarding whether to stay in small clinics, provide good care and be an example, or to work in existing health institutions in order to pressure for change from within. There are no easy answers to this issue and our collective priorities will continue to evolve from our experience.

• •

Pelvic Self-Examination

Several women's health collectives are operating in the Bay Area. I first learned how to do a pelvic self-examination at the San Francisco Women's Health Collective in one of their regular classes on Monday evening. Seven or eight women were in the group, plus two women from the collective to show us how to use speculums and to talk about identifying different vaginal infections. We each had our own disposable plastic speculum which we bought from the collective. (You can order plastic speculums in bulk from any medical supply company at about thirty-five cents a piece.) Initially the two women from the collective talked about the reasons they were teaching pelvic self-exams: to correct the lack of knowledge many women have of their own bodies, to erase some of the mystique and fear many women experience during a doctor's pelvic exam, and to teach women a means of detecting obvious vaginal infections. Then one of the women from the collective demonstrated how to use a speculum on herself, and any woman in the group who wanted could try to do her own self-exam. A monthly pelvic self-examination does not obviate the need for a regular professional gynecologic exam (at six month to one year intervals) where pap smears can be taken, but it serves as a means of early disease detection and of attaining greater self-awareness.

When I examine myself I try to follow a set routine. First I urinate. This makes the ensuing exam more comfortable and thorough as a full bladder will obscure findings. I lie comfortably on my back on a firm surface (floor or table) and let my knees fall gently apart, or sit on the edge of a chair. Using a goose neck lamp and a hand mirror, I examine the external genitalia. I look for growths and skin changes such as rashes, discoloration, etc. I look for any noticeable discharge coming out of the opening to my vagina. Next I pull back the outer lips (labia majora) and expose the smaller inner lips (labia minora). I look in the crevace lining the inside of the labia majora for cysts.

Then I do a speculum examination. I use a plastic speculum which I sterilize before and after use with alcohol. I put the speculum in tepid water to bring it to body temperature for comfort. I carefully lubricate the blades with surgical jelly. KY jelly or Lubrifax are the most popular and can be obtained without prescription at any drug store. (Don't use too much because the jelly can be easily confused with vaginal secretions.) I put the hand mirror down for a moment and, pulling the lips apart with my left hand, insert the blades of the closed speculum with my right hand. The blades should run perpendicular to the floor. (If they are inserted parallel to the floor they will press your soft vaginal tissues against your pubic bone causing pain.)

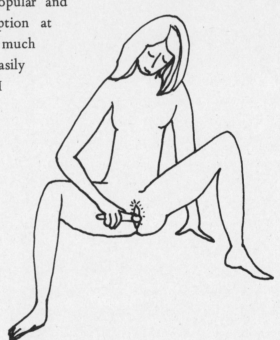

When the speculum is firmly inserted, I turn it so that the blades are now parallel to the floor and I squeeze the two outside arms towards each other. This spreads the blades open, inside my vagina. With proper insertion there is no discomfort. The teeth on the handle will lock in an open position. Gently I push the blades further in to expose the pink cone-like cervix, the opening to the uterus. The cervix moves around a bit. If it is out of view I can massage my lower abdomen to gently push it back to center.

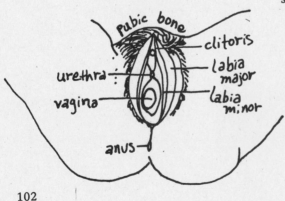

Using the hand mirror, I inspect the mouth of the cervix (the os). I look for red moist areas around the opening (cervical erosion); I look for discharges coming out of the cervical mouth. Discharges from the cervix are signs of an infection in the uterus or fallopian tubes, such as gonorrhea. Discharges from the vagina but not from the cervix are signs of vaginal disease such as trichomonas vaginalis or fungus infection. Next, I slowly release the teeth of the speculum and remove it, closing and turning the speculum sideways before removal to avoid discomfort. Then I wash and sterilize my speculum.

An excellent book useful for identifying different infections is the *CIBA Collection of Medical Illustrations,* Volume Two, The Reproductive System; Frank Netter, M.D., Ciba Publications. Also see the *Handbook of Obstetrics and Gynecology,* Ralph Benson, M.D.; Lange Medical Publications, 4th Edition.

Movement

In ancient Tahiti, a matriarchal society, there were no sexual inhibitions and no frigidity. Sex was an integral, open part of the Tahitian culture. Women were taught a dance, similar to belly dancing, at a very young age. The dance was done primarily to stimulate the woman's own sexual feelings, but also to excite her man.

For the Tahitians there was no foreplay as we know it before intercourse. If a woman desired a man she danced in front of him. If the man was not aroused enough for intercourse the two people would sit down facing each other and begin tapping each other's bodies lightly with their fingertips. The tapping was their foreplay. It would get gradually harder and turn into slapping the more excited they got. Then they would make love.

Women were the aggressors sexually, approaching the men first. The sex roles were reversed from our culture. The women were always "pestering" the men to make love. Tahitian men were less interested in sex, and preferred to go off in their fishing boats or talk among themselves.

What is especially interesting to me about this sexual pattern is that Tahitian women were brought up to believe that they turn *themselves* on. They danced to heighten their own sexual feelings.

They were not brought up to wait for touch stimulation from a man to open the feelings in their own bodies.

Women in our culture are taught few activities to help them feel good and sensual in their own bodies. We are taught to make ourselves *appear* sensual — with make-up, clothes, hairstyles, figure exercises, mannerisms. All these outer mechanisms are geared toward molding women into an unnatural, odorless, hairless, weak "little girl" stereotype which is supposed to be opposite and "sexy" to men. None of these rituals help the woman feel good or more tuned in to who she is as an individual. Most of them are a lot of trouble, expensive and uncomfortable. The woman must wait for male approval to feel rewarded for her efforts and reassured that she is "sexy."

I certainly acted mostly within this framework until just a few years ago. I get in touch with the places where I am still acting the stereotyped woman when I can notice the difference between what I am doing and what I am feeling, between the person I am and the image I am acting out. Pay attention to what qualities women you know project. Do you feel that they are trying to reveal themselves or to project an image of the woman they are supposed to be? How many women do you know who feel as sexual inside their bodies as they look?

Belly Dancing for Yourself

We can take some customs from other cultures to help us here. A friend of mine, Barbara Clemans, is a masseuse, a movement teacher and a belly dancer. She teaches belly dancing classes for women, oriented towards dancing for themselves. I talked with her about the history of belly dancing, about exercises from her classes and why she decided to teach belly dancing.

Barbara: I've studied many forms of ethnic dance — Afro-Haitian, Tahitian, Hawaiian and Barat Nat Yam South Indian Dance. I have found belly dancing to be the most female of these expressions. Belly dancing, or Beledi, is an ancient Middle-Eastern art form traditionally performed by women. It began as a dance of empathy for women in labor rather than as a seductive dance for men. The women of a tribe would gather and emulate the rhythms, contractions and abdominal undulations of the woman giving birth. Middle-Eastern women were originally not allowed to perform in public or for strangers. Through the Second World War belly dancing was performed publicly by young boys.

I use belly dancing in my women's groups now as a kind of movement therapy. There should be another word. I don't like to use the word "therapy" because it suggests correcting a disease. I feel simply that our culture has not given space for some kinds of expression. There are ways our bodies can move which we don't use because the movement isn't socially acceptable or taught and patterned in our culture. A lot of our originality, spontaneity and creativity is blocked by these conditioned responses. Moving in new ways can help to free the body of restricting patterns.

Me: Why do you teach these classes especially for women?

Barbara: Belly dancing is so female, not cute or "feminine" or passive. Female. It has to do with creation, nurturing and birth. It is a statement of passion and energy, of pride in the fullness of form.

The first time my teacher saw my belly he told me he would be very upset if I lost weight. He said "Don't! I really like that belly! It's beautiful to see your belly and hips vibrate. The Bedoins would go crazy over you!"

Well, that was the first time I'd ever had positive reinforcement for my body condition. To belly dance you need a belly. To shimmy, you need flesh to shake. Many women go through life and think they ought to flatten out their natural form. Belly dancing is a celebration of our natural femaleness.

I emphasize getting in touch with your feelings in the pelvis and lower half of the body, and opening up your body image. Belly dancing is very grounded and centered. All the movements are made from a firm position of flexed knees and contact with the ground. The movements are supposed to originate in your center, your hara, and flow up and out to the rest of your body. You learn to feel that even your hand movements begin at your center.

It is an improvisational dance. There are basic movements to learn, but after that the dancer combines them any way she wants, to express herself. In the tribes the dance evolved away from being only a childbirth ritual. When the tribe was gathered together any woman would enter the circle to dance when she felt moved by the music. She became part of the music, in addition to the drums, flutes and violins — the movement of her hips, her finger cymbals and the noise of the coins on her dress became percussion instruments. She and the other musicians communicated rhythmically through her dance, in tune with the universal rhythms. That's why the dancing is extemporaneous; it should come as a response from within.

Me: That's such a different orientation from most Western dance and movement where the patterns are imposed from the outside, and the performer is taught to tighten her body and constrict it. "Pull your belly in. Tense your muscles." It's so different from release and opening to the spontaneity within.

Barbara: That's why I think it's a universal dance that all women could do, might want to do for themselves, whether they perform or not. My classes have a very tribal quality — women getting together to reinforce our female energy.

The release of constriction in one's pelvis is fantastic. During sex is probably the only time an American woman moves her hips very much. There is opening up of feeling in that area, but she is still having to respond and pay attention to someone else. And she's probably moving in preconditioned ways.

During any movement, I stress getting into pelvic feeling for yourself, and releasing the energy in your lower half so that you move from your center.

Me: What about the music?

Barbara: Picking something that you really respond to, that really turns you on is important. You can use anything you like. I've used jazz and rock, sitar music, anything sensual. You can buy American records called "belly dancing" records. But if possible find Greek or Arabic music, music from the Middle-East. Listen to them. The music is different from ours. See if you like it and respond to it.

The traditional instruments are: the oud, a 12-stringed instrument; the dorbakek, Arabic drum; a Kanoon or violin; the raye or flute; and zils and fakashats, or Turkish castanets and finger cymbals.

Banging the Pelvis

In the classes we do warm-up exercises to relax and loosen our bodies. I do a Reichian exercise which releases tension in the pelvis.

Lie on the floor on a rug. Be on your back, with your knees bent, feet on the floor. Bounce your pelvis up and down on the floor, firmly. Do all the work for the exercise with your leg muscles; the pelvis should be loose and relaxed. Lift by pushing up with your feet. Let your chest and shoulders be loose too.

The Spine Roll

There is an exercise in this same position for increasing flexibility and rhythmic movement in your spine. Keeping your head, shoulders and feet on the floor, raise your body up into an arch. As you lift, your pelvis should come up first. Coming back to the floor, lower your spine down gradually from neck to tailbone. The pelvis comes down last. Do this quite slowly as though you could feel each vertebra separately.

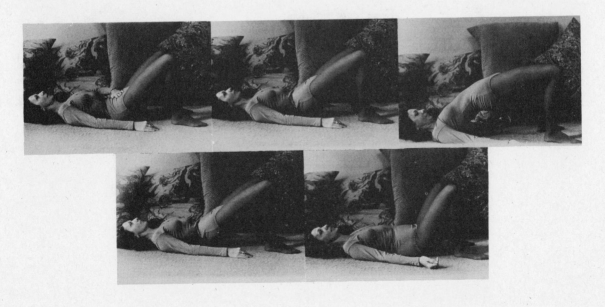

When you lift the pelvis to start again, curl it upward pushing from your feet and rotate the pelvis forward. Raise the rest of the spine, articulating each vertabra as you go. This movement is basic to belly dancing. Try it standing up also.

The Floating Pelvis

This time when you raise your pelvis off the floor stay there awhile and rotate your pelvis in the air. Try to allow the rest of your body to relax while you move your

pelvis in circles and from side to side. Keep your weight on your shoulders and feet, so that you get the sensation that your pelvis is floating.

Let your eyes be closed and tune in to any kinds of movements your pelvis would like to make. Pay attention to how you feel doing the movements. You probably only allow your pelvis to move this way during sex. How do you feel directing your focus to your pelvis for your own enjoyment? Try to allow yourself pleasure in these movements.

The Hanging Abdomen

A good breathing exercise can be done on your hands and knees. The spine is straight. Try to let all the muscles of your torso, abdomen and pelvis be loose. Let them relax and droop towards the floor with the pull of gravity. How do you feel letting your belly hang down? Do simple abdominal breathing in this position. Let your belly relax more and more.

This is a yoga breathing exercise which helps develop coordination of the abdominal muscles. Stand with your feet wide apart and firm on the floor, knees flexed. Place your palms on your knees and rest the weight of your torso on your arms. Now inhale **and** suck your belly as far in and up toward your ribs as you can. Exhale and release the muscles so your stomach comes out again. Repeat several times. Do this slowly.

The Four-Point Pelvic Rotation

This exercise is a basic belly dance movement. Stand with your feet apart and knees flexed. Have your arms outstretched to the side, slightly curved. Move in a square pattern at first. Once you get accustomed to the direction of the movement you can make it more flowing and circular.

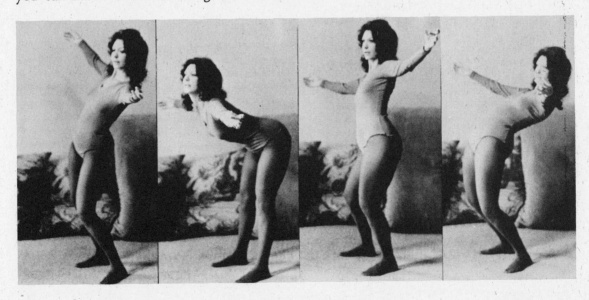

Imagine four points around you, one to each side and one in front and back — north, south, east, west. Move your hips toward one point at a time. Let your torso lean slightly in the opposite direction from your pelvis (as your hips lean to the left your torso leans to the right). Keep your focus in your pelvis. Let the motion of the movement come from your feet and legs.

The Shimmy

Stand in the basic position, feet apart and firm on the floor, knees flexed. Let your arms be out to your sides, or slightly rounded up over your head with your palms facing outward and wrists touching.

The movement of the shimmy comes completely from the motion of your feet and legs. Shift your pressure on the ground from foot to foot in a piston-like motion without lifting your feet. Your buttocks, hips and abdomen need to be loose and relaxed in order to shake. Tilt your pelvis slightly forward and backward until you find the place where your pelvis can comfortably hang without tension and your genital muscles feel relaxed. Your feet are are stationary on the ground and not stomping. The flexing of your knees and the changing pressure in your legs makes the hip and abdominal area shimmy.

When you can easily shimmy standing still, try it in motion. Take slow steps across the room, shimmying each time you move one leg forward. You can do this stepping on your whole foot, or faster on your toes.

Basic Hip Walk

This is the basic belly dance walk. Stand with your weight on your left leg and foot. Step out with your right leg and thrust that hip up, forward, and a bit around to the left. Then shift your weight onto your right foot and bring the left leg out in the same manner. Keep doing this "walk" until you've moved across the room.

Hand and Arm Exercises

It is helpful to do some simple exercises to loosen your hands and arms. Begin with the fingers one at a time articulating each joint. Then articulate your wrists, elbows, shoulders. Fold and unfold each part of your arm and hand slowly and deliberately. Open and close the joints.

Now undulate the arms and hands instead of folding them. Follow the contours of your body with your hands. Sculpt the space around you.

Women With Women

Women With Women

Being female, I am different from a man. I am not just a "soft boy!" My real differences are not my learned outer feminine, rather than masculine, mannerisms, such as wearing dresses and flirting with men. The most important differences are not even that I have full breasts and a vagina. The differences happen at the deepest feeling layer of my being; with every man I have ever known intimately and long enough for many of our social roles to drop away, our critical communication goes on at a deep rhythmical level.

The closer he and I move to opening our natural selves to each other, the more I experience this basic difference. Sometimes this difference feels alienating to me and sometimes attractive. It is this factor which for me, and I think for many other women, gives me a sense of exploring the unknown when relating to a man — and which satisfies me when I connect with his maleness. I want to know this foreign land which is not me.

I do not feel this same basic rhythmic difference with other women. There is a body rhythm of being female which I feel in myself, and in other women. When I tune into another woman at this level I feel connected to and understood by someone who experiences me automatically past all superficial traits; the feeling is that of communion with a member of one's family. There is a sameness at our roots which makes me feel at home. Sisterhood is a biological connection.

I value my close friendships with other women highly. I feel an affinity based on our common experience of being female. When I want to tune in to it the connection is deep, and allows a different communication from that which I experience with men. I have to explain less. She knows my pleasures. She knows my bullshit. She knows the important nuances of my problems. I am understood at a depth and level which only comes between old veterans.

Now that I am beginning to appreciate other women at a deeper level, I need to discover new and purely female ways of relating. I no longer have to define myself and my relationships only in reaction to men — I do not have to be the "opposite" sex. I do not need to restrict my connections with women to roles defined only in relation to men's roles. I can start to be myself, defined and validated by me. I can look to old close relationships with my mother and my sister for some help with new patterns. I can also look to history and to other cultures for possible female models.

A fascinating book, *Mothers and Amazons* (Julian Press, cloth), is a history of several races written from a female point of view. It contains discussions of female symbolism and accounts of Amazons and the matriarchal cultures of Greece, Tibet, Maylaysia, Central America, Egypt, Africa, Babylonia, Europe, North America, and the merry wives of Kamchatka. It is amazing how prevalent matriarchal societies have been, and amazing that they are virtually left out of our history books.

I have the choice of relating to another woman in ways previously restricted to men without buying into a male role. I can let my woman friend rub my back when I'm tired, catch me when I trip, hug me when I'm down or when she feels affectionate. Physically taking care of another woman does not have to be a sexual relationship. I can experiment with receiving physical contact from other women without assuming a sexual intent.

If the connection between me and another woman is sexual, I can relate as myself. I do not need to be her "opposite;" I don't need to fit my feelings into the old masculine/feminine role structure. That superficial role structure is stifling enough to the natural individuality of heterosexual couples! I am a woman relating sexually to a woman. That is new. That is different.

There are exercises late in this section for you to share with other women to help you become aware of your attitudes about each other and to explore new avenues of connection and nourishment between you. Some of the exercises are specifically significant for women. Others are simply everyday activities which women don't often share. You may want to try out some of these new areas of relating, talk over your feelings about them with friends, or just read them.

Pay attention to what your fantasy is about the experience you'd have if you did do them. Be conscious of your expectations and your concept of your sex role. If you do try out the exercise with a friend, you will probably find your fantasy is quite different from the reality!

116

Closeness and Competition

What has our traditional relationship been as women to each other's achievements? Since most women are brought up to play the role of the good loser and man's best helper, woman to woman relationships have been largely the comraderie of the underdog — supporting each other when we're down, when I break up with my boyfriend, when I don't get that job, when I'm depressed or bored or lonely — I can call my girlfriend to share the blues. Support from friends when you're down is invaluable and important — but how do we relate to each other's triumphs?

Phyliss Chesler in her excellent book, *Women and Madness,* (cloth, Doubleday) makes some vital points about how the traditional female underdog role is getting in our way during our new stage of development. Happiness is viewed with suspicion. "What are you doing out having a good time? You must not be experiencing your female plight if you're so happy." There is a tendency among women in the movement to want to keep each other down.

Perhaps these critical attitudes come from fear of new risks, or of being left behind while a sister "gets ahead." They are based on competitive comparisons which follow the negative masculine model for "success" and can only complicate our growing pains.

We need to learn to support each other's successes, as well as our failures — we need to break out of the subtle oppression of competition and the myth of the dignity of the underdog. I need to no longer feel glory in being a martyr.

I need to quit viewing the success of another woman as somehow taking something away from me, to feel that it is threatening or detrimental to me for another woman to be pretty, happy or successful. I need more such women — she's providing me with a better model than the "martyr" or the "male ego trip." And hopefully her success will clear the path some to make mine a bit easier.

I need to be wary of blaming a sister for my problems. Blaming and fighting among related organizations has unfortunately been the pattern and downfall of most radical groups. Rigid emphasis is put on sameness; and a great deal of attention is focused on the differences or "flaws" of other radical groups. The groups spend their energy blaming and blocking each other and have little effective energy for their real opposition.

Let's start supporting each other's differences. I see diversity in the women's movement as a strong point. It reflects the reality of the many aspects of our female living which need to be dealt with. One group can't cover all these aspects — we need

Lesbian Liberation and Political Liberation, Health Liberation and Personal Liberation — and on and on! We are fighting against homogenization, and *for* the freedom to be our diverse natural selves.

I see a particular problem for women here because women are not really accustomed to confronting men directly. (It is much easier to criticize Mommy than Daddy.) Women are taught to bitch and complain, but those are passive and ineffective attitudes. We need to learn to act and confront. In many families the mother ultimately takes the blame for the family problems. Let's quit spending our valuable energy fighting and putting down our sisters, and focus on the real and more important obstacles.

In the women's movement today, many women are starting to act out new roles — more aggressive, more active, more overtly powerful. This requires an adjustment from me. I need to get used to experiencing another woman in this new role. I need to learn new ways of being in that position myself — powerful and "successful" without competing, without being paranoid, without having to put others down and without sacrificing myself for the cause along the way. Unfortunately I have very few good models for this now.

To me *a new model for group interaction* could be one of the great human contributions of the women's movement — the collective spirit of working and achieving without false hierarchy, without the fear of sharing, without the necessity to step on someone else on the way "up." Can I learn to let go of the concept of "up" and "down" — which necessitates creating a "loser" so I can "win?" Do I need someone else to feel "down" so I can feel "up?"

Recognizing and accepting myself, my body, as unique and valuable is the beginning step toward interacting in a new way. I can enjoy another woman's difference if I feel confident of my own worth and effectiveness. I can work together collectively and successfully with others if I let go of the concept of "winning" and "losing," and recognize that there is room and need for us all. Can we learn this in time?

The focus of the exercises and interviews in this section is on learning to do this — to become aware of the competitive and conditioned attitudes in yourself towards other women, and to try out new models of behavior based on cooperation and sharing. Some of the awareness exercises you can do by yourself, and others are done with a partner or in a group.

Consciousness Raising Groups

A small women's group can be a supportive and enlightening atmosphere in which to start examining and working on your feelings. Anica Vesel Mander is a friend of mine who is currently spending much of her time working at Alyssum, a Feminist Growth Center in San Francisco, doing women's workshops, and helping start women's consciousness raising groups. I talked with her about how she came to be active in the women's movement and about how to start a consciousness raising group.

Ani: I was born in Yugoslavia, and I lived there until I was nine. That was during the Second World War. I'm Jewish. My family left Yugoslavia because of the Germans to live in Italy for six years.

I came to this country in 1949 when I was fifteen. Terrible time to come here — just ready for the fifties! Later I went to the University of California in Berkeley and did graduate work in Comparative Literature. I was working for my doctorate when I got married the first time. I never finished my doctorate, however, I taught French and Italian at Boston University and at Harvard for about five years.

When I came back to the West Coast, I taught at San Francisco State College several years part-time and also remarried and had two children. When the student-teacher strike broke out at San Francisco State my life was transformed. I had not participated in college union activities before, but when the strike broke out I joined. That was a long, tedious, painful strike which lasted five months. Afterwards I asked that I be given a full-time job, which I got as an assistant professor of French. I taught there for two years and then I was fired. I'm about to file suit.

Me: How'd you get fired?

Ani: My department recommended unanimously that I be retained, but I was fired by the dean. The reason given was that I didn't have a Ph.D. I brought up the fact that a man in the same department who didn't have a Ph.D. was given tenure. I'm suing partly on the basis of sex discrimination, but I think it was more than that. It was broader political discrimination — everyone who went on strike who wasn't tenured was fired. I stopped formally working last June. Since then I've been supported by my husband.

Me: That's nice.

Ani: No it's not nice, not at all. It's very bad. I don't like it. Until then I was economically independent at least in my mind. I had lived alone for many years. And I worked after I was married. This is really the first time that I am not financially independent.

Me: What were the main issues of the strike?

Ani: Well, the black students were asking for an autonomous Black Studies Department. The faculty joined the strike for their own reasons, and also to support the black and other ethnic groups' demands.

The experience of the strike really politicized me. I was fired and that politicized me even further — and brought me into the women's movement. This was in my consciousness already, but I didn't center on it until this happened to me personally. When I was working and trying to effect change within my work it was very easy to limit myself to that area. I was busy reforming the French curriculum, teaching courses so that the distance between teacher and student was diminished. But I hadn't really branched out until this happened to me.

Me: What kinds of things did you start doing?

Ani: It was very informal. I talked to several women similar to me, in that they were professional women active in the man's world, and I suggested that we start a group. We started very haphazardly, sort of social and chatty, but quickly it jelled into a very serious, very intense group of women. It was a consciousness raising group, but we didn't call it that. I don't know if any of us knew the term.

I had always had close women friends, but there I was talking personally to strangers. Talking seriously about women's problems rather than chatting really affected me.

When the group came to its natural end after eight or nine months, I wanted to go on from talk into action. Some of us started a collective called the Good Works Collective: The Women's Center for Growth and Action. Consciousness raising is one of the main areas we work on, but we also work on other projects, and films.

Me: What would be the difference between your collective and a group of women who do charity work?

Ani: It is a self-help approach rather than helping the poor or the "disadvantaged." The focus in other groups like that has always been that somebody else has the problem. "The people across the ocean are in trouble. Let's send them money." We realize we all need to help each other to help ourselves.

That's what's so rewarding about being involved in this collective. I can bring any of my problems and relate them to the other people's problems and pool a kind of communal energy from it. I see women's problems politically, that is, in terms of what happens to women in a male-structured society. The problems I have and you have are not unique to us. And they're not solely my responsibility. I have a very strong feeling that to throw it all back on the individual is harmful to women and in general. As a woman, it's not helpful to my mental health to say, "It's all my problem."

It's different from conventional attitudes, and connected with the Radical Therapy approach — I'm interested in "Change Rather Than Adjustment."

Talking About Men

Begin the group by allowing bitching and complaining about men and "oppressors" for several sessions. Be detailed and specific — policemen, mates, fathers, brothers, bosses, sons. Get into your feelings about doing this and hearing it. Do you feel embarrassed? Do you feel guilty? Do you want to "protect" your man and defend him? Keep each other from protecting men and oppressors. Show your anger and pain.

Watch for the line where the complaining seems to become avoidance. You can easily spend all your time focusing on men (again) and not get around to yourself. You won't get anything done this way.

Go back to yourself. The group should agree when you no longer want to talk about them and need to talk about us.

Some Topics

How you feel about your name, first and last.

Define real and imagined oppressors and problems.

Share reading material.

Invite guest speakers to contribute their experience, *after* the first meetings.

Do some "body work" — massage, sensitivity, movement, breathing.

Sex

Start from scratch. It's important to assume you know nothing, because most of your basic premises are probably misinformed. Notice where ideas come from.

Talk about *female* sexuality. Notice how most talk about sex is from a male standpoint. Talk about *female* arousal, female orgasm, masturbation and homosexuality.

Share your feelings about lesbianism.

Talk about the attitude that only women "unsuccessful" in their feminine role join women's groups.

Why are you choosing to be with women?

Does your man have negative reactions to your being in the group? Does he feel left out or threatened? Does he fear you will reveal his sexual inadequacies?

Differences Between a Consciousness Raising Group and a Therapy Group

Bitching and Complaining is initially encouraged. In a therapy group the focus is usually brought immediately back to you.

Leaderless — self-help orientation rather than leaning on authority.

Don't analyze. Accept what a person says as what she wants to communicate.

The emphasis is on *sharing and supporting* each other — rather than on confrontation — without qualifying analysis.

Each person decides for herself how far she wants to go. *Don't push.*

Don't "call" a woman every time she "plays games." Trust that she is doing it for her own valid reasons and needs to get her feelings out.

Wait to call her on her process until she's become stuck and interferes with the progress of the group. There will be women who don't really want to move and change. This will become clear after awhile. Make a group contract beforehand to call each other on this point. The woman who continues to refuse to change will probably drop out.

There is a collective commitment to each other as women, which creates a special kind of sharing and support, a focus on getting someplace together.

The Cycle

1) *Initial energy* — from new deep sharing, discovering commonality of experience and new aspects of your female identity, and from receiving support.

2) *Getting stuck* — when you first feel your resistance to change. When you have worked through your resistance to opening up and have shared and supported and learned from each other for awhile, but begin to feel like moving on.

3) *Moving On* — consciousness raising groups have different natural life spans, but most reach a stage when the members feel they would like to either stop the group because nothing new is coming out of it, or because they feel tired of discussing subjects and want to do something about them.

You can: end the group and implement what you've learned in your own life, see a private verbal and/or body therapist, or join a different kind of therapy of group.

Imagine

This exercise was written by Theodora Wells, a feminist and a business communications and training consultant working in Los Angeles, California, who has written a book called *Breakthrough: Women Into Management* (Van Nostrand Reinhold, cloth). Her exercise is designed to help a woman imagine a world without the myth of male superiority as a working premise. It could be a powerful exercise to use in a consciousness raising group to start people thinking about their female self-image and its practical effects on our living.

We need to protect and nurture our connections with other women. Female alienation is encouraged by male chauvinism. I need to watch for places where my own attitude is altered by cultural prejudices which distort my self-image and my perception of other women. How much of the social feminine stereotype do I accept and take part in?

Woman — Which Includes Man, Of Course: An Experience in Awareness

There is much concern today about the future of man, which means, of course, both men and women — generic Man. For a woman to take exception to this use of the term "man" is often seen as defensive hair-splitting by an "emotional female."

The following experience is an invitation to awareness in which you are asked to feel into, and stay with, your feelings through each step, letting them absorb you. If you start intellectualizing, try to turn it down and let your feelings again surface to your awareness.

★ Consider reversing the generic term Man. Think of the future of Woman which, of course, includes both women and men. Feel into that, sense its meaning to you — as a woman — as a man.

★ Think of it always being that way, every day of your life. Feel the everpresence of woman and feel the nonpresence of man. Absorb what it tells you about the importance and value of being woman —of being man.

★ Recall that everything you have ever read all your life uses only female pronouns — she, her — meaning both girls and boys, both women and men. Recall that most of the voices on radio and most of the faces on TV are women's — when important events are covered — on commercials — and on the late talk shows. Recall that you have no male senator representing you in Washington.

★ Feel into the fact that women are the leaders, the power-centers, the prime-movers. Man, whose natural role is husband and father, fulfills himself through nurturing children and making the home a refuge for woman. This is only natural to balance the biological role of woman who devotes her entire body to the race during pregnancy.

★ Then feel further into the obvious biological explanation for woman as the ideal — her genital construction. By design, female genitals are compact and internal, protected by her body. Male genitals are so exposed that he must be protected from outside attack to assure the perpetuation of the race. His vulnerability clearly requires sheltering.

★ Thus, by nature, males are more passive than females, and have a desire in sexual relations to be symbolically engulfed by the protective body of the woman. Males psychologically yearn for this protection, fully realizing their masculinity at this time — feeling exposed and vulnerable at other times. The male is not fully adult until he has overcome his infantile tendency to penis orgasm and has achieved the mature surrender of the testicle orgasm. He then feels himself a "whole man" when engulfed by the woman.

★ If the male denies these feelings, he is unconsciously rejecting his masculinity. Therapy is thus indicated to help him adjust to his own nature. Of course, therapy is administered by a woman, who has the education and wisdom to facilitate openness leading to the male's growth and self-actualization.

★ To help him feel into his defensive emotionality, he is invited to get in touch with the "child" in him. He remembers his sister's jeering at his primitive genitals that "flop around foolishly." She can run, climb and ride horseback unencumbered. Obviously, since she is free to move, she is encouraged to develop her body and mind in preparation for her active responsibilities of adult womanhood. The male vulnerability needs female protection, so he is taught the less active, caring, virtues of homemaking.

★ Because of his clitoris-envy, he learns to strap up his genitals, and learns to feel ashamed and unclean because of his nocturnal emissions. Instead, he is encouraged to keep his body lean and dream of getting married, waiting for the time of his fulfillment — when "his woman" gives him a girl-child to carry on the family name. He knows that if it is a boy-child he has failed somehow — but they can try again.

In getting to your feelings on being a woman —on being a man — stay with the sensing you are now experiencing. As the words begin to surface, say what you feel from inside you.

Eyeballing

If you tried the exercise called "Looking" in the Body Awareness section, you are familiar visually with your genitals and may want to explore your feelings about "being seen" further. "Eyeballing" can be a helpful exercise for this.

If you are in a women's group that has been meeting regularly for awhile and you are frank with one another, you might want to try this exercise in your group. I would choose a time in the group's cycle when you are feeling quite close and candid with one another and preferably after meetings in which you shared some physical contact, such as massage or sensitivity exercises.

The basic format of "Eyeballing" is for one woman to sit down with her legs spread apart in a position so that her genitals are easily seen. When a woman from the group comes up to her, the seated woman says, "This is my vagina." The woman who is looking says, "I see your vagina." This interchange is repeated with all the women in the room, so that eventually everyone who wants to has looked and been looked at. Take time to share your reactions.

This group experience can be a direct way of learning about your own shame feelings and any other attitudes connected with your genitals. People usually start out timidly, but by the end of the exercise many women have emotionally worked through their feelings of embarrassment and have come to the place where they are proud of their genitals, saying loudly, clearly and happily, "This is my vagina!"

How to Choose a Therapist

One way of dealing with problems can be (private or group) therapy. Many different schools of therapy exist — Freudian, Jungian, Reichian, Bioenergetic, Gestalt, Psychic, Behavioral, and on and on. Each technique emphasizes and focuses on a different aspect of human personality.

If you are considering doing some kind of therapy, first check into the differences and choose the one whose focus seems most relevant and balancing to you. If your dreams feel meaningful, and you have images often, Jungian therapy, in which one works largely with image interpretation, might make most sense to you. Or Behavioral therapy might be the framework you want to work in if you experience the world in a very linear cause-and-effect way. Freudian psychotherapy emphasizes one's early sexual relationships. Gestalt therapy involves a great deal of role-playing and emphasizes acting out repressed parts of your personality. Psychic therapy might make the most sense if you are very intuitive and tuned in to events on this level. Reichian and Bioenergetic therapies both approach the personality through its physical manifestation and would be appropriate if you want to explore your body life.

On the other hand, choosing a therapy whose attitude is opposite to your normal orientation has its advantages — you may want to do something opposite to your normal patterns in order to experience a new dimension and to balance yourself some. For instance, if you normally are quite analytic and "head" oriented, some kind of non-verbal or body therapy might open up new parts of you and be very balancing. Where I am coming from is that there is no one therapy which is best or better than all the rest. The judgement about which therapy is better for a person comes for me from their deciding what focus they want, what fits them best at the time.

The following conversations come from a transcript of a talk with Roberta Ellner, a trained marriage counselor who does private therapy and groups in Walnut Creek and Berkeley, California. She and other psychologists in Walnut Creek have formed The Hilltop Psychology Group. They see clients privately, run groups in verbal therapy, and also do Masters & Johnson Sexual counseling. Roberta and I talked mainly about what to consider when choosing a therapist.

Roberta: My practice is mainly of women. That's not accidental because there's an obvious resistance on the part of people in the community to see a female therapist. I see couples and individuals and families. I also work with a male therapist at Hilltop doing Masters & Johnson sexual therapy; we are just starting a sex therapy *group* which, as far as I know, has never been done. I think it's important for people to share the problems which arise out of the sexual dysfunction with each other. This would be possible in a group.

Me: How do your clients come to you?

Roberta: Mostly they come through a referral from another patient — which makes me feel good! They don't usually come in at first specifically for sexual problems but for some other connected difficulties they are having.

Me: I think a lot of people *expect* to have problems sexually. They don't have a high expectation about their sex life.

Lise, Roberta, Erik, Julie

Roberta: I think that's true. And depending on where you are living, believe it or not, there are still fantastic myths about women's rights as sexual beings, about how much pleasure women are entitled to. When you get into a conservative area the sex role concepts are very Victorian, and people don't have any real sense that they are entitled to experience as much pleasure as possible. They don't expect much. They let little things go by. Dissatisfaction builds up. And finally they come to a crisis point where they need a therapist.

Me: Let's talk about that. There are so many different kinds of therapy and certainly many different individual therapists; it would be difficult to know how to choose one.

Roberta: It's a complex problem if you don't have any familiarity with therapy or a particular therapist. A person should have time to sit back and explore the field for what's available and what fits them. That doesn't usually happen because when people seek out therapy, for the most part, they are in a great deal of distress and urgency.

Ideally there would be an agency where people could go to talk with someone and get information. You could talk about, first of all, what therapy is — what the process is like; what the therapist does; what kinds of changes to expect in yourself; that there will be ups and downs and there could be times when you'll feel a lot worse than when you started; what resistance is; what transference is; the theoretical basis for why therapy "works;" that the process of learning new things about yourself can be disorienting; what the differences are between the techniques. That way you could decide if therapy is what you want or not, and if it is, which kind fits your needs best. You might decide therapy's not what you want at all. You'd rather do something else.

Me: That kind of information center is a wonderful idea!

Roberta: Wouldn't that be great? There isn't such an agency now, so a person has to do her own exploring. You can read some psychology books to get a sense of what's available in the field, and talk with your friends who have gone to psychiatrists or psychologists. Often a person in need will call up a psychological association they find listed in the phone book, or go to a clinic. This does not seem ideal. Preferably you would get a referral from a friend, someone who's psychologically sophisticated and who you feel has benefited from her therapy.

But if you're in a crisis situation, you might not have time to do this carefully and you'd need to take a referral from a minister or doctor or clinic. The direction you're given under these circumstances is to someone who's competent; it's not all a matter of competency that makes therapy work. The thing to do is to go to this competent person to get through your crisis. Then you have the option to either continue therapy with them or to look around. That initial contact does not have to determine the whole course of treatment, but once you're in the therapeutic relationship, because of the inherent power structure, you tend to forget you have the right to make a judgement about the therapist.

Me: You have the right to shop around.

Roberta: Yes. It isn't so bad to make a change. According to most traditional therapy, this is looked upon with horror — you lose your "transference" and the therapeutic relationship is broken. This may be true, but you can also make incredible gains if you feel a different direction. It's very, very hard to do, but the client should always be acutely aware of her own intuition, intelligence and individuality.

A good way to approach choosing a therapist would be to get three or four names from friends and make one appointment with each therapist to "interview" them. Tell them that you are "shopping" for what's right for you. Formulate some questions to help you decide whom you could work with best. Also ask the therapist if she has a feeling about whether she can work with you. This way you will find out whether your therapist is willing to answer questions directly. Many traditional therapists would avoid a question completely and try to use it in the therapeutic process. Some will answer very directly and personally. You need to decide whether this is the way you want to be answered, or do you want to be in a more ambiguous situation where things are left more up to you.

The most important thing is to respect your own gut reaction to the person — is this the kind of person I could work with on what I need? Ask the therapist what direction she pushes her clients in — a Bioenergetics person will have a different kind of goal than a Freudian analyst. Is this the kind of therapy which will challenge some of my defenses? Distinguishing these things will be fairly clear with therapists who label themselves obviously, but there are many therapists who take an eclectic approach to their work.

You need to pay attention to your first reaction — it has to do with a sense of trust. Can I trust this person? After that, the choice of a therapist isn't particularly important in some ways, because if you want to go in therapy, you are "set" on therapeutic gains. How much you are going to move is so much an internal matter rather than how much the therapist is going to accelerate you.

Me: I think it's important to be aware from the start of the "risks" of personal growth.

Roberta: That's especially important with couples. There's no guarantee where the therapy is going to end, and if a couple comes in to therapy saying, "We want to save our relationship," it's the obligation of the therapist to let them know she can't guarantee that. They have to make the choice. You can't put your choices on the therapist.

Something else to consider is that there is no "agenda" for the meetings. Unless something particular is bothering you, you don't pick a topic before you come in; that would cancel out some important feelings which might come up but don't fit the topic. It's important to talk about whatever is uppermost in your mind when you are there. Anything can be grist for the mill! It's also good to be aware of the topics you are censoring during the hour and of what you are doing to "please the therapist."

Demystify the relationship in terms of the power structure and be aware of the places where you buy into the authority-patient role. I heard a therapist in San Francisco describe his method for getting clients hooked on him. He sits and waits and just as a patient is about to make an interpretation, he makes it for them! The clients get dependent on him for problem-solving. Even so, the clients tend to get better. But it's very serious. They idolize him and don't feel they've done it themselves. In actuality the therapist is just a guide and the client has to do the real work for herself.

Me: It's a human relationship the way any other relationship between two people is.

Roberta: Yes. Even well-intentioned therapists are subject to their own prejudices which need to be recognized. The therapist's attitudes are to be taken very specifically as the therapist's attitudes. Every therapist has unconscious subtle ways of making judgements and influencing the direction of the client.

Me: I need to keep in mind that I'm not going to an authority with the answers, but to someone to talk things over with.

Roberta: And don't think of yourself as a "patient." I'm not "crazier than" this therapist. She has thousands of prejudices too.

Me: You're there to work together.

Roberta: Yes. And whatever you do, make up your own mind! That brings me to the particular problem of women in therapy. You need to be very aware of the sex role attitudes of the therapist and what his or her models for a woman are. My attitude with my clients is that a woman's self-concept is changing today and I am exploring that with the client; we learn together. You should think about this in choosing a male or female therapist. Some female therapists might have as Victorian a concept of womanhood as a conservative male therapist. And some male therapists who have worked through this role concept could be clearer.

It's important to get a sense of how well the therapist can handle differences. You might be able to work with a male therapist and "educate" him about what it's like to be a woman (or what it's like to be in a certain religious or ethnic group) if he's willing to learn. It can be a growth process for you to work with someone who doesn't necessarily agree with you but who is open to differences.

Me: I can deal with some male relationship areas with a male therapist which I can't approach as directly with a woman therapist. And there are definitely things about my own femaleness which I feel I could only deal with deeply with a woman. I've found that men therapists tend to be patronizing at some level to women clients no matter how "liberal" or "liberated" they see themselves. It's part of their upbringing.

Roberta: It can be good to switch sometimes from a male therapist to a female one. At Hilltop Psychology Group, we often have our clients see a therapist of the other sex in the office to deal with a particular problem and then come back to the original situation.

The topic of choosing a therapy and a therapist is difficult because it's so complex. And the problem we're trying to deal with, of course, is the super-human therapist!

Good therapy can be invaluably important, but it's critical to realize that there are many other things in this world that are balancing and "therapeutic" besides therapists!

Alyssum

Women who have been active in the Women's Movement for some time are beginning to feel the need for tools to implement ideas and changes they talked about in consciousness raising groups. It is usually necessary to create our own organizations to fill this need, as there are few such existing resources. A group of nine women in the Bay Area around San Francisco have created an organization called Alyssum: A Center for Feminist Consciousness. They see it and other organizations like it as an alternative to traditional adjustment and male-oriented therapy, and as filling some of the current gaps in public resource centers for women. The groups are leaderless as much as possible, and the orientation of the groups is self-help. The women who organized Alyssum include some female therapists who feel they can learn something different from the feminist focus than they usually experience in their other group work, some women oriented toward consciousness raising groups, and women experienced in body therapies.

Alyssum is a hardy Greek wild flower whose name means "without madness," and which can grow in any environment. The location is now on Union Street in San Francisco.

Alyssum

a center for feminist consciousness

Due to the centuries of living in societal female roles, women have either given away their power (to men, to the establishment, to their parents and even to their children), or used it in devious, manipulative ways, thus losing much of their aliveness.

Our aim is to help women take back their power, use it fully and openly, and experience their uniqueness in the process. We are women trained in gestalt therapy, family therapy, body work and massage and experienced in leading women's groups.

Lois Brien, Cindy Brown, Shelly Dunnigan, Pat Grosh, Lisby Mayer, Cynthia Werthman Sheldon, Anica Vesel Mander.

I've just begun to pay attention to how I am with other women; and to what these patterns tell me about myself. My attitudes about other women reflect my feelings about myself and my own womanhood.

Do I feel insecure and threatened when my partner is attracted to another woman? What is it about the particular woman that worries me? Do I think she is "prettier" than I am? Do I see her as sexier than myself? What do I think she has as a woman that I believe I lack?

Closeness between women is often regarded as less important than the closeness between a man and a woman, as filler companionship until one of them connects with a man.

Do I regard women as less interesting companions than men? Do I regard myself as less interesting than my man? Do I automatically look to a man when I want an expert or authority? What kinds of social customs — such as career norms, educational slants, and social roles — perpetuate this state?

Is there part of me that believes I can only satisfy my need for intimacy and contact through a relationship with a man? Do I value my male friends more than my female ones? Do I cancel a "date" with a girlfriend if a man asks me out at the same time?

Do I look on other women as my enemies and rivals? (Women are not to be trusted.) Do I at some level believe that a person would only befriend me for a sexual connection? How would my interactions be different if I started looking on other women as allies instead of competing?

Do I believe women to be generally less sexual and passionate than men? Do I feel myself to be less sexual than the men I relate to? Do I criticize other women for not being "feminine?" How does my feminine sex role image impose limitations on my conduct?

My sexual attraction to other women at some level reflects my feelings about my own body. Do you regard other women's genitals as disgusting or unattractive? How do you feel about your own genitals? Do you like to touch yourself? Do you like to touch other women? Why do you think a man may like to touch you?

Experiment with including your sexual feelings for a woman you meet along with the other qualities about her you take note of. "She is open and direct and easy to talk to. We have a lot in common because we are doing the same kind of work. I like the way her skin feels. I like the way she touches firmly." Or, "I don't like the way she looks. She has an interesting career but she bores me. She doesn't excite me physically because her body seems lifeless and dull."

How do you feel tuning in to your physical reactions to another woman? In most situations any kind of sexual response is considered anti-social. Can you accept these feelings and enjoy them? You probably don't feel you have to relate sexually to every man who turns you on.

Touching and Talking

The exercises in this section are oriented towards helping you become more aware of your feelings about touching other women and how these attitudes reflect your self-image. They are also aimed at breaking down some of the learned barriers in our culture so that you can have the choice of moving closer to other women if you want.

Deep Tension Release

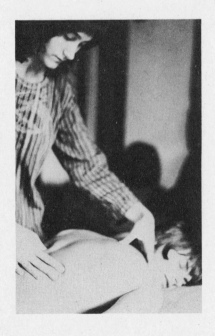

Two kinds of Oriental pressure point massage are: Reflexology (or Zone Therapy) and Polarity Therapy. Reflexology is quite easy to learn and do. Polarity is a more complex body treatment. It requires much training and experience to do well as a therapy; however, there are some basic Polarity points which are simple, safe for anyone to use and which release deeper muscle tension than light massage does. You will not get a sense from these exercises of the whole body reactions resulting from long, complete Polarity treatments, but you will get pleasant local tension release.

Reflexology

Reflexology massage can be done on yourself as well as by another person. It is explained in detail in a paperback called *Stories the Feet Can Tell* by Eunice D. Ingham (P.O. Box 948, Rochester, New York) which is available in most health food stores. It is based on the idea that there are nerve or (electro-magnetic) energy connections between all parts and organs of the body which connect with the feet. By pressing firmly on the spot on your foot which corresponds to your problem organ you can have a positive influence on the ailment, possibly by improving the circulation to that organ by stimulating the energy and nerve connections.

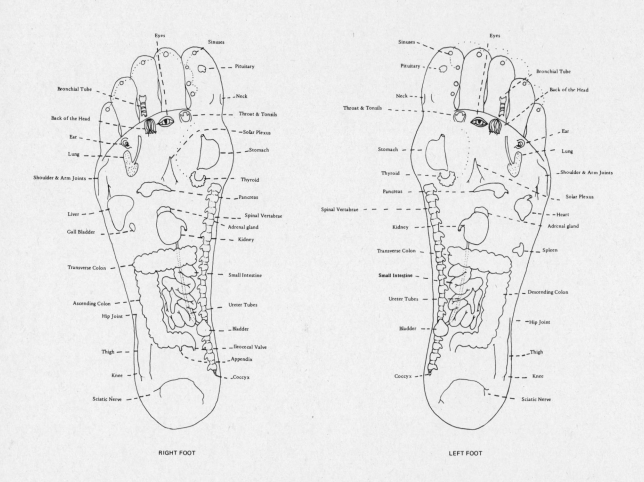

Press in all over the soles, tops and sides of your feet with your thumbs. Press firmly and hard. Some points will feel good or neutral, and some may be quite sore. Check the foot chart for the connected organ or body part to see if there are any problems in the connected area. Because you can stimulate all parts of the body simply by working on the feet, a reflexology foot massage is very refreshing, for yourself or for someone else.

140

Polarity treatments for the head and neck are extremely relaxing. You need a partner to work with and preferably a table with a pad on it for your friend to lie down on. Have her lie on her back. You stand at the end of the table behind her head.

The Net

This relaxation technique requires that you place each finger of both your hands on a different acupuncture point. With your elbows pointing out to the sides from your body, spread your fingers wide apart. Place both your thumbs in the top center of the skull. Place your two index fingers on either side of the bridge of the nose just under the boney eye socket ridge. Place your second and third fingers to the side of the nose under the cheekbones. Your little fingers go on either side of the face at the jaw hinge. (If your partner opens and closes her jaw several times, you can feel this joint.) If your partner has a large face in proportion to your hands you may have difficulty reaching all the points at once.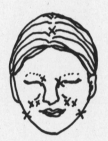

When you have all your fingers in place simply rest them there on your partner's face about a minute making contact without pressure. Try to relax your fingers and hands in position.

Now take your hands away slowly. Go back to each point separately; press and stimulate the points one at a time. These places may be a bit sore on your partner, but after you work on them she will feel less tension in her facial muscles. The key to working on these spots well is to apply your pressure *very* gradually and evenly and just to the point of soreness not pain.

The Occiput Release

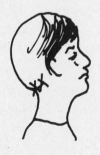

The occipital ridge is the boney shelf at the base of the skull. It is full of nerves and tendons going into the head, neck, eyes and face; releasing tension here relaxes all those areas.

141

Stand to the right side of your partner's head. Lift her head gently with your left hand. Place your right hand under her neck. Your wrist should be at right angles to your arm, and should be positioned against the base of your partner's neck. Your fingers will naturally be pointing up your friend's neck toward the occiput.

You want to eventually lower her head onto your thumb and forefinger, so that your fingers are pressing into the occiput and her head is resting on them as on a fulcrum. Place your thumb under the occipital ridge on the right side of your partner's spine and your index finger in the matching place to the left of the spine.

Slowly roll and lower her head onto your fingers. When the head is in position, move your left hand from under the skull, and rest it lightly on the forehead. When the weight of her head presses onto your fingers, the pressure may feel sore to her at first. Stay with the position. When your friend gets accustomed to the pressure and relaxes her neck some, the soreness will gradually disappear, and your partner's head will relax back over your fingers onto the table.

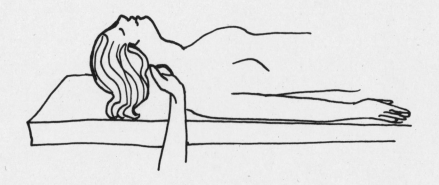

If you press on your own trapezius shoulder muscles (which go behind your collar bone from the side of your neck to the outer tip of your shoulder) they will probably feel rather tight and hard. Press in deeper and you might feel soreness and small lumps in different places along the muscle. These lumps are what you want to work on to release the tension. Many headaches and arm pains begin from muscle contraction in this area.

Have your friend lie down on the table on her back. Stand at the end of the table behind her head. Rest your left hand lightly on your partner's

left shoulder. Use the fingers of your right hand to explore her right trapezius muscle for tense hard tissue or lumps. When you find a place along the muscle which is tight, that is, not pliable and loose, *very gradually* apply pressure with the ball of your thumb. When you reach a depth where it is sore, stop increasing the pressure. Stay where you are and maintain the pressure you have. Wait for your partner to relax. Tell her to focus her attention on the sore spot and to imagine she can breathe into it. As she relaxes, the soreness will disappear, and you will feel a slight softening and spreading of the tissue under your thumbs. This is your signal to move gradually deeper in on the muscle, until you reach another sore layer.

Keep with this process until you feel your partner has relaxed the sore area a lot and you can feel more softness and flexibility in the muscle. Then move on to another area of the trapezius muscle to work on the tension there.

When you have covered the length of the right trapezius, relax your right hand and rest it lightly on your partner's right shoulder. Now begin looking for tight places on her left trapezius muscle and apply the same technique for releasing those lumps using your left thumb or fingers.

Reichian Massage

Wilhelm Reich used body contact techniques in his work to release deep muscular tension. Described here are two simple exercises for loosening constriction in the thighs, the spine and the pelvis.

Thigh Shake

Be sitting on the floor. Have your partner lie down and rest her left foreleg across your lap so that you can reach her upper thigh muscles without straining. Spread your fingers apart and place one palm on the inside of your partner's thigh, the other on the outside. Hold her thigh between your hands and shake and vibrate the muscles vigorously. Move and sit beside your partner's right leg and repeat this on the other thigh.

Releasing the Legs and Hips

Let your partner be lying on the floor on her back. Stand at her feet and grasp her ankles. Slowly raise her two legs lifting from the ankles until both legs are

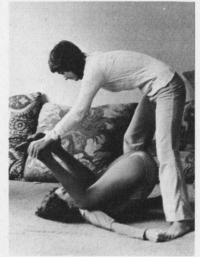

held in the air but the pelvis is still mostly resting on the ground.

Wait in this position a moment until you feel your partner relax and give over the effort of lifting to you. When you have this done to you, try not to tense any of your muscles as your partner lifts. See if you can remain loose while she does the work.

When your partner has released her legs, move your hands palms down onto the soles of her feet. Begin leaning your weight onto your hands and pressing down on the feet. If your partner's legs are relaxed, the knees will bend and be pressed toward her chest. Her pelvis and spine will raise off the floor a bit. If your partner is quite flexible, you will eventually be able to move her knees to the floor over her shoulders. But don't push anyone beyond their flexibility. Move *very* slowly, evenly and gradually. Help her relax and curl up in a ball.

Then, just as slowly and gradually, reverse the movement and lower her legs to the floor again.

You can trade off and have your partner do this to you.

Sensuality and Relaxation Massage

Because of a nervousness about any touching being labeled "sexual," most women shy away from physical contact with other women. We tend to reserve all our

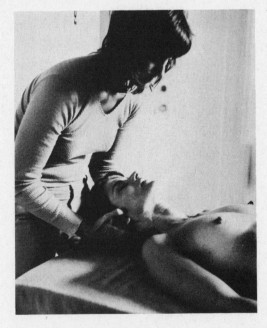

energy for physically caring for and relaxing someone for men and children. This cuts women off from sharing pleasurable ways of taking care of each other which do not need to be sexual.

Massage is a simple effective relaxation technique. It can feel good to do and to get. It can be a means of exploring feelings about touching and being touched by other women without sexual pressure. If you are in a woman's group of any kind, spending some of your meetings massaging each other is a good way to begin to feel closer as a group, and to trigger a lot of feelings about your body and physical contact with other women which you can talk about in later meetings. (Usually you'll be so relaxed from the massage that you won't want to focus and start "analyzing" until the next meeting!)

Esalen massage is the name given to a kind of massage developed originally by two women, Storm Accioli and Molly Day Shakman, who formerly worked on the massage staff at Esalen, Big Sur. Esalen Massage is now taught at Esalen Institute in San Francisco and Big Sur and at other growth centers where massage is considered an important sensory awareness technique.

This kind of massage is quite different from its European ancestors and from the stuff that's done in most American "massage parlors."

In its new form Esalen massage can be a powerful body awareness tool and many verbal therapists are combining some massage work with their other techniques. Aside from that it feels very wonderful and is a useful skill to have to share with lovers and friends.

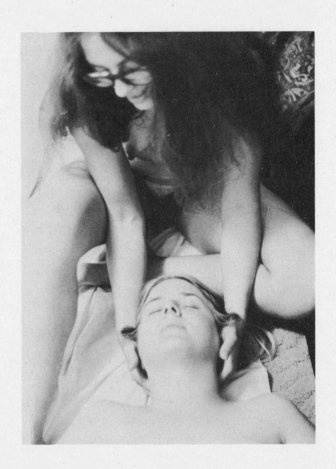

In massage parlors no consideration is given to the comfort or feelings of the masseuse; all the emphasis is on pleasing the client. A basic premise of Esalen massage is that it is just as important how the person giving the massage feels as how the receiver feels. In learning Esalen massage you are taught ways of tuning in to the feelings in your own body while massaging, and ways of using your strength easily so that you don't get tired or strained. It is a wonderful exercise for learning how to keep tuned in and centered yourself, while paying attention to someone else. This seems particularly important to me as a woman since I was brought up in a culture which stresses the nurse-martyr role for women — I should sacrifice my comfort and time and energy to take care of someone else. (This nurse role is a large part of the stereotype of a "good" wife and mother.) If you experiment with this philosophy in massage you will find that *both* the giver and the receiver get less satisfaction. Besides the masseuse getting tense and tired and less pleasure from doing the massage, her friend receives a less relaxing massage; she can feel the tension in the hands and arms of the masseuse and that feeling is transmitted to her.

Free Form

Arrange a comfortable massage area for yourself and your partner in a quiet, very warm room. Place a pad or several blankets on the floor large enough for you to sit on comfortably alongside your friend who will be lying down. (If you are on a rug you want to protect from the massage oil you can get large sheets of painters' plastic or gardening plastic to put under you.) Cover the padding with a sheet or several beach towels

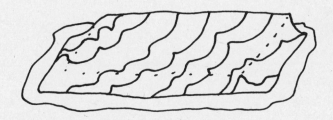

Massage oil that's good for your skin can be made by mixing grocery store vegetable oil (cold-pressed safflower, soy, olive, almond) with several drops of a concentrated scented essential oil. You can buy scented oils at head shops, or you can use a tiny bit of oil of wintergreen from a pharmacy, or food oil (oil of peppermint, lemon, clove) from a grocery store. Pour the oil into a clean shampoo or cold cream squeeze bottle that has a flip top.

If you both feel comfortable nude, doing the massage without clothes makes it easier to work without worrying about getting oil on your clothes. More importantly, one of the central ideas about this massage is to make some space for letting go of some of the embarrassment we often feel about our bodies and to celebrate our naturalness and uniqueness.

Have your friend lie down on her stomach. Sit facing her on her left side, so that you are parallel to her back (and could put your hands on the middle of her back without straining). Close your eyes a minute to tune in to how you are feeling. Pay attention to your breathing. Shift around in your position any way you want to make yourself more comfortable.

Tell your friend to close her eyes and relax and to only talk if she doesn't want something you're doing to her. This is a space for you both to communicate non-verbally and to tune in to the universe of touch.

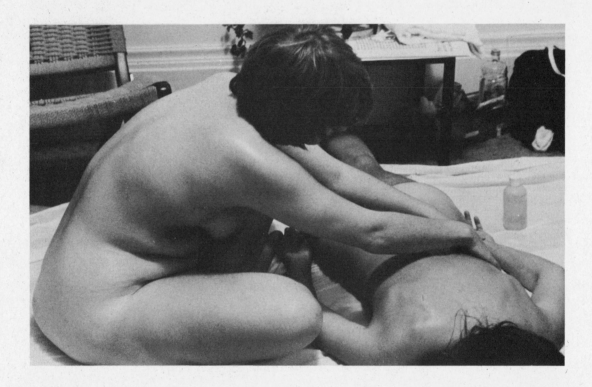

Squeeze some oil into your palm and rub your hands together until the oil feels warm. Place both your hands down in the middle of your partner's back. Be still there a moment. Then begin spreading the oil over your partner's back. Eventually you want to oil your friend's back, buttocks, backs of the legs and feet. Be slow.

When you need more oil, don't lose physical contact with your partner. It is important to stay touching because she is now in the world of your touch and breaking that contact is disorienting and surprising. You can do this by resting your left elbow or forearm on your partner's body and squeezing the oil into that hand with your right hand.

When you have covered the back of your partner's body with oil begin experimenting with different kinds of touch. Try fingertips and fingernails, deep and very light pressure, fast and very slow rhythms. Try using different parts of your hand and forearms to massage as well as your palms and fingers.

Don't focus on pleasing your friend. Focus on the feelings in your own body and how you can make yourself feel good. Is your breathing relaxed? Are you sitting comfortably? Rather than trying to tense your muscles and push, can you *use your weight* to lean into your partner's body for pressure?

Do the whole massage with your eyes closed so that you learn to "see" with your hands. Let your hands rather than your head decide how to move and touch. Listen to your hands and let them do what feels good to them. When your hands move over different kinds of tissue do they want to do different things? Do they feel good pressing in deeply on large muscles? Kneading on soft tissue such as the buttocks and thighs? Molding around the shape of the bones?

Massage the back and then move down across the buttocks, thighs, calves and feet, exploring and experimenting as you go. What does your friend's body communicate to you by the way she feels? Is she firm and smooth? Hard and muscular? Soft and pliable? Bony and angular? What parts of her body seem to want you to press in deeply and which want light pressure, or none?

When you have spent some time massaging each part of the back of your friend's body, try some long strokes which go from neck to ankles. Let all of you sway with the strokes; lean and dance. How does it feel to you when the movement comes from your whole body, not just your hands and arms?

Now bring your hands again to the center of your partner's back where you began. Rest your hands there still for a moment. Now gradually move them away from your partner's back. Stay sitting with your eyes closed and tune in to how you are feeling now inside your own body. Where is your breath? Where are you tense or relaxed? Notice any sensations you are feeling in your body as a result of doing the massage.

If you were receiving the massage, let yourself be still a moment before getting up. You don't have to jump up right away. Take some time to tune in to how you are feeling in your body now as a result of being touched.

When you are ready, sit up and tell your partner how the massage felt to you, what you liked and didn't like.

If you were giving the massage it's your turn to lie down now and receive. Trade places with your partner and repeat the exercise.

This is a good exercise to begin getting into massage with. You learn the relative unimportance of technique, and the importance of enjoying yourself, feeling good in your own body while massaging. You learn that almost anything you do feels good! Specific strokes are for variety and new ideas to add to the kind you make up on your own.

If you are interested in exploring getting into other women sexually, you can use massage as a very early step in perhaps becoming gradually more comfortable physically with other women. Massage is a helpful place to start tuning in to how you feel about touching and being touched by women.

The deepest key to tuning in to women sexually is opening up the feeling and awareness more and more in your own body. The better you feel about yourself as a woman the better you will feel about other women.

150

If you have done the free form exercise, you've learned that you can make someone feel wonderful without knowing any massage strokes at all. The real key to massage is the relaxation and sensitivity in you, your hands and body, to what makes you comfortable and to the flow between you and your partner.

I have included techniques in this section for different parts of the body which need detailed work. Another pleasurable type of stroke in massage is one which covers large areas of the body, and runs along long muscle groups. I like to alternate between strokes which concentrate on small areas and long broad strokes. This gives your partner a sense of the wholeness of her body.

There is no set way or length a massage should be. I try to let each massage be different, an expression of how I am feeling at the time, what I feel for my partner, and spontaneously what flows between us.

For thorough, detailed and very fine massage instruction, see *The Massage Book* written by George Downing and illustrated by myself (Random House/Bookworks, paper and cloth). In this section I want to describe a few strokes not in *The Massage Book* which focus on areas of special interest or high tension for women.

The Figure Eight

Your friend is lying down on her back. Sit on her right side about parallel to her waist, so that your left arm can easily reach her chest. Spread oil all over your friend's torso. The pattern of this stroke is a figure eight on the muscles supporting the breasts. Your right hand should be resting *lightly* on your partner's abdomen.
Use your left palm and fingers to
describe the figure eight. Begin on the
sternum bone in between her breasts,
your fingers pointing away from
you. Lean some of your weight onto
your left palm and slide it around the
lower edge of your friend's left breast.
Move around her side, and up onto the
pectoral muscles. Now move your hand,
heel first, down under your friend's right breast, up her right side, and back onto the upper chest by way of her right pectoral muscle — until you end up touching the

151

place on the sternum where you began the stroke. Keep circling continuously around the breasts in this figure eight five or six times. Let your whole body sway with the movement.

The Slide

Brenda Sales, who is an especially fine masseuse working at Esalen, San Francisco, showed me this stroke. When done right it is one of the most pleasurable strokes in massage to me and reaches some areas other strokes don't.

Be on your partner's right side parallel to her hips and facing her right shoulder. Spread oil on her chest and arms. Lift her right shoulder and place your left hand under it palm up. The fingertips of your left hand should be between her spine and right shoulder blade at the base of the neck. Lower the shoulder onto your hand. Your palm is under the shoulder blade. Your right hand goes opposite your left on her chest, like a sandwich.

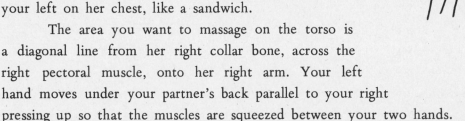

The area you want to massage on the torso is a diagonal line from her right collar bone, across the right pectoral muscle, onto her right arm. Your left hand moves under your partner's back parallel to your right pressing up so that the muscles are squeezed between your two hands.

When your two hands are in place on the back and the chest, press them toward each other and begin sliding them diagonally out toward her right arm. When you get to the arm, lift your hands and go back to your original position. Do the slide again. With both hands press in firmly not only with your palms but with your fingertips. Repeat the stroke five or six times. Now sit on your partner's left and massage her left shoulder.

Overlapping Thumbs, On Upper Chest

Be sitting behind your partner's head. The basic stroke is an overlapping motion with your thumbs pushing away from you. Begin on your partner's right pectoral muscle and move out toward her shoulder. Press in with the ball of one thumb and slide it away from you a few inches. Pick the first thumb up and do the same with your other thumb. You are rubbing the same few inches of skin with both thumbs alternately. What makes the stroke feel good is to get the motion going so that your thumbs overlap — just before you lift the first thumb your other thumb begins the stroke. It's like massaging by twiddling your thumbs.

The area to cover is the pectoral muscles and the upper chest. The stroke should fan out from the edges of the breasts onto the shoulders. Across the upper chest the motion is down from the collar bone towards the breast. Move from the right side across the body to the left shoulder.

Pinching

The basic motion of this stroke is to grip a fold of skin between your thumb and fingertips, lifting and squeezing the skin. This should be done firmly and gently. Pinching is very effective and relaxing because you are stimulating the tiny nerves in the skin. You can do a whole massage this way all over the body, but there are certain areas where it feels especially good. One of these is the lower back.

Your friend should be lying on her stomach with her arms to her sides. You can either straddle her and sit on her thighs; or sit at her left side parallel to her hips and facing her head. Begin the strokes on her buttocks with both your hands and continue the pinching across her sacrum (the arrowhead bone at the base of the spine), the lower back, and as far up onto her back as you want. The area around the sacrum is full of nerves which spread into the pelvis and is often tense. Be more thorough here. Work like an inch worm lifting folds of skin between your thumbs and fingers all around the edges of the sacrum bone, on top of it, and up around the waist. If you lift the next piece of skin before completely letting go of the first, you can make it feel as though you are rolling one long fold of skin all the way up the spine. Mmmm.

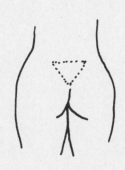

153

Pockets Around the Pelvis

Your friend should be lying on her stomach. You can be either straddling her legs or sitting beside them.

The area you want to work on (on the surface) is the area around each leg where the thigh moves into the pelvis. Deep massage here is very relaxing for the pelvis and the legs. Use the balls of your thumbs or your fingertips. Work on one leg at a time and be thorough. Once you receive it and learn how good it feels you'll have the patience to work slowly. You want to find depressions at the top of the thigh which are small pockets around the pelvic bone or sitting bone.

Press in with your fingertips up toward the pelvic bone. When you are in as far as you can go, rotate your fingers in small circles on the spot. Work systematically from the crease of the inner thigh up across the back of the leg and onto the side of the hip.

The Foot Squeeze

Massaging the feet is especially relaxing because of the many nerve endings there and their connections with other parts of the body. When I am in touch with feeling in my feet I have a pleasant sense of awareness through my whole body, and with the ground.

This milking stroke is a particularly relaxing one which covers the whole foot. Let your friend be lying on her stomach. Use more oil on the feet for this stroke than you normally would. Pick up the left foot slowly with both your hands. Have your thumbs on the sole of her foot and the rest of your fingers on the other side of her foot. The movement of the stroke is an overlapping squeezing motion. Start with your left thumb at the base of her heel. Squeeze the foot with your left hand and drag your hand down the foot to the base of the toes. Press in hard with your thumb. Just before your left thumb reaches the base of her toes, begin the same squeezing and dragging with your right thumb. Now pick up your left hand and start the stroke over at the base of the heel.

Keep up this squeezing in overlapping strokes as long as you can without getting tired. (That probably won't be long because this movement is quite tiring for your hands!) This is one of the few massage strokes which feels good to me if done very fast. Try it at different speeds.

Now put your friend's foot slowly down again. Any time you move your partner's limbs while massaging, do it slowly and thoroughly. Otherwise she will be surprised by the switch in mood from the rest of the massage and tense against your touch. I also experience having my limbs lifted for me as a delightful luxury that is just as pleasurable as any massage stroke. Repeat the Foot Squeeze stroke on your friend's other foot.

Women With Men

magical touch, coats my average-feeling body with delightful and rare exciting feelings — he "turns me on!" It doesn't happen that way for me.

Functioning from the Midas conception of excitement is functioning from a passive position. I am dependent on an outside person for when and what and how much pleasure I feel.

Most women and men I've come in contact with seem to think of sexual excitement in these terms. I've talked with some male therapists about the reactions of their female clients to doing tension-releasing exercises which can also create a heavy sexual charge in the woman. Most women react to the feelings during the exercises with nervousness because they think that they are "turning on" to their therapist. It doesn't occur to the woman that the charge is a self-generated energy which is internally accessible and at her command — because this goes against everything she's been taught about the nature of her own energy. It doesn't usually occur to her that she is "turned on" by the pleasure and excitement of releasing her own energetic powers.

I've been paying attention lately to where my feelings of being "turned on" seem to start. I notice whom I turn on to, why, and especially to the changes I experience over a period of time in interest and excitement about them. I've found that my feelings for somebody almost always change when *I* do in some way, and not because the other person is any different.

Because of the monopoly of male sexuality models in our culture it is difficult for me to develop my own female sexual identity. The concept that men are sexual beings and women are their neuter playthings prevents the development of any independent female sexuality culture. Where are my models for female orgasm, female pornography, independent female sexual energy?

I read a Question and Answer column in a local newspaper recently in which people were talking about where they learned about sex. One woman answered that her husband had taught her "everything he wanted her to know." When asked where her husband learned about sex, she said she didn't know how he got to be an authority. All the other women replied similarly that they had learned from a man. Where did you and do you "learn about sex?" How come we are playing into the game that our men are sex authorities, sex teachers, the sources of woman's concept and definition of sex? How does it change my conception of myself, my man, and alter my interaction with men to think of myself and other women as authorities on female sexuality? Can I explore and find female models that are not degrading and do express my naturalness? Can I begin to explore the premise in my own life that all energy is sexual energy — that is, a drive towards life and nourishment and self-regeneration?

160

Reichian Therapy, Bioenergetic Therapy and Kundalini Yoga are three disciplines very similar in their approach to energy flow in the body. The next three exercises come from these disciplines and are aimed at increasing muscular flexibility in usually tense areas and increasing the energy charge throughout the body. If you experiment with these exercises, you will find the effects quite different from gentler, more peaceful yoga or breathing exercises.

The Cow-Cat

Be on your hands and knees on a carpeted floor or firm pad. Breathe through your nose.

Inhale while you: arch your head and neck back so that you are looking at the ceiling; let your spine and your abdominal muscles relax so your back and stomach curve down toward the floor (the cow).

Exhale while you: let your neck relax and your head fall forward down toward your chest; tuck your buttocks under and forward, arching your back up like a cat.

Alternate the cow and cat positions as you inhale and exhale. Begin slowly; gradually alternate faster and faster as you speed up your breathing. Do this as long as the movement is comfortable. Stop as soon as you get tired; lie down on your back with your eyes closed and let your breathing relax. Pay attention to any changes in sensation which you may feel moving inside your body.

The cow-cat exercise particularly increases flexibility in your lower spine and pelvis. This is the "joint" of the "upper and lower halves" of your body. Often movement is segmented here so that while a person moves her legs (for example in walking or running) she may hold her upper body rigid, or when she gestures using her arms and head, she may unconsciously hold the lower half of her body still. These are learned tension patterns that can be released by practicing movements in which your upper and lower halves move together. Pay attention to your upper and lower half movement pattern and experiment with responding with your body as a whole.

Leg Vibration

Lie down on your back with your arms at your sides. Raise both legs at once straight up and hold them about a foot apart. Stretch your legs towards the ceiling, heels leading and pressing upward. Your legs may begin to shake (vibrate) a little; this is tension releasing. Experiment with moving your legs different distances apart to see at which distance they vibrate more.

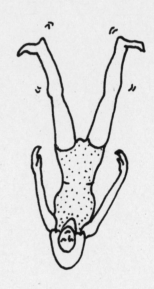

Do this stretch just a few times and then relax your legs on the floor again. Tune in to any new feelings happening inside your legs.

The Ego Breath

Stand firmly with your feet wide apart. Breathe through your mouth. Stretch your arms out to either side at right angles to your body, palms facing forward. Make fists. Inhale and stretch both arms backward (in a straight line). Exhale and bring your arms to their original outstretched position. Keep repeating this movement cycle very rapidly with your breathing until you feel tired. Lie down on your back and relax. Tune in to the feelings in your chest and arms.

You have a friend. You've known her for a while. You finally meet her boyfriend. And it blows your mind.

They don't seem to go together at all! What does *she* see in *him*?

I realize I usually expect a friend to make an intimate alliance based on her strengths. But often we make close alliances based on our weaknesses; we choose a partner who will go along with protecting us from confronting our deepest insecurities because opening up unconsciously brings back early childhood fears about what it was like to get close when we were small and powerless. (Luckily, these deals don't always work and we end up having to face the conflicts anyway!)

Silent Contracts

Couples make half-conscious, unspoken agreements about their conditions for mutual protection. These silent contracts make up a crucial part of the structure of most couple relationships. It is important to become aware of what the fears and contracts are in your relationships and to make them overt. It is usually easier to see these contracts in operation in other people's relationships. Which of your friends have a parent-child relationship? (She'll play helpless little girl, so she won't have to assert herself, so he feels strong and wise.) Which of your friends have a tyrant-victim role relationship? (She'll boss him around so he can complain that he can't "do anything" because of her.) Many contracts are identifiable if you can label the roles you get into. Super-masculine/ultra-feminine is another role which allows the man to play strong and tough and the woman to play pretty and delicate. I see the sado-masochistic couple pact as simply an extreme variation of the traditional masculine-feminine team in which the husband takes all the aggressive power traits and the wife accepts the passive, anything-you-say-dear role.

Another interesting agreement is the brother-sister role or "pals." The mood of this contract is usually functional, light, focused on fun and "freedom." It often masks a fear of deep emotion and a belief that intimacy has to mean a loss of freedom.

Within the larger general role contracts are smaller more specific ones based on whatever individual fears a couple might want to trade boycotts on. "Let's not fight because I'm afraid of being angry." Some common sexual protection pacts are: "I'll pretend not to turn on to other people if you will too," and "I won't tell you if you won't ask."

The basic attitude behind all these silent agreements is, "Let's both pretend it isn't there." The catch comes when one partner breaks a silent contract, because inherent in "I won't bring this up if you won't make me face that," is the threat "If you dare bring *this* up, I'll for sure bring up *that*." Each partner needs to be keeping a vindictive beast somewhere inside of them, ready to attack the other if betrayed. It's a system of mutual blackmail, which is destructive to closeness, trust and a sense of freedom within the relationship. These kinds of contracts increase the tension and fragility of a relationship because the connection is so conditional. Without these contracts, there can be a feeling of stability and commitment which is not conditional to any contracts and, therefore, makes infinite space for individual expression, growth, and freedom within the couple connection. "I love you not because of what you do or what role you play or what you fulfill for me, but because you are you. I am happiest when we are both feeling most free to be ourselves."

Sit down with your partner periodically and try to verbalize any silent protection contracts you feel you have. Talk over your fears together and see if there are other ways you can support one another where you feel afraid and help each other deal with these feelings openly.

The List

A fun exercise I've found helpful for getting in touch with my patterns in choosing partners is to make a list of major intimate relationships I've had up to the present. I make five columns: (1) my partner's name (2) his or her basic personality type (3) their body type (4) my characteristic role in relation to them and (5) why we split up. You can make this last category one general category about a mutual problem, or two categories (one, his crucial contribution to the split; two, your crucial contribution to the breach).

1	2	3	4	5
N	intellectual, sensitive	small, boyish	intellectual, sensitive	didn't fight
J	exotic, crazy	tall, wiry	ethereal poet	too unstable
L	intellectual, sensitive	stocky	sexy	too possessive

I can look at the list and see how my preference for certain types of people has changed. I've found that I often unconsciously choose a partner to be an extension of myself, that is, someone who I feel possesses characteristics which I want.

164

So I look at my list to see how my choices reflect my balance needs. I ask myself: What kind of partner do I prefer? What type of person do I attract? Do I attract the people I want to? What does the type of person I attract tell me about what kind of image I must project? Do I choose people who will consistently make the same kinds of contracts with me? How am I different when my partner's not around? What parts of myself am I shutting off to be with them? What is my fantasy about what would happen if I did not hold back? What are my fears about being alone? What are my fears about being open and intimate.

Breathing Together

Some of Magda Proskauer's breathing exercises can be done in pairs and are useful for becoming aware of how you alter your naturalness to be with someone else.

Sit back to back with your partner on the floor with your legs comfortably crossed. Sit so that as much of your two spines is touching as possible without straining. Now tune in to how you are leaning against each other. You may have sat automatically so that neither person is exerting more pressure than the other; the two of you are sitting comfortably so that you support each other without strain.

You may not automatically have this relationship. Is one person exerting more pressure than the other? Are you the "leaner" or the "leaned on?" Does this feel comfortable to you or not? Is this a relationship which is typical of the two of you at other times?

If you are feeling uncomfortable, too leaned on or too leaning, without talking, indicate to your partner how you want to shift positions. Rearrange yourselves so that you are both comfortable. There will be a position in which neither of you feels pressed, and both of you feel supported.

165

Now close your eyes and notice where your breath is in your body. Relax the muscles of your abdomen and let your breath sink a little deeper into your pelvis. Can you feel any movement in your lower back as a result of your breathing? Stay tuned in to that feeling a moment — the feeling of the in and out motion of your lower back as you breathe.

Now tune in to your partner's breathing. Can you feel your partner's breath at all — or can you only feel your own? Can you feel any movement in your partner's back as a result of his or her breathing? If so, stay with that feeling a moment. What happens to your own breathing when you pay attention to your partner's? Do you lose track of your own breath? Or can you feel your partner's breathing, and still keep aware of your own?

Now move slightly away from your partner. Does any sensation from your partner's breathing continue even though you are not touching?

Now move back to back again and lock arms at the elbows. Lean against each other firmly and stand up together!

Sex Roles and the Real Me

Tuning in to your sex roles is an important step in awareness of your patterns with men. I talked with Stella Resnick about her feelings on women's and men's sex roles and what kinds of Gestalt exercises are helpful for sex role awareness.

She is a clinical psychologist and a Gestalt therapist who works at the Gestalt Institute of San Francisco and is in private practice doing individual and group therapy.

Me: I'd like to talk about what you experience as the difference between being treated in a sex role and not being treated in that role.

Stella: My own interest is in how I treat *myself* within a sex role. My role behavior comes from learned expectations of how I *should* behave and how I'll be treated, possibly rewarded, by someone else as a result. On the other hand, behavior which comes from my own motivations is much more in tune with *my* desires, with what nourishes me.

Me: It's hard to distinguish sometimes between the two. I've found I need to frequently ask myself: "Am I doing this thing for me or for someone else?" My conditioning to make "little" concessions is so intricate and pervasive. It's the little concessions that add up to a general feeling of not being myself.

Stella: I'm conscious now of some of the places I operate within role expectations. In my own psychotherapy, it became apparent to me that I wanted to be a "good woman." A good woman stays home, I thought; a good woman is a wife; a good woman is a mother; she serves her husband; she's always giving.

I had a lot of guilt because obviously I wasn't doing those things! I wasn't a wife, or a mother. I was into my own work, my excitement, my creativity, enhancing *myself.* That wasn't a good woman at all! By my definition, I was a bad woman. So what I felt was, "I don't deserve to be loved." What guilt!

I can trace it back to learning it from my folks. Those attitudes are very insidious and deep. They adhere because they're learned at such as early age when we are defining our identity. These role attitudes become very much a part of the self concept.

We all need some sort of structure in which to operate and by which to define our self. Letting go of some of this structure can be very frightening. When we let go of role behaviours, without replacing them with solid attitudes based on self-awareness, we feel a void — "Who am I?"

Me: It takes me awhile to get in touch with what is under my structure. For me, being "a good, nice person" was a big deal. Often I didn't do what I wanted, but I thought I was being "nice" to other people and that was more important. Then I realized that I wasn't nice! My behavior was dishonest and manipulative. I'm letting go of some of these controls, but it's disorienting and scary. "Who am I if I'm not 'nice Kent?' She knew how to get people to like her. How will people react if I act the way I am?"

Stella: Changing brings out our conflicts between approval and loneliness — because we assume, I think, that if we are not whatever we see as 'a good woman' or 'a nice person,' we will not be loved. That is always the greatest fear. To be loved seems to be a basic need of the human animal and make us social animals.

The greatest sense of self comes when I recognize that the feeling of approval comes from the love of self in its plainness, rather than from what I can *do.* (This is also true with self-love or self-acceptance.) When you love me for my attributes — because I am so and so, or can do such and such — I'm never satisfied. The satisfaction of love really comes when you love me for my plainness, for my simplicity, for what I am, not for what I can do. That's a satisfying kind of love. That goes way beyond roles.

Me: You know, the same struggle is there even with friends. I have a new friend. We met recently. We talked. We had lunch a couple of times. We liked each other. Among other things, she teaches tennis, and she felt she had to give me a tennis lesson so I would like her, because she's good at that. It was really hard for her to believe that I could just like her before she demonstrated her skills. And I felt the same kind of thing! I wanted to do some 'body work' on her, so she'd be impressed. What a distraction! It's so deeply conditioned that approval comes from demonstrating "accomplishments."

Stella: Yes. And it's important to recognize that it takes two of us to perpetuate the system. All role behavior is complementary. One role fits against another. Like the role of mother to child, teacher to student, wife to husband, weak to strong, victim to aggressor.

When you talk about a woman's role, the complementary man's role is implicit. That's why there can only be limited women's liberation without man's liberation.

Now women are becoming more conscious and focusing on self-importance instead of role importance. I see "sex-roles" undergoing an evolving change, but I don't see the whole thing going at once, by legislative act, new customs, or even by simply an awareness of the oppression behind the role.

To abandon some of those expectations of rewards — to allow the recognition that the old patterns of behaving are not rewarding or fulfilling — comes very slowly and with pain. There is always a feeling of loss in giving up concepts lived by so deeply for so long. Abandoning expectations so tied up with our concept of self feels like ripping a part of ourselves away.

Me: I have so many dreams, or fantasies, connected with those reward expectations! I'm attached to them sentimentally, that is, unrealistically. It's difficult to say goodbye to them even when I see they don't work. But I sure feel better when I do!

Stella: Here you need to be sure to distinguish which role behaviors are self-nourishing and which are not; simply because you experience something as role behavior does not mean that you ought to give it up. Things like motherhood, cooking, sewing can be outwardly rewarding *and* internally satisfying.

Probably as a result of my being a woman, I've learned to cook and I enjoy cooking for people I care for. To give that up because that's a "woman's demeaning role" would be ridiculous.

Me: I think a lot of women are really confused at that place now because they think they ought to give up every role.

Stella: You also need to be patient. It's important also to appreciate that the labeling of self as a particular sex happens very early and is very deeply engrained: "Congratulations, Mrs. Smith. It's a boy!" By the age of two, the child has already learned to "be" a boy or a girl by behaving in certain ways. Kids learn there is boy behavior and girl behavior, boy play and girl play. One of the worst things you can say to a little boy is that he's like a girl. And it's an affront to call a girl a tom boy. This continues into adulthood. Generally one of the worst things you can accuse a person of is "un-role-like" behavior.

This comes up in psychotherapy. People often indicate that the worst thing they can imagine discovering about themselves is that they are homosexual. They're saying the worst thing they could find is that they are a masculine woman or an effeminate man. There's so much cultural stigma attached to abandoning role behavior.

Me: It seems to me there's no faith that your organism will simply just be itself. That if you're biologically a woman, you'll be a woman whether you're consciously playing out your sex role or not. There's a feeling that you have to learn to do "feminine" things, conditioned mannerisms, and then you will be a woman.

Stella: Most of those things are irrelevant, but I think some of them are realistic. Higher animals do learn some kinds of sex roles which are important to species maintenance. Harlow discovered that monkeys raised in isolation did not carry out appropriate mating behavior. Or they were lousy parents, if they ever got it on.

A lot of sexual behavior is learned rather than innate for humans too. We mimic how our parents and other models relate physically. People need to take baby care classes and can profit from seeing sex films. What can get in our way are unnecessary, unsatisfying and rigid cultural role mannerisms; these are what are in transition now.

When we talk about the current sexual revolution we're really talking about an isolated behavior, fucking. In the broader terms of sex roles, liberation is coming but a lot more slowly.

We need to recognize the difference between the expectations we have and what it is we want, what nourishes me, what feels right, what feels good. Learning to differentiate is important.

Again, much of that is learned so it takes time to sort out my deepest preferences, and it takes time to go through the pain of being unable to achieve reward in the learned ways.

Me: Are there any Gestalt exercises I could do to get in touch with my roles and my feelings about them?

Stella: Well, one thing to do is to recognize what your "shoulds" are. Sit on one chair and face an empty chair. Imagine that there are two parts of you, one on each chair. Tell yourself all you should be to be a good woman. Talk to "yourself" on that empty chair and say, "To be a good woman you have to: bla, bla, bla." List all your requirements, and listen to yourself as you talk. This is a way to discover the expectations you lay on yourself. Now switch chairs and answer with how you feel about trying to live up to those expectations.

A Good Man Should

Any demand I put on myself puts a complementary demand on someone else. If I have expectations of myself as a "good woman,' you can be sure I have expectations of what a man ought to be in order to be a 'good man' to me!

Men and women are constantly making unspoken 'bargains' and 'contracts' to complement each other's roles. An exercise to tune in to your role expectations on others is to imagine that a man you are close to is sitting on the opposite chair; tell him what he should be and do. (You can also share this directly with the man.)

Then switch chairs. Imagine you are that man, and experience how these expectations make you feel. How would you respond to your demands if you were him? You'll probably discover what a burden it is to attempt to live up to someone elses expectations.

Me: It takes a lot of special effort to act unnaturally!

Stella: And the man's role is a burden to himself, though differently than the way a woman's role is a burden. The roles are complementary, and the burdens and freedoms of the two are complementary.

If a man has to be "someone to lean on," he's carrying a lot of weight. "I can be passive because my man will be strong, aggressive and assertive. My man will take care of everything — and he better! If he doesn't, he's a sissy. He's no good. He's not a man."

A man has to be a breadwinner. It's culturally accepted and much easier today for a woman to decide not to have a job, not to make money. Personally she may want to go out and work, but she has a choice. For a man, making the choice to stay home or not work still goes very much against his role.

Reversing Roles

Me: Are there exercises couples could do for role awareness?

Stella: They can reverse roles and play each other; then make demands as though they were their mate. This helps you experience how your partner sees you, and how it feels to receive the demands you put on him or her.

After that you act out how you would *like* your mate to be. She, playing him, might say, "You're so beautiful tonight, dear. I love that dress on you. You make it lovely!" Playing her, he might respond, "Darling, I'm so glad you're home. You must be very tired. Let me massage your head a little. Here's this wonderful dinner I've made for you."

Matching Strengths

Sometimes in couple therapy I have the two people get into a physical battle to exemplify the power struggle between them. You make a contract not to physically hurt each other but to focus on matching strengths.

The husband of one couple I worked with recently was always complaining about how his wife pushed him around. I had her lie down on her stomach. Then he lay on top of her on his stomach and held her arms down. Their instructions were for her to get up on her feet and for him to keep her down. It was a very interesting exercise for them — their patterns became very clear. She started pulling all her tricks; he responded to them, even knowing they were tricks! He kept insisting that we give her a handicap. He said, "Well, it's not fair. I'm too strong for you. Perhaps I should use only one hand."

It was very clear what his 50% of the contract for their weak/strong role game was. He wanted her to be top dog. In a relationship that's always the case — 50% one, 50% the other. It just isn't 90%/10%. Whatever they are doing is always by mutual agreement.

Me: One thing I do when I hear myself making some sort of an accusation about my partner is ask myself, "Hey, What am I doing to perpetuate this? What's *my* complementary role?" Are there some techniques couples can use to get in touch with their mutual contracts?

Stella: You can have these mock fights. But it's really very hard to get outside your process. I think the best thing a couple can do is go into couple therapy together. They get a trained and fairly impartial observer that way.

You know, understanding yourself in a relationship is very tough. I can't understand how I am in relation to someone else unless I really understand who I am

172

alone, what I want, what is good for me, what my basic undisturbed rhythm is. It's very important to get in touch with my own self-permissiveness, or lack of it. How do I hold myself back? How do I not grant myself permission to do or to enjoy? What are my specific anxieties about how much pleasure I experience?

I'm discovering that pleasure anxiety is one of the greatest limitations that people place on themselves. We're much more willing to experience pain than pleasure! We all have it. Superstitutions — like knocking on wood — come from pleasure anxiety. I have it. Last week I was so happy that I started bumming myself out by saying, "I know something is going to happen to make this bad." It was my way of dealing with my own pleasure anxiety.

Me: I get scared that I'll lose what is making me happy. I don't want to feel that pain of losing pleasure, so I hold back on my pleasure. Crazy!

There's also simply discomfort in change and a need to adjust. I feel disoriented by change, even if the change is for the better. It's in me, and I see it in other couples who try to hold each other back unconsciously, from fear of upsetting their balance and not being able to adjust to changes.

Stella: Yes. And there's so much guilt about feeling good! "I'm not supposed to feel *this* happy. I'll be punished." To me that is a major change we have to confront in our modern world.

We are getting closer to our body preferences. Getting away from role behavior is part of this process. Role behavior limits *my* pleasure because it is prescribed. The more in touch I am with my deepest feelings, the more pleasure I experience; along with that I experience pleasure anxiety which I need to work through.

We are an enlightened civilization gradually becoming more enlightened. Our culture is basically moving in the direction of more pleasure acceptance. That's why role behavior, along with other behaviors, is in evolution right now. When we talk about the difference between 'straight' people and 'hip' people, a lot of that distinction is in terms of role. Straight people are seen as more oriented toward their outer role, while hip people are seen as more oriented towards their inner motivations.

Me: I think a lot of people think they're not as clear or sharp or "together" when they're happy as when they're unhappy. For me it's a feeling of being 'off-guard.'

Stella: Many artists have that. "I have to be miserable to create. If I'm happy, there's no motivation." Until recently artists had to leave the society and struggle physically to allow for their creative expression which came from pain. We need to do that less and less, and a lot of modern art comes from a more positive place. Picasso was certainly no struggling artist like Van Gogh or Gaugin. Many artists today are well-to-do, successful. They are beginning to express the joy of life and the experience of an enlightened existence rather than pain and alienation. And change is becoming the rhythm and rule of our society rather than the exception. Rigid role behavior doesn't fit this fluidity.

The women's liberation movement is part of the whole transformation to self-awareness apart from one's role. It's a move towards greater creativity and individualism. The women's movement in that way is like a number of other movements saying, "I've been labeled and it doesn't fit or feel good. I want to get out of my role with all its fixed associations."

Any group which revolts against their role, also revolts against the role of their complements. The blacks who started the Civil Rights movement are not the only ones who have reaped the benefits. The ones who experience the oppression revolt first, but all of us have benefited from freeing ourselves of some of our role behavior and becoming more ourselves. Revolutionaries aren't any more oppressed than other people; they just experience their oppression more. That applies to women's and men's liberation being complementary.

Me: I know of almost no men who have the concept of themselves as oppressed by their roles.

Stella: I think males often don't recognize their oppression as sexist. It is usually dealt out by other men, while women usually experience their oppression at the hands of men. Take the draft. That's obviously male sexist oppression, but it's administered to men by men. Or the career pressure on men. The pressure of being a husband and a breadwinner.

The oppression of having to pay for a woman when he takes her out, even though she may earn more money than he does. The feeling of inferiority, insecurity and unworthiness that comes if he doesn't pay for her. The oppression that comes from having the physical burden in a relationship. The man opens doors, parks the car, and carries heavy bundles, as though men don't experience the discomfort of "heavy." Men are not supposed to show emotion, softness, sadness. They are supposed to be aggressive and objective. They're not supposed to be affectionate toward each other, which cuts off a whole area of support and warmth that women are more allowed to share with each other. These areas have not been identified as male oppression, but they are.

Me: I was talking with a friend of mine recently who's very active in the women's movement. She said her husband has been changing his feelings. He decided,

"I'm going to stop buying my male responsibility role." He quit his job which was mostly supporting them and 'dropped out.' She wasn't really prepared for that! Now they are working it out together and both feel better.

Stella: There are so many responsibilities women put on men! There's oppression in both sex roles, but because women feel their constriction more, there's going to be uneven development.

That's a big problem for a lot of women right now who don't want to compromise. It's hard to find a man to spend time with who isn't attached to his limited sex role.

Beyond the biological sex difference which dictates social behavior to some degree, we need freedom to choose our experiences by preference rather than by dictate. It's very exciting to project a world where there is awareness of one's own inner self as enlightened parents raise their children to be more in tune with their selves.

My fantasy is of a society of gentler people and more satisfactory individual experience because people will be more tuned in to their own individual inner natures. Once we are more in tune with ourselves and more allowing of ourselves as a result, we'll be more allowing of others.

Balancing the Female and Male Parts Within Ourselves

Most of the exercises in this section are to be done with a partner. They offer ways of exploring together behavior patterns which you might ordinarily consider outside your sex role. If you stay with these experiments past your initial feelings of awkwardness at doing something new, I think you will discover how much more pleasure you could allow yourself. (See Alan Watts' essay "The Future of Ecstasy" in a paperback called *The Pursuit of Pleasure.*)

Each of the exercises is designed to reverse your masculine/feminine roles as they are probably now set up. As you do them, notice what your specific fears and discomforts are about acting "unfeminine." What feels exciting and pleasurable about it? How does your mate feel getting into unrole-like behavior? How do you feel about him or her acting in this new way?

It is likely that as you get more into your own confidence and aggressiveness, your partner will begin to experience some insecurity which, because of the burden of his male in-command role, has not been allowed to surface before. How do you feel about your partner showing vulnerability? Do you react with "You're weak!" or can you receive it as an important sharing from your partner which could bring the two of you closer? Recognize that it takes strength to be willing to be open about one's fears and vulnerability and to trust that you won't be judgemental. Openly sharing your fears is a way of confronting them with someone else and dealing with them so that you can help each other grow.

You: Female and Male

A basic place to start is by exploring your own feelings about femininity and masculinity. Divide the room you are in by an imaginary line down the middle into a "feminine" side and a "masculine" side. Be standing on the masculine side. Talk aloud about how you feel being masculine. "I am big and tall and loud. I yell a lot. I most fast and decisively. I stomp. I am in charge. I'm in command of the things around me." As you speak, let yourself act out these qualities by talking loud and stomping. Let your body move in what you feel is a masculine way.

Now walk over to the feminine side of the room. Feel the difference. Let yourself verbalize the difference in the qualities you feel as being feminine. "I move more slowly. I am aware of my long dress moving against my legs. I am talking more softly and musically. I have a different relationship to the objects around me; I want to touch them and smell them; I feel a kinship with the plants and the textures. I want to sit down now."

How does it feel to play each role? Think about people you see frequently and your regular activities. During which situations do you act particularly "feminine" and which "masculine?" Experiment with opposite roles in each situation and notice how the new role feels. Are there traits which you would consider "masculine" which would be useful to you in a situation you normally term "feminine?" Experiment with mixing the two types of role behavior in the same situation, alternating to fit your needs.

176

Passive/Active Exercises

In their studies of human sexual behavior, Drs. Johnson and Masters found that the inhibitions of rigid role behavior are a major block to sexual pleasure. An exercise they give for opening up some of these behaviors is called Sensate Focus. I am including a variation of this exercise here.

Sensate Focus

There are two basic aspects of Sensate Focus: one is to give each partner a chance to experience being totally aggressive sexually, and also totally receptive; the other is to learn to forget time clocks and goals.

Choose a time when you both feel relaxed and unhurried and will not be interrupted. The basic activity of Sensate Focus is massage so the room you use should be comfortably warm for both of you to be nude.

If you are usually the more receptive and responsive of the two of you in lovemaking, it is your turn to take the aggressive role. After a hot bath or shower, have your partner lie face down on a massage table, the bed, or a pad on the floor covered with a sheet. Spread warm oil all over your partner's body and then begin to massage their feet. Work extremely slowly and intricately. *Don't worry about technical strokes.* You are touching your partner to communicate your feelings, not your expertise. Do what you hands want to. Include lots of feather light stroking along with smooth firm strokes with your palms and fingers. Work you way slowly up the legs and back.

Now have your partner turn over. Massage from the feet up the legs slowly to the hips. Bypass the genitals and massage the stomach, chest, and face.

It is important as you do this that both of you have a desire to forget about time and the "goal" of orgasm. If you are receiving, let yourself be massaged without directing it and get into the current feelings you are having in whatever part of your body is being touched. If you can do this you will discover new areas and dimensions of pleasure. Paradoxically also, if you do have an orgasm, it will be fuller and more powerful for your having allowed relaxation and more feeling to flow into every part of your body.

Finally you as the giver of the massage do massage the pelvic area and the genitals. By now your partner is probably feeling extremely relaxed and sensitized so that your lightest touch on the genital area will be felt. Massage all the intricate contours of your partner's genitals very slowly and carefully and gently. Now and then use one of your hands to massage another area of your partner's body simultaneously. If you had agreed at the beginning of the massage to continue until orgasm, keep massaging the genitals and other particularly erotic areas until your partner reaches a climax. Try to be open and responsive to your partner's own individual rhythm. If you are receiving the massage try to see what happens if you let yourself relax and go completely *at your own pace* without any thought of hurrying for someone else or pleasing them.

After you are done share your feelings about how the massage was to do and to receive. On another day, trade places and you be the receiver while your partner is the giver. In which role are you more comfortable?

Connecting

Most of us consider only a small portion of our bodies (the pelvic area and the genitals) erotic. This seems to me to be a learned adult state far different from the natural total responsiveness of a young child's body. "Connecting" is a technique by which you can learn to re-eroticize your whole body so that your pleasure is not so localized. It is a good exercise to use with men who have desensitized their nipples and chest (thinking that it is not manly to be sensitive there) and want to allow more feeling in this area. You can also use connecting to open up erotic feeling in any other part of the body.

When you are making love and touching your partner's genitals begin with your other hand to gently massage one of his nipples. (If you already know which nipple is more sensitive, choose that one.) Keep massaging the two areas simultaneously until your partner reaches a peak of pleasure. Then remove your hand from his genitals while continuing to massage the nipple. Repeat this sequence several times.

If you do this frequently when you make love or share massage, eventually the nipples and breast area will become as sensitive and excitable as the genital area.

Talk over with your partner later how he feels about allowing more sensation into this area.

Here are two erotic massage strokes I learned from Shirley Lewis and Wilbur Hoff, which are inventive "connecting" strokes. To feel best they require covering your partner first with a light film of massage oil. The proportion of how exquisite these strokes feel seems to increase with how light your touch is. The speed will vary some with each individual's taste, but should be quite slow.

178

Your partner should be lying on his or her back on a bed, massage table, or covered pad. Be sure the room is warm.

Sit on your partner's left side facing his or her abdomen. Place both hands, palms down, on your partner's abdomen and begin *very* lightly and *very* slowly making large circles on this area with your whole hand. Continue these circles for a while.

Now slowly separate your hands, moving one palm down the inside of your partner's leg and the other up the chest. Your right hand going across the chest traces a line from the abdomen, across the ribs, over the left nipple, over the left pectoral muscle arc, and into the armpit. *At the same time* your left hand moves from the abdomen, over the hip, down the inside of the thigh, inside the calf, across the ankle, ending up in the arch of your partner's left foot.

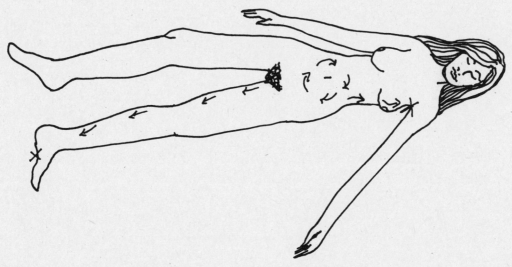

Much of the success of this stroke depends on timing: your hands should be crossing the thigh and ribs at the same time and should also reach the armpit and foot arch simultaneously. Now, make slow *light* circles in each arch with your two hands in time; stay with this light motion awhile.

Now begin the return trip. Retrace your paths toward the abdomen, moving still slowly and feather light. (Cross the thigh and side simultaneously.) End with a few more circles on the abdomen.

Repeat this stroke on your partner's right side.

Two V's

Your partner is lying on their back. You will need to be sitting, facing toward your partner's head, about parallel to his or her left knee. Place both hands on the left foot. Position your hands so that  your thumbs and fingers form a "V" cupping the top of the foot. Move slowly and lightly. At first move both hands together side by side over the ankle and onto the calf.

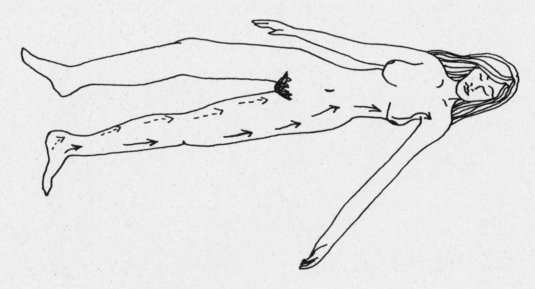

Now pace your outer (right) hand faster than your inside hand (because you want your right hand to reach the armpit when the inside hand reaches your partner's crotch). The path of your right hand is up the outside of your partner's left leg, over the hip, over the abdomen and ribs and left nipple, until your fingers are on the left pectoral muscles.

All the while your left hand has been moving even more slowly up the inside of your partner's left leg so that your fingers touch the crease between the thigh and pelvis *just as* your upper hand touches the crease of the armpit. Now comes the peak of the stroke — your two hands are going to simultaneously do the same light squeezing stroke on each "crotch." Do this by moving both sets of fingertips simultaneously down the crease of the armpit and the crease of the pelvis. As your thumbs slide toward your fingers in this motion, "pinch" thumbs and fingers together lightly as they move down the two creases. Particularly pleasing about this stroke is the "rolling" sensation created by the repetition of stroking the two areas, once with your fingers and again with your thumbs — and the internal sensation that the two areas being massaged are somehow the same.

Now quite slowly retrace the path of both hands down your partner's left side, ending as you began with both palms resting on the foot. Repeat the stroke on your partner's right side.

Other Connections

You can also try inventing your own strokes for connecting: the mouth and the nipples, the perineum and the navel, the perineum and the back of the neck, the mouth and the genitals, the palms of the hands and the bottom centers of the feet, the asshole and the bottom centers of your feet, the tip of the nose and the nipples.

Anger and Sex

I've found that resentment from repressed anger very often comes out as sexual coldness. It is unfortunately traditionally a feminine "weapon." Holding out in bed seems to be one of the few strongholds a woman who sees herself as powerless falls back on. This process cuts deeply into your own pleasure as well as your partner's.

The next time you feel distant and annoyed when your partner approaches you sexually, ask yourself, "Am I angry and resentful about something now, or about something which happened at another time? Am I holding out here because I did not express myself fully there?" Share your feelings with your partner.

181

If you feel you have trouble including your resentments along with your other communications, here is an exercise you can do with your partner to become accustomed to voicing them.

Anger Awareness

Sit opposite each other and choose one person to be the listener and the other the talker. If you are the talker, start by listing some things you are angry about connected with your partner. Don't worry about how silly they may sound. The object of the exercise is not to be "reasonable" or "right" but to share your feelings so you can deal with them, let go of them, and move on. "I feel angry when you . . . don't help with the dishes . . . don't feed the dog . . . come home late without calling . . . make fun of me . . . try to tell me what to do . . . clam up and don't show me what you're feeling." Phrase your sentences so that you make it clear that these are your feelings and not an accusation about how horrible the other person is. Saying "I feel angry when you don't call" leaves space for the other person to hear you without feeling defensive. It evokes a different response than, "You are a lousy unthoughtful creep for not calling last night!" One is a way of communicating your feelings and offering to work something different out. The other is simply name-calling, which usually makes the other person resentful and argumentative.

If you are the listener, keep in mind that what you hear is not so much a statement about you as *a statement about how the other person perceives things.* Answer each statement with only "I hear you." Pay close attention to your own reactive processes by noting when you want to defend yourself, be judgemental and reasonable, make excuses, or when you want to counter with accusations of your own.

Now switch roles with your partner and repeat the process.

George Bach has written a helpful book on fighting and couple relationships called *The Intimate Enemy* (Morrow, paper).

Couples and Communication

Good communication, being able to send direct messages and also to listen clearly, is an essential element of a growing continuing relationship. In my talk with Cynthia Werthman Sheldon of the Gestalt Institute of San Francisco we discussed communication between couples, and I have included that part of the tape here. (See the section called *Talking To Yourself* for her discussion of Gestalt Therapy.)

Me: I'd like to talk about patterns you've observed in women clients.

Cyndy: In my practice I've noticed that it is often the woman in the couple relationship who comes into therapy first: she's upset, and usually more dependent on the relationship with her man for her satisfaction — she has the kids, has taken the role of cook and housekeeper, and may never have developed any of her own creativity outside these areas. She may come in with complaints of being very bitchy lately and taking it out on her kids, being depressed, turning off to her husband sexually and turning on to others, or being physically sick a lot.

Therapy can help her get in touch with her own strengths. She may take back the power she has given her man — to approve of her, or not — and she may begin asserting herself without playing games. So instead of making nagging statements like "You never help out," or "You're always late," (these are blame statements) she may begin to tell him more how she feels and what she wants. "When you come home late I get upset, angry, hurt, and I'd like you to call me ahead of time if you're going to be late." Or "I know I complain a lot. There are things you do which infuriate me. Instead of complaining, I'm going to let you have it!" Or, she may realize she isn't angry at her husband. "I'm not really mad at you and the kids even though I've acted that way. I realize I just spend too much time at home. I need more space to do my own thing. Maybe I'll take that real estate course after all." So during the course of therapy she gets clearer about her underlying feelings of what she wants for herself and how to communicate these in a more direct and clear manner.

This shift in her behavior is often quite threatening to the man. He is not used to his woman being so straightforward! At this point he may come into therapy.

If the man comes in and also learns how to be clear and direct, then you can end up with two people who want two different things at the same time. How do they get along? Often each person insists on their way; to give in to the other is seen as giving up, losing or copping out. A power struggle ensues.

Me: Does that include competition about who's the more powerful sex?

Cyndy: Yes! Each time the man does his own thing, the woman may feel she's less of a woman; when the man gives in to the woman, he may feel less of a man.

Me: As long as they stay within that framework, they have to be working against each other; for one to "win" the other has to "lose." There's no place for getting together; it's an endless loop.

Cyndy: Yes, the loop is endless and so alienating. The $64,000 question is, "How can I take care of myself, be assertive *and* be open to your love and care about you without competing?" So often this seems like an impossible task. To me it isn't, but it also isn't easy! And being "in love" may have nothing to do with it at all. Only after you've gotten clear what you need and want for yourself can you then know whether you and your man can provide a setting for you both to get what you want.

Me: To break the loop and come together, it would be necessary to be aware of the role I was playing. Are there some Gestalt games to help me become more aware of where I'm stuck in self-defeating roles?

Cyndy: A good place to start is to try to communicate basic feelings. I saw this exercise on an educational television show: Sit opposite your partner on the floor and alternately trade feelings you're having, in one word, such as "happy, depressed, nervous, excited, anxious, numb, insecure, wondering." Say, "nothing" if you don't feel anything at the moment.

Stay away from all thoughts. If a thought comes, try to get in touch with the feeling behind the thought. If you *think,* "I don't like how you are looking at me," ask yourself how that thought makes you *feel.* Sad? Scared? Angry? Pay attention to your process as you do the exercise; notice which emotions you avoid and when you want to qualify and judge. Leave out explanations and judgements.

It may sound quite simple but it is hard to do. We tend to move away from our feelings without even noticing. You could have a third person observe and bring you back by saying, "Stay with your feelings."

The Four Elements of Communication

Anytime two people talk, there are four things happening: what I say, maybe a message underneath, what you hear, and what you think my intent is. Most of the time we miss what people are sending and hear our own imagined intent. For example, if I compliment you, you may think, "She's just saying that because she wants something from me."

Another helpful exercise is to sit down and have a conversation *including* all four of those communication elements in what you say: one person says what she wants to communicate; the other answers with what he hears her saying; then she says what she really means.

If he says, "I want to go out to dinner tonight," your response might be, "I hear that you don't like my cooking and you don't want to tell me." If he doesn't feel that, he might say, "No, that's not what I am feeling. I want to go to a restaurant because both of us are tired from working all day and I think it would feel good to have someone else wait on us tonight!"

Me: What are some common misunderstandings?

Cyndy: The "simple" process of talking and listening is so often confused. A classic misunderstanding is the communication when a husband tells his wife he's having an affair. She has many choices as to how she hears that! The intent might be to provoke her; the intent might be to relieve his guilt; he may want to be honest and explore the meaning of this to their relationship; he may want to be close to her again; he may want her to mother him. The possibilities are many. The only way to know his real intent is to check it out by asking.

Another common miscommunication goes on when the husband comes home at night and the wife hits him with all the things that went on with the kids that day. He can hear that as a bunch of silly, irrelevant nonsense, or maybe as complaining. "You have a good time all day with all those other people and your secretaries, and look what I've been doing." Well, it's very important for him to find out her intent. I've found that often the wife's intent is to make contact. She isn't particularly interested in talking about the kids but she's using that to start a conversation. She may not know how to make contact in more meaningful ways.

The man often does the same thing. He comes home from work upset about his day and talks on and on. The wife doesn't understand his business. She gets upset. She feels left out. She feels he's more married to his business than to her. His intent may have been to make contact and share.

Me: The more we talk about all this the more I feel the ridiculousness of trying to make contact with somebody who has so little commonality of experience — mainly because of the rigidity of the roles!

Cyndy: Well, there are basic cultural and social differences which make relationships difficult, but in my experience everyone comes from a unique background and this means that the role assumptions will be different for everyone. One man may have grown up assuming that women are supposed to act in a quiet, reserved manner. His woman may have grown up assuming that women are supposed to be bubbly, cheerful, outgoing. They'd have trouble understanding each other and getting along, perhaps, if they didn't work on their different perceptions and come to some understanding. Otherwise everytime she is bubbly and outgoing he might feel upset.

Expectation Awareness

Our family and origin have given each of us hundreds of little rules about men, women, family life, children — many of these rules are out of our awareness. Yet in a relationship we may unconsciously bring these rules in as "expectations." "If you really loved me you'd bring me not just a cake for my birthday but flowers too (like my father used to do for my mother)."

A fun thing to do would be to make a list of all the rules and expectations for sex roles and love you can remember from your family or origin. Also list new ones you've added. Share the list with your partner. See if the two of you can understand your differences, rather than put the other down for them. It can be very helpful to bring out these unstated expectations because they often function as unspoken tests. If the man doesn't come through with those flowers, he's failed (without knowing)! It's a destructive miscommunication.

Me: There's a special woman's culture that we grow up with too which comes from magazines and advertising. "If a man really loves me, he does all those things it says he does in *Ladies Home Journal.*" But he's never even read *Ladies Home Journal!* He doesn't know about those expectations.

Cyndy: Yes. And a man probably has a whole list for his woman too. You can learn a lot about each other by sharing your expectations. Then you need to talk them over and find out which ones are agreeable to both of you and which ones aren't. Your husband may love you very much and still not want to give you flowers for your birthday! Fritz Perls often said we marry our expectations, and we don't see the person. We see our ideal.

I Like/I Don't Like

Me: Something helpful I've done is to sit down with the person I'm living with and start talking about all the reasons I do and don't like living with him. We each make a long list of the negative things and then the positive. Both are useful information. It gives him a picture of what it's like for me to live with him that often doesn't get verbalized. Then it's his turn. I like to end with the positive because when he starts listing all the good things about living with me, it's great to hear them and feel really appreciated.

Cyndy: The negative feedback is helpful too. But you need to learn how to say the negative things you feel without disqualifying the other person or closing off yourself.

Me: I can really feel now how much of an act of love it is for someone to stay vulnerable and open to me while feeling angry.

Cyndy: It's so crucial to keep the connection open while fighting — that is, if you want to work things out! Things such as labelling and namecalling cut the connection. "You're a bitch. You're lazy. You're stupid." They are ways of closing off that leave no room for response except defensiveness and argument.

We're brought up in a very judgemental society. We're taught to believe that there's such a thing as right, wrong, good, bad, better, worse, smart, dumb — and then we go around putting everyone in boxes (including ourselves) which cuts us off from each other.

One popular label of husband to wife is "You're just being emotional!" That cancels her out and the whole discussion! She may not be coming across clear and straight. She may be whining and bitching, but she may also be genuinely upset. It's important to differentiate between your partner's manner and what she wants to communicate. The husband could say, "Hey, wait a minute. All I hear now is whining and complaining. What are you really trying to say to me?" The other half of that is the wife who says, "You're just being withdrawn and unfeeling again" — rather than saying "I don't like your pulling away from me. I'd like to be closer to you. What are you really feeling?"

So many people don't know the difference between game playing (manipulative emotion) and deep feelings.

Me: Yeah. A lot of women label themselves as the feeling emotional one and the man as the cold one.

Cyndy: And she may be playing as much of a game as he is! I'm thinking of the woman who insists her husband

listen to her feelings since her friends or therapist have encouraged her to express her feelings more. And what often happens is she splashes her feelings all over the room. She whines and crys and rages, etc. She usually feels unsatisfied anyway. No wonder. In women (and many men too) like this, their feelings are often surface pseudo feelings that don't come from deep within one's center.

In my experience someone who is angry on the surface a lot, may be feeling a lot of sadness and pain way down deep. And many who seem sad, fearful and helpless on the outside may feel a great deal of anger and rage down deep.

Many of us have been brought up to avoid those deeper feelings. We may not know they even exist. And we think our surface feelings are all we have.

Me: I've been assuming you've been talking mainly about your experience doing therapy at Family Therapy Institute of Marin where your clients would mostly be married suburban couples. You work with other couples too, younger, hip, unmarried. Is there a big difference in these relationships?

Cyndy: No. I find very little difference. The younger couples may have a lot of experience in the growth movement, Esalen Workshops here and there — and so they "sound" open. They know the language, but they don't know much about relating openly. They get "stuck" just like everyone else. Often it's more difficult to work with couples who know the language and gestures — the therapist can think they're aware and they aren't.

I've worked with couples who live very different life-styles from what we usually mean by suburban. I'm thinking of couples who reverse roles: husband stays home, wife works; or same-sex couples; or threesomes, foursomes; etc. Within all relationships I find everyone has the same kinds of problems relating.

Jealousy and its Alternatives

Lynn Smith is a social psychologist and a sex researcher who lives alternately in Berkeley, California, and New York State. She has been studying "consensual adultery" since 1966, and is currently writing her doctoral thesis, at the University of California, Berkeley, on some of the psychological aspects of co-marital sex (consensual sexual relations among couples). She and her husband, Jay, are currently editing a collection of research articles on Sexual Alternatives in Marriage and are also writing a book on their own research of the last six years entitled *Consenting Adults: An Exploratory Study of the Sexual Freedom Movement.*

In the course of this research Lynn has become interested in the dynamics of sexual jealousy and especially in discovering how individuals and couples manage to reduce and resolve their jealousy feelings. Jealousy has unfortunately received very little scientific attention, yet it often causes severe conflicts for anyone involved in an intimate relationship.

I talked with Lynn about some of the things the couples she interviewed had found useful in dealing with jealousy. Though she and I are talking mainly in terms of actually opening up a couple relationship to other sexual partners, I think her suggestions can be very useful on an emotional and idea level for any couple who simply wants to be more open with each other about their fears and their sexual feelings in an effort to find some alternatives to jealousy.

Me: I'd like to talk today about jealousy. Let's say I'm in a couple relationship in which I feel a lot of jealousy tension, and I want to start dealing with it. Where do I start? What steps come first?

Lynn: Do you want to talk about a couple who is or isn't committed to open sexual relationships with others?

Me: Let's start with a hypothetical stable couple who are not sure about that question, but they know they want to start dealing with their feelings, and hopefully decrease them.

The First Step

Lynn: First, because jealousy seems to be so closely tied with personal security and how you feel about yourself, you need to sit down and get into your own feelings.

- What exactly are my jealous feelings?
- How would I *like* to feel?
- What kind of intimate relationship do I want?
- Why am I choosing to deal with these feelings now?
- How do I feel about myself in general?
- Do I like my body or not? The better you feel about your body, the less likely you are to get jealous.
- How do I feel about making love?
- How do I feel about "how good I am in bed?"
- How much do I enjoy making love? If you don't enjoy making love, you may feel jealous if your partner's with someone else because maybe she enjoys it more, maybe they enjoy it more, and you're left out of these good feelings.
- What are my feelings about deep intimacy?
- Do I want to have multiple relationships because I don't want to put all my eggs in one basket? Am I afraid to get even closer, more vulnerable, and more deeply involved with this one person?

190

- Do I feel like sharing my partner because I respect their individuality, or because I don't really value them too much?

One of the criticisms that some people make of not being monogamous is that then you don't tend to progress and deepen your own relationship. The theory is that there's not as much need to because you get more spread out and you tend not to work on problems between the two of you. I think this is only so if you have decided that you don't want to get closer, or that you're not very happy in the relationship.

Getting involved with other people shouldn't be considered a panacea for marital problems! But new relationships may well alleviate some of the feelings of isolation and boredom, the interpersonal intimacy impoverishment that the isolated nuclear family tends to suffer from, and some of our inhibited and thereby exaggerated desires for sexual variety.

Instead of reducing the energy directed toward the growth and development of your primary relationship, secondary relationships may in fact feed back into and contribute to the depth of your primary relationship. Getting involved with other people can thus be an intermediate step to breaking up — or moving closer.

Examine Your Beliefs

Once you sort some of these feelings out for yourself, you need to communicate your feelings and share them with your partner by:
- beginning to talk about how you feel about other people sexually,
- sharing what relating to someone else means to you,
- and listening to that information from them.

The two of you need to examine your beliefs about situations in which you might get jealous. For example, if your partner is attracted to someone else, or perhaps actually becomes involved with someone else, what interpretations do you put on this situation?

- If you believe that someone can only love one person at a time, then you'll probably react to the situation by thinking your partner doesn't love you anymore.
- Do you think your partner's attraction to someone else implies that you are sexually inadequate?
- Do you suffer all kinds of self-doubts and think that you are not meeting his or her needs?

191

- Do you think that jealousy is a measure of love? If your partner's not jealous when you're interested in someone else, do you think they don't care?

It's notions like that you need to start thinking about, sharing with your partner, and (after clearing away your misconceptions) eventually rejecting in order to relate to other people without feeling jealous.

Me: To me, just the step of sharing my sexual feelings about other people with my mate has been really important. I started noticing about a year ago that I would talk about all kinds of other things that happened to me during the day, but somehow I never included, "And I met this terrific person I really turn on to!" That was a blank in our sharing.

Lynn: You can come to know each other much better if you will share these feelings. Often people find that when they start talking about their sexual attraction, their desires, their needs, what they like and what they don't like, it really opens a feeling of being able to talk to each other about almost anything which they might not have felt previously. It also gives you a chance to check out your interpretations of why the other person's doing something, and what it means to them. It's likely it means something different to your partner than it means to you, and you may lay a whole fantasy thing on it that just isn't there.

Being able to accept having relationships with other people, even close friendships, means expanding a conception that we have in every other sphere of life into the sexual sphere — the idea that one person cannot meet all of your needs. You have business friends, you have intellectual companions, you have people that maybe you play tennis with, or you do this or that with. Yet in the sexual sphere we expect it to be all one person. This puts a lot of pressure on our sex life with that one person. You can ask yourself:

- Do I put the demand on my partner that they meet all my needs? Do I feel that's realistic?
- In terms of my own sexuality, how does holding back my attraction to other people affect my feelings for my mate? For myself and my own sense of energy?

On The Spot

Once you start talking about being attracted to other people, when you're out in public and you see someone you think is attractive, or your partner sees someone they think is attractive, you can point them out to each other. Share these feelings on the spot. You will begin to get a sense of what other people you're each attracted to. This gives you an opportunity to share these feelings in concrete non-threatening situations where you know nothing is going to happen but where you can acknowledge, "Hey, he's attracted to her," and begin to see how you feel about it. I can remember doing that at the beach with Jay.

Why Her?

If you find you feel jealous of someone, it may prove enlightening to try to figure out why you feel jealous of them in particular and not of someone else. You may think they're more good looking, or more this or that. Or maybe you don't like them. Ask yourself:

- What is it about that person which makes me jealous?
- Does that in any way reflect feelings I have about myself?
- How can I make myself feel better in that area?
- Can I accept differences among people and enjoy them?

Me: I know when I'm in a particularly unhappy place myself and I've been kind of grumpy and shitty to my partner for a while, and then somebody, some other woman, is really warm to him, I feel threatened. I feel like, "Oooh, I've been really horrible to him and somebody else is being nice to him, and he'll like the way he feels with her better."

Why Now?

Lynn: That's one of the things that I think that is a worry for some people, realistically in some ways. If your partner's having an affair with somebody it's not a daily thing, it doesn't have the responsibilities that living together has. It doesn't have the routine or the pressures and thus may seem quite exciting and carefree by comparison with daily relationships. Often when one partner makes a switch, it doesn't work out when they get into a daily routine. Because of this, it's important for a couple to talk about how they feel about their own relationship and why they are choosing to open up about other people now.

- How secure or insecure do we feel together?
- How satisfied or dissatisfied? How dependent?
- Do we want to see other people because things are bad, or because we feel happy and open?

- How committed are we to keeping our primary relationship together, no matter what else is happening?

Protecting Your Limits

You can also think of ways to structure your outside connections to protect the primacy of your own relationship. There are a number of different agreements which couples in our study have entered into. Many have effectively set up ground rules to govern their relative freedom within whatever, for them, are desirable, manageable limits, with the understanding that these rules may be redefined over time as their limits change. Examples of some of these agreements are:
- Let me know before you do anything —
- Not too often
- Only if I like the other person
- It's okay for you to have sex if I'm similarly involved
- What we do, we do together; no separate outside dates
- When I'm out of town, we both do what we like — and so forth.

Ask yourself what kinds of arrangements would make you feel safe. Some people start by only involving themselves with other couples who obviously have a good primary relationship. This way you know they aren't looking to take your partner away. Some go even further than that, and try to discourage any emotional involvement. "Just make it sexual." However, that seems to me to defeat part of the purpose of opening your relationship because though it may be less threatening, it probably won't be as worthwhile or rewarding either.

My feeling is that if things are good at home, realistically you've got the edge on anybody else because you've got a history which isn't easily replaced. You've grown together in various ways. Unless something big is wrong at home then your partner isn't likely to make a change, even if they're enjoying somebody.

Me: I've found that to be really true. Connections develop over time which can't be formed quickly. That makes me think that it would be quite important to give yourselves time and space to get to know each other first and to build a solid connection *before* opening up the relationship to others.

Lynn: Yes. That points up an interesting quality about jealousy. It seems to be situational and you have to learn how it operates for you and how to deal with it. It doesn't seem to be an emotion you can "get rid of" totally.

The part of jealousy that's related to insecurity and mistrust has to be dealt with in each new relationship. A base of trust is necessary between two people in order to eliminate jealousy from the relationship. Even if you got over feeling jealous with one person, you'd still need to go through an initial monogamous period with your new mate to develop together your own base of intimacy and trust.

It's also my impression that jealousy is to a great extent person-specific, or more exactly, relationship-specific. For instance, I know several couples who were comfortable in a sexually open relationship with their mate and who eventually split up and regrouped with different partners. In each case they found they were quite jealous about their new partners, and they went through a monogamous period again before opening the new relationships up.

Something which seems to help allay jealousy feelings is believing that you are irreplaceable and that your relationship has a unique quality to it. If you take whatever steps you can to make yourself irreplaceable, to really satisfy diverse needs of the other person, without making the mistake of assuming it's up to you to satisfy *all* of their needs, then you're less likely to have reason to fear loss. If your relationship has developed to the point where you are really relating to each other deeply as individuals, then you know that somebody else couldn't possibly replace you because they can't be you. I'm mostly aware of that from my own feelings. I feel that way, and that really makes a difference in wondering whether my partner would go off with somebody else. Even though I might get jealous at times, I don't really fear total loss.

Me: That would certainly help decrease the intensity of the feelings. Something which really helps me when I find myself feeling jealous and negative towards someone else is to remember that jealousy has mainly to do with me, and little to do with the outside person. My jealousy is really an expression of my feelings about myself.

Lynn: Jealousy usually masks a fear of losing control. Jealousy is intended to be protective,

although it is often destructive. It's used as a defensive emotion, so that if you feel threatened, or fearful that you're losing control of the situation, you get jealous in an attempt to bring the attention and power back to yourself.

The issue of control is really an important one. We all seem to have been programmed that it really is possible to control someone else, to essentially own and possess another person, that this is a good thing, and that probably if we don't, something bad will happen. These feelings must be worked through thoroughly, and gradually discarded if you want to let go of the jealousy struggle in a relationship.

But in learning to overcome your jealousy feelings, you may find it important to feel that things are not going to get out of hand, especially intially, so that you won't feel threatened and mobilize your jealous defenses. Mutually agreed upon ground rules seem to help here.

Many couples succeed in getting through the first phase of working on jealousy, the phase of sharing their feelings and opinions about other people. After straightening out the ideas, many people get stuck on the next phase, changing their feelings. So many people say, "It's a nice idea, but I just can't feel that way!" Our conditioning is deep and based on fear. It has to be worked through very gradually with a lot of love, a lot of support and consideration between two people.

Developing Ground Rules

- The first step is to give each other the feeling that you each are in control of the situation. That means being very specific about what you each want and making mutually agreeable "ground rules," about which steps you are each ready for now and which you aren't. These rules provide a certain feeling of security. "I won't be surprised."
- They also allow you to move at your own pace, only changing the rules when you feel ready for something else. It is important not to push and pressure your partner or feel that you are being pushed.
- Ground rules give you the feeling that you're in control; you partner's not doing anything you didn't agree to. One rule that many people find helpful is to agree to check with each other before they do something. This way you have the chance to get used to the idea before it occurs; you have a chance to exercise your veto power. You develop an atmosphere of mutual thoughtfulness.
- Ground rules keep the focus of effort on your primary relationship. The assumption is that your present couple relationship is primary and most

important to you and that you are making changes to enrich it. Any other connections you make are seen as "secondary relationships." If there is ever a conflict between the needs of your primary and secondary relationships, the needs of your primary connection take priority — or else jealousy, will reappear.

- This fosters a feeling of trust. You are working together on something with love and consideration for the feelings of your partner. You can learn to trust your partner because you see that they stick to your agreements when you need them to.

- Remember that you are experimenting with relating to other people and that if it doesn't work out, or maybe this is not the right time, the decision is not irreversible. You can close back up until you may or may not feel like trying again.

- Don't move from a philosophy, from what you think you should do, or what you wish you felt. Move only when you feel at one with the changes, realizing and accepting at the same time that growth may be somewhat painful. Remember that this may or may not be the best path for your relationship. You have to decide what you want and how well that fits who you are.

- Accept that the process takes time because you have to learn that what you've been taught doesn't necessarily happen. Doom doesn't necessarily descend. Disaster does not befall you in the relationship. You don't inevitably split up. You still care for each other, and it is possible to love more than one person at a time. But you really have to learn that from experience.

Alternatives to Competition

And then there's the question of competition.

Me: Ah, competition . . .

Lynn: Competition places the whole matter of control, that is, feeling like you're in control, in question. When you're competing, somebody's going to "win" and somebody's going to "lose," and therefore there's a real fear of loss involved! If the person that your partner's seeing sees herself as a rival and acts that way, it tends to draw you into it. There have been some studies done on competitive behavior which have shown that if one person competes in a relationship, the other person, even if he or she tries to cooperate, is usually coopted into a competitive position. You are forced to withdraw or to relate within the competitive structure. There are several ways that couples have told that they use to avoid this kind of atmosphere.

- Make certain the outside person understands that you and your partner have an open relationship which allows what is happening.
- Let them know that you don't see them as a rival so they won't feel the need to compete. You and your partner need to talk about any areas where you feel you are competing with each other. Do you use other people against your partner? Do you feel the need to be "even," so that if he's seeing someone you need to too?
- It's important to know if there's a difference between what you say and what your partner is telling the other person. Does he say, "I love my wife and I also care for other people," or "My wife and I don't get along so well . . . ?"
- Another possible way to deal with rivalry feelings is for the three of you to spend time together. This can change some of the basic causes for jealousy: feeling lonely and "left out of the fun," and also the fear of the unknown. You can check out your fantasies about the other person to see how they match up with reality.
- If you are comfortable with a sexual threesome, you can bring the outside partner into a situation where you are cooperating together to please your husband or yourself, rather than acting as rivals.
- One psychoanalytic explanation of jealousy is that it is a defense against your own desire to be unfaithful, either heterosexually or homosexually. You see that your partner is getting something you want but have denied yourself.

Me: I feel a lot of that — that the feelings I call jealousy in myself come when my partner does something I'd like to do but which I fear. My jealousy is really envy. That's easier for me to see when I think about situations of jealousy which are not sexual. It's very clear to me that my jealousy feelings for, say, a movie star or a very talented person or a very beautiful person, come from desire to have what they have and frustration that I don't. For me, sexual jealousy comes when I see a partner doing something I'd like to do but for some reason have forbidden myself, either out of fear that I would be punished or fear that it would ruin my primary relationship. My fear is often largely fear of breaking up our couple structure. "If he or she can do that, so can I. But how can we keep our connection solid if we run around doing things like that which divert our focus?"

I'll often accuse my partner of pulling away from me, even though it is I who is closing off from them for fear of being hurt. To pull away when I most need my partner's nourishment and support is a terrible feeling.

Lynn: That's how jealousy is destructive — it makes people move away from each other.

What's my Purpose?

Another thing that's important in getting rid of jealousy is to think whether it is serving any purpose for you and whether or not you are ready to let go of that.

- Jealousy can be an outlet for sadism; it supposedly gives you the right to be cruel and vindictive. "He hurt me, so I'm going to hurt him at least as much, maybe more!"
- On the other hand, if you tend to brood over your feelings of jealousy and ask for details and confessions, you have to ask yourself, "Am I enjoying the pain and the martyrdom? Am I choosing to prolong the situation and getting some satisfaction out of it?"
- You need also to examine your own sense of pride. Am I acting outraged partly because if I didn't, I think other people might think I was a patsy, a dummy? This factor is quite important in dealing with the outside partner. Do I feel I need to "save face" in front of her by competing?

Me: Dealing with "the other woman" is so complex! I've learned some things about my tendency to want my partner to always feel the same which have helped me. I used to have a strong tendency to want my partner and myself to like the same things and to be together constantly. Now I feel much more interested in my partner's individuality and my own and in how we can live together without feeling pressured to become a unit.

This individuality is really put to the test if my partner is attracted to a woman I dislike! More and more I've learned to accept my partner's separateness from me, his privacy, his right to have different feelings and opinions. If he turns on to someone I don't like, I don't feel the pressure I once did to do something to change him or me. "Friends don't have to be mutual." And I don't feel pressured to like the other person. It's always nice to like the other person, but if I don't, I figure that person is part of his life with which I don't want to be involved; we are different there.

What have you found is important in dealing with outside partners?

Lynn: The biggest thing is probably leveling with the other woman, coming across straight with how I feel. If you feel jealous, acknowledge it, and then talk about it with the other person. If you find that the other person is straightforward, cares, shows some concern with how you feel, then that seems to make a big difference in how you feel about the whole thing. They might do something to make you more comfortable, or they might acknowledge that they don't want to do whatever you feel uncomfortable about, that they don't want to threaten you. Partly it makes you realize that the other person's not out to do you in — unless, of course, they really are!

Me: Right! That's important to find out too! Do you have feelings about how much involvement is helpful? Do you think that the more you know the other person, the better off you are?

Lynn: Some people make the ground rule that "It's okay for you to be involved with somebody else but I don't want to know about it," or "I don't want to know who it is." But that seems to indicate that you're not really comfortable about the situation and would really prefer to avoid it as much as possible. You aren't really coping openly with your feelings together. I think, unless you find you don't like the person, that probably the better you get to know them and the closer you feel to them, the happier you will feel about your partner relating to them.

- You have to start by being open and honest with each other, at least to the point of having a talk about relating to your husband.
- It's important for you and the other woman to sit down and talk without the man there. This takes away some of the threat of feeling as though the two of them are conspiring against you. This also gives the two of you a better chance to get to know each other and indicates a willingness on her part to be open and considerate.
- Then the three of you can talk together.
- This is important because often the outside person is wondering, "Gee, is it okay with his wife? I don't want to cause a big mess or sneak around or feel guilty myself." This gives her a chance to be open too.

Me: Yeah. I imagine there are more people around today who would want to work the relationship out openly. The traditional role of "the other woman" is so lousy! A sneaky homewrecker. We need a new book of etiquette — A Manual for the Liberated Other Woman!

I'm wondering if there are any blatant misconceptions most people have about opening up their relationship which you've noticed? What are some surprises?

Lynn: People often report renewed sexual interest at home! If you extend a certain amount of freedom to each other, there's a certain amount of appreciation from your partner that goes along with that. Many people find that they appreciate each other all the more, in general, and also sexually, because they don't feel as tied and restricted. Their own relationship recaptures a more voluntary spontaneous rather than obligatory quality. It's my personal belief that the way you keep someone's affection is like this (open palm gesture) rather than like that (closed fist gesture). Because love is something that's freely given, and if you try to trap it then the person will naturally resist.

It's also a frequent surprise that the grass is not necessarily greener on the other side of the fence, once you take the fence down. Often people find out that they've got it better at home than they thought. They tend not to fully realize that it takes awhile to get to know a person sexually. They just expect that immediately it's going to be outstanding with somebody else, and that isn't true! They often find that the new experience doesn't have the quality of intimacy or the depth of really knowing each other that sex with somebody you've been close to for a long time has. You've been together for awhile and maybe your sex doesn't have the excitement of the first time, but it has a lot of mutual learning about what each other likes, and often you find that you're more satisfying to each other as sexual partners than someone else is. You're not used to your new partner. You don't know what they like and they don't know what you like.

Me: It's been my experience so far that what I crave in a relationship is the feeling of freedom, much more than actual outside sexual encounters. And I have strong feelings about what I want to base my actions on. I don't want to be motivated by fear; I don't want to decide to live some way because I'm afraid. That seems to me to be a really destructive place to be moving from. I want to live from a different base than that. I have to protect myself in some way, and respect my limits. But I don't have to work from those fear places. Just accepting them and say, "Okay, I'm really afraid and I'm not going to try and work on it" makes me feel very despairing. I put so much attention on protecting myself that the fear gets bigger and the paranoia gets worse; it makes me think of myself as more fragile than I am.

I also would like to have a lot more feeling towards my partner of pleasure about his or her enjoyment, more pleasure about their having a good time.

Lynn: It's a very positive feeling for me when I can appreciate someone's relationship with somebody else, when I don't feel jealous and can take pleasure in the fact that they had a good time. That feels good. And there's a certain relief to it, too!

It really does seem a part of loving someone else to not cut them off, and to take pleasure in their happiness with other people, instead of saying "You're only going to have good things with me, not with somebody else!"

Fly/Welcome

Charlotte Selver is a wonderful and wise woman. She is one of the few people I have met whose dominant quality is of wholeness. This is a difficult quality to describe because so few people I know are whole, that is, congruent. The opposite quality is segmented, which I perceive most people to be. The closest feeling I can relate is the feeling of oneness watching a beautiful animal like a panther gives me. When such an animal moves, the movement comes from her whole body as all her reactions, do, in streamings; her head is no more emphasized or important than her tail — unlike most people whose parts often seem to be separate entities! Most people give me the feeling of uneven development so that much of the time they are in a state of tension and conflict internally between the parts, in a continuous attempt to be balanced.

Charlotte is one of the few teachers I have experienced whose work is pure, real, and beyond technique. She and her partner, Charles Brooks, have been teaching classes in their unique kind of Sensory Awareness for many years. A good deal of their work and exercises help you come closer to a sense of balance and wholeness within yourself, and with the energy around you.

This exercise is a simple one which stood out for me during a week of work with her and Charles. It can be helpful for uniting the parts of myself which are sometimes at war when I feel jealous.

Stand in a room, preferably with high ceilings and little furniture, holding a rubber ball. Choose a ball whose color, size and weight feel good to you. Let yourself think about the ball and its pleasant qualities. Feel how this ball rests in your hands. Think of some ways you might like to play with it.

Now toss the ball high in the air. As the ball leaves your hands, say, "Fly!" Follow its flight with your eyes. Can you let your feelings soar with the ball? Can you feel joy in its movement?

As the ball begins to head toward the floor again, prepare to receive it. Can you tell where you need to be standing so that you will catch it easily? Feel its motion toward you. As the ball comes into your hands, let yourself experience the return of its shape and weight. When it is in your hands, say, "Welcome!"

Repeat this sequence ten times or so, experimenting with different moods of letting go and receiving.

Now try a variation with a partner, someone you like. Stand side by side. Your partner starts to run very fast away from you. As they leave your side, say, "Fly!" How do you experience their leaving? How do you experience their flight? How do you experience yourself without them?

As your partner reaches the edge of the room, he or she should turn and begin running toward you. How are you preparing to receive them? As they move closer, open your arms to them. When you two meet, embrace and say, "Welcome!"

Repeat this sequence several times, paying attention to your feelings about letting go and receiving. Now trade roles with your partner, so that you run and he or she stays still.

Carmen Lynch was born in Australia and came to this country when she was twenty-two. She is a psychotherapist, teacher and consultant trained in social work, Family Therapy, and group therapy. She is currently in private practice in Berkeley.

Carmen and I talked about working as a co-therapy team with a man who is also your mate in your private life. The particular kinds of stresses and closeness created by this situation quickly bring out deep issues. I find that my working relationship with a man is an enlightening capsule of my patterns in other areas of our relationship.

Carmen: Currently Preston Wright and I work together as a co-therapy team. We do intensive psychotherapy and describe our way of working as a Process Psychotherapy. By that I mean we focus on the feeling stream, with the process of what's going on between two people as they're talking rather than on the content of what they are saying. For example, a couple may be talking about a social experience they shared but as they talk, their actions, voice tone, etc., tells you they really want to make close contact with each other — the process is one of getting close, the content of their speech is just a vehicle of expression for their inside wish.

We see people as having many layers of feelings; we try to go from one layer or level to another. For example, anger may cover hurt, and underneath the hurt the person might experience terror or helplessness or outrage. A person often puts out one feeling as a protection against another feeling. An obvious example of this is being angry in order not to feel hurt and vulnerable.

Many Layers

Me: How do you use these concepts of levels of feeling for tuning in to your own process?

Carmen: I usually get a clue by noticing something funny about what I am doing or saying. For example, if I notice I'm getting into judging, I say to myself, "What's going on that I feel I need to handle it this way? What is the layer underneath that I am not letting myself feel by judging?" Often I find that I am threatened or scared. Something may have been triggered that I don't feel I can deal with.

And sometimes I'll notice I'm nervous because my voice is high-pitched, or I'm talking very fast. Then I try to make space for myself by closing my eyes, going inside and letting myself float to see where my feelings go. Frequently something will come back to me from yesterday or last night that I hadn't finished with yet.

The other day Preston and I were teaching a training class I usually like, but that day I was very tense and I didn't know where the feeling was coming from. I went through my check list. I liked the class. I was doing what I enjoy. There was nothing between Preston and me that would make me nervous. Then I remembered some criticisms from another class which had upset me and were still bothering me now. When I realized what it was and that it didn't have anything to do with my present situation, I could relax. Sometimes it's enough to just realize what I'm really feeling. Sometimes I need to stop and work through the incident by fantasizing.

Me: How do you apply the Process Therapy to your work with couples?

Carmen: With couples it's easier than with individuals because you can see the two parts happening separately. Say, a couple comes in and the husband starts telling us what happened last night. The wife looks away. He goes into criticizing — and we stop right there. What was going on before the judging? What did he feel when he saw her look away? What was she feeling? We ask them individually; then bring them back to interaction. "Tell your wife what you feel like when she seems to be bored with you. What does it feel like to tell her that? How does she feel hearing it?"

We cut the exchange down into all its parts. This helps two people connect and open up in a way they never have before. This process is a tool they can use on their own to decipher all the things that are going on at once to avoid misunderstanding.

I really like to help my clients learn tools for themselves outside of therapy. They'll always have problems to deal with and hopefully they're not always going to be in therapy.

Me: I'm interested in what happens between you and Preston. What are some of the positive and negative results of working together? The first problems I have working with a man I live with are competition and the pressure of being together so much.

Carmen: Often in an intimate relationship with a man, my expectations, fears and hopes get in the way of experiencing him for him, but working together as professionals it's difficult to distort.

When we first met, Preston and I related as friends. Going through the hassles and fun of working together without intimate overtones enabled me to be free and spontaneous. We developed a basic trust for each other that we've built on. There are times when we are having conflicts with each other personally, but when we work together we dip into the trust layer and work from there.

Another positive aspect is sharing so many intense, sometimes poignant, sometimes joyous moments together. We have more opportunities for sharing times of really feeling your own and other people's humanity. From working together we have an appreciation of how competent and giving we each can be. I like that! I'm touched

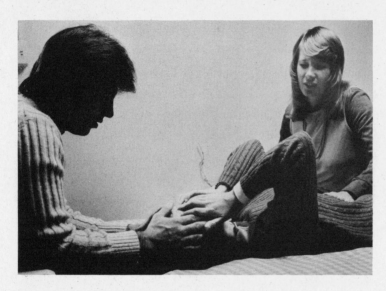 when I see Preston being sensitive, tuning in to a person's pain or vulnerability or whatever. We also appreciate how taxing our work is, and I think that makes it easier to make room for each other. For example, if he's had a draining day and wants to go upstairs and be alone rather than talk to me, it's easier for me to appreciate his reaction than it would be if I didn't do the same kind of work or were waiting around all day for him to pay attention to me.

An important part of working together also is developing ways of nurturing each other. When you put out together as a couple it's crucial that you can take in too. A simple analogy of this process is a couple working hard side by side to give a party and after it's all over, being together, appreciating what they each did, sharing different memories from the evening, etc.

A negative is that there are times when you really need to be away from each other and you're scheduled to work together! At such times an existing problem may be heightened. I may be feeling picky and critical and need to be alone. If I can't have that time away, the critical part of me may start working overtime while we're together, and, boy, three hours later, I'll feel like a volcano and have a greater need for distance and perspective.

Another negative is that working together limits opportunities for meeting new people. Many married people I know draw a lot of social life and friends from each of their places of work. When you work together and especially form a private practive as we do, it's much harder to meet new people.

Not exactly a negative but something I have to watch out for is making a conscious effort to develop other relationships so that Preston and I don't end up on a little island of our own.

I've found that the most essential ingredient for working together is a basis of trust. If you don't have that, you're never going to have a working relationship. You need that in your personal relationship as well, plus you need to just enjoy each other as friends, as people.

Me: Developing the trust required to really successfully work with a man I'm close to has put me in touch with places I hold back in my personal relationships. I realized when the issue of trust came up in work that at a deep level I was still protecting myself. My partner and I had to sit down and deal with the places in our relationship outside of work where we were still holding back and not trusting each other. Somewhere I still felt, "He's the enemy and I need to keep a reserve to protect myself." It was a new attitude for me in a relationship to say, "I won't hold a reserve. I'm not protecting myself. I'm all here with you and there's not a little part of me somewhere that's secretly ready to pack up. I'm committed to working this out."

Carmen: That's really important. Having fairly consistent rhythms is also an important ingredient.

Me: That's certainly been important for me. I've worked with people whose pace is faster than mine. They'll come up to me and say "Nothing's happening!" When I knew a lot was happening. I'd say, "You're going too fast. You're pushing people." We were both responding to the difference in our rhythms.

Realizing that carried over into our personal relationship too. It cleared off a lot of the judging we'd been into about our different ways of doing things. We learned to notice that if the other person was doing something different, it wasn't necessarily "wrong." Some people in the groups liked my rhythm; and some liked his. We learned to appreciate that. Before that, we'd argue all the time!

Carmen: Preston and I have basically similar work rhythms so when I get picky about his work I know to ask myself what else is upsetting me. I may be nervous about not looking good. I tell him he's not doing a good job instead of telling him about my nervousness.

I think the most important key to why Preston and I have worked together so successfully is that we trust each other not to act out our private hassles while we're working. No matter how much we hate each other, or have been fighting, or are in the midst of something we didn't have time to finish, we can make that separation. Even though he may have called me all kinds of names fifteen minutes earlier, when we go in to teach or to work with a family together, we can plug into our deeper connection and harmony.

That's one way we apply the level concept in our own work. We work from our deep trust layer — no matter what else is temporarily going on. In fact we can even give each other appreciation for doing a good job and sympathize with each other over a tough session.

Me: I have that sometimes. It's a beautiful place to be.

Carmen: Working together as a team really requires clarity there. Often we'll work with someone who doesn't respond to one of us. Because of some past experience with his mother, a guy literally may not be able to hear me. Preston can say exactly the same thing I do to him and he'll understand right away. Or there may be a time when it's important for the client to work with a male therapist and I need to sit back and be quiet. Preston and I need to be out of the power struggle so that we can do these things in response to the needs of the client, rather than our own egos.

After a session we may spend time giving each other feedback and talking over how we work together. I trust that his feedback is about what was going on in the session and not misplaced from some conflict we had before.

Early in our working relationship, he and I spent a lot of time sharing all kinds of infantile, irrational feelings that we needed to work through in order to function well together. "They liked you better than me. I did all the work and you got all the appreciation. I really felt jealous. That guy was really looking at your legs — were you aware of that?" We would get into the fears we felt when all of those things happened. Sharing all this, even though it was hard to do, brought us closer and nurtured our trust layer.

Me: Figuring out some kind of non-verbal communication system between the two of you seems like a good idea to me.

Carmen: Yeah. I especially hate to have criticisms pointed out to me in front of people. That belongs to me, but for Preston not to honor that while we're working together would be difficult. When we first worked together, we used to sit opposite each other so we could make eye contact. We would check each other out verbally, and give each other little nods. Then we got to read each other so well that if he was

going in a direction I didn't like he'd know how I felt just by looking at me. Now our timing is so worked out that we work smoothly. When I work with someone else, I really miss Preston. I reach a place where I wait for him to come in, and he's not there!

Also, being able to share when we feel competitive has been really important. Preston

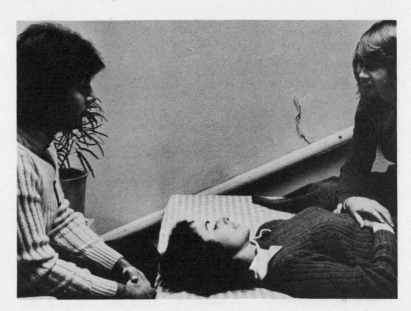

is a fairly special guy in terms of his relationship to a female co-therapist. Most male therapists I've come in contact with need their female partner to hold back and not be as strong as they are. They feel threatened. When we first co-led groups, Preston was a lot more experienced than I was. I grew and reached a point where I shot into my own power and strength. I'd been scared. Now I was dying for him to go on vacations so I could do the group alone! He handled it by sharing with me the times when he felt threatened by it.

Mainly he really appreciates my power. I feel this is pretty unique in a man. That is one of the ways he gives to me. He doesn't give in a lot of the gifty ways, but he really gives by letting me have as much room as I need and really digging my excitement in my own power. It's very hard to let someone move beyond you. That is really a gift.

Underneath Competition

Me: What's a way I could work on my feelings of competition?

Carmen: When you find yourself competing, recognize that it's usually a cover up for being scared or threatened. You could ask yourself, "What is threatening to me? Why am I nervous? What am I scared is going to happen?"

Me: What are some of the problems you have working with someone with whom you're *not* involved in a long-term relationship?

Carmen: One of the most difficult aspects of working with someone you don't have a long-term relationship with is not wanting to put time and energy into working out all the hassles and details involved. Sometimes I enjoy confronting, giving and receiving feedback and discussing the work relationship for hours. At other times I feel like putting my energy into another part of me besides work, and at those times I don't feel like getting into deep discussions with my co-therapist. In fact it would feel like an intrusion if I did. I think this limits in some ways the potential of a non-intimate working relationship.

Another aspect is that the kind of sharing which comes from working together closely leads to intimacy, with a man or with another woman. There are invariably sexual feelings. It's often hard to express this intimacy in a way that feels appropriate. It's crucial to pay attention to timing, waiting to act on feelings until it is appropriate and congruent with where you are at.

Me: Otherwise there are a lot of gaps in your connection.

Carmen: Yes. This applies to all kinds of relationships. It's a critical point. Most people skip a lot of steps and then wonder why the relationship isn't solid.

At each step, you can ask yourself, "What do I really feel ready for? Am I doing this just beacuse it's my image of what's groovy? What do I really want? If you're into a place where you just want to go to bed with a man, do that! If you want a solid connection, you need not be afraid to stay with where you are. Go with what fits rather than how you want it to be.

Pacing ourselves has been a struggle personally for Preston and me, but experiencing the struggle and staying with it has helped us to help other couples. There's a part in both of us that would like to have a child together but we know that doesn't fit yet, although we wish it did. I was wanting to live with Preston and was ready for it before he was. We had to deal with each other's feelings about that whenever it came up, but we were determined to move only when the time fit for both of us. We believe we have some chance of making it together if we make decisions and go into action when the time is right and not before.

Me: The tendency to skip steps in a relationship is really strong. It seems to me to be related to a conception that as soon as you have a feeling you should act on it and culminate it immediately.

Carmen: "Go with your feelings" is a popular phrase. But that means going with your feelings — separate from your actions. It's an important distinction.

Me: I see that pattern often in massage workshops. People come in with different sexual expectations. Our conditioning is that if we're sexually aroused, there's no other possible response than to have intercourse, or really act on it. What I'm concerned with in workshops is recognizing that conditioning and saying, "There are other choices. You could stay with your feelings and see where that leads. Just because you're turned on doesn't mean you have to sleep with the person — or even that you want to!" Usually people move into another place of feeling very relaxed and energized.

Carmen: So many times people have intercouse when what they really want is simply to be held. Couples usually feel a lot of pressure to move fast. I had two people, adults in their thirties, in a group do a fantasy about that. They sat next to each other and acted out driving home from a movie. I had them deal with every small feeling. She was very nervous because her hands were sweating and what if he wanted to hold her hands? He was worried, "Will she still like me and think I'm strong if I don't make a pass?" I helped them share those private thoughts and fears with each other and how scary it was to say them.

After a while they felt they needed a break from each other but it was really hard to say goodbye. "I really want you to go now, but I'm scared I won't see you again." It was very touching. The group felt very close, because everybody feels these things. We're all worried about coming off sophisticated.

It's so important to examine every step of a relationship, to pay attention to all the parts: the fears, the expectations, the childish things, the deep feelings. When you do everything just clicks into place.

Me: You're ready.

Carmen: And when you're ready, things just flow.

Long-Term Relationships

Long-term relationships take a kind of self-awareness and interaction consciousness that is not necessarily required in other situations. It is also a topic which would require writing a whole other book to discuss thoroughly! The best and most deeply helpful material I've ever read on developing a nourishing, growing connection with others is in the last four chapters of Shirley Luthman's book, *Intimacy: The Essence of Male and Female* (Nash Publishing, cloth). Shirley, as the Co-director of the Family Therapy Institute of Marin, has worked for years with families, couples and individuals. In her book she outlines eight steps to intimacy which she thinks are critical, and discusses them at length with examples.

The first step is to reveal yourselves as you are without bending to inner or outer pressure to fulfill someone else's conceptions.

The second step is to give and receive each other's expressions as statements about yourselves rather than demands or judgements.

The third step is to experience and express your differentness and conflict as chances for growth and learning, rather than as rejection.

The fourth step is to be committed to sticking with any feelings that arise until each of you feels openly heard and understood.

The fifth step is to be responsible for your own boundaries and limitations so that you do not pass the blame for what you do onto your partner.

The sixth step is to respect each others limitations.

The seventh step is to understand that though you may unintentionally irritate or disappoint each other, you do not intend or want to hurt each other, and you do not see manipulation or punishment as even a possibly productive alternative.

The eighth step is the mutual feeling that your intent is to give all you can to each other wherever you can without hurting your own selves.

The next chapters talk about trust, about not measuring the giving, about commitment to openness and contact even during fear, about listening and creating a non-judgmental atmosphere between the two of you, which allows for mistakes and, therefore, growth, about a true shared feeling that you do not want to change who the other person is. The last chapter is on what she calls "Supra-Intuitive Communication" or the deep non-verbal communication which often develops between two people who have known each other long and openly. I suggest you read her book.

Intimacy and Fear

An important step in self-awareness is to realize that each move toward openness and connection with another person is accompanied by some feelings of fear. We are almost all raised in an atmosphere where to reveal oneself wholly without caution is considered dangerous and foolish. The capacity to prevent others from knowing our real feelings is admired and cultivated. We are encouraged to be "cool" and "in control." No matter how desirable increased intimacy with someone else feels to us on one level, there is always that other voice which is saying "Watch Out! Be careful! Don't be too open. Keep something in reserve."

If we recognize and accept these fears each time we feel ourselves unfolding a bit more, we can open ourselves even more deeply to our partner and achieve a richer intimacy. Simply checking in with myself from time to time for these fear feelings and then sharing them with my partner is the best way I've found to erase any unconscious attitudes that he or she is "the enemy." To be able to say, "I love you and I am moving closer to you, but I am also afraid that you will reject me (laugh at me, hurt me, not like me)" brings the two of us even closer.

Boundaries

This is an exercise which is useful for getting in touch with where you feel threatened by closeness. Choose someone to do it with to whom you are emotionally close, or let them act out the part of that person. You can also choose some classic male/female roles to play such as aloov vs. pleading, to experiment with the dynamics of intimacy between two people playing those roles.

Sit on the floor facing each other, about three feet apart. If you choose Pleading and your partner chooses Aloof, begin talking to each other in those roles.

Mary: I sure would like to see more of you. I really like being with you and I don't know you very well.

Martin: I really like you too, Mary, but you know how busy I am. I've got a job all day and in the evenings I have my music which is really important to me. I'm spending as much time with you as I can.

Mary: Maybe we could plan sometime during the next week when we're both free to go away to the woods or the beach or just be together here.

Martin: I don't like to make plans like that. These things should be spontaneous, not scheduled.

Mary: Well, maybe when we are together, we could spend less time with your friends and more time with just the two of us. I'd like to move closer and really get to know you.

Martin: Right now, Mary, I'm going through a period when I feel as though I need to be alone a lot. It's not that I don't like you or want to see you, but I really feel I need to be by myself now. When I do see someone, though, it's you.

. . . Where do you go from here? If both people stay in these roles they are deadlocked — and probably don't want to get any closer anyhow. If either of them did, they would change. There are several alternatives which you can act out. Mary could begin to be more assertive, less pleading, and more independent. "Well, Martin, if you can only see once a month, that's not enough of a relationship to satisfy me. Either we allow ourselves more time or I don't want to see you (or I'll allow myself to get involved with other people). I won't promise to be available at your convenience." Martin could react in a number of different ways to break the stalemate. Use this exercise to experiment with alternative roles for yourself in situations where you often feel stuck.

Along with the verbal exchange during the exercise experiment with different distances between you and different amounts of physical contact, keeping up a constant dialogue about how each change in distance feels to each:

Mary: I want to be closer to you (she moves toward him one foot).

Martin: That feels o.k. to me.

Mary: I want to sit right in front of you so our knees are touching (she does).

Martin: That' too close! I don't like that. I feel crowded. I want to move away this much (he does).

Each of you moves back and forth different distances to find the place which you feel allows the right amount of contact between the two of you. There will be a place where you feel best and others where you feel too far away and too close. Pay

216

attention to what body reactions (breathing, muscles, tension, etc.) accompany these changes. You can also move to different spots around the room (behind, lower, and higher than Martin) and experiment with those relationships.

Orgasm

I realize that I've gotten almost all the way through this book without talking about orgasm. That is because *the whole book is about orgasm.* Orgasm as I understand it is an emotional and physical response to openness and contact; it is an ongoing approach to the world, an expression of my own aliveness. I think there is a higher percentage of non-orgasmic women in our culture because women have been repressed from expressing themselves not only as sexual beings but also in every other aspect of their naturalness, especially their self-assertion. Holding back your ego and the expression of your power cuts down your chances of being orgasmic. (From talking with women and men, and from my own experience, I would speculate that a lot more men, however, are non-orgasmic than is statistically reported. The fact that a man can ejaculate sperm, can "come," yet experience little emotional or physical release throughout his body is not commonly talked about!)

Orgasm is an energy response of the whole being. From my own experience, however I am feeling at a given time is how I respond sexually. Therefore, my orgasms range from not-at-all; to frantic and forced feelings of pushing out and releasing tension; to relatively mild and local sensations in my pelvis; to deep slow very powerful feelings of inward-receiving contractions; to very active electrical sensations moving through my entire body. They are expressions of my own energy condition, my feelings about my partner, and the quality of relation between us.

The most important keys for me in broadening and increasing my sexual pleasure have been: learning to express my anger directly; respecting my pleasure preferences and directly asking or communicating these to my partner; gradually coming to know my own body better, through different body therapies and awareness practices.

The books of Drs. Johnson and Masters, *Human Sexual Inadequacy* and *Human Sexual Response* (Little, Brown; cloth) are extremely helpful. I also recommend highly a paperback by Jack Lee Rosenberg (Random House — The Bookworks) called *Total Orgasm* which describes excellent breathing and movement exercises for individuals and couples for release of tension and sexual energy. Stanley Keleman's book, *Sexuality, Self and Survival* (Lodestar Press, paper) is the best and most helpful theoretical book I've read on sexual aliveness and the whole person.

Body Techniques For Increasing Orgasm In Women

- Masters and Johnson position: the woman sits in front of partner between his or her legs, leaning back and resting on their chest. Her partner uses a warm oil or cream to massage her torso, and then genitals.
- Hatha yoga
- breathing relaxation techniques
- massage
- "connecting"
- knowledge of own and partner's anatomy
- direct anger
- vaginal push ups and outs
- masturbation
- clearly communicating what you want and like

Some Body Techniques To Help Men Prolong Erection

- rhythmical contraction and release of the muscles of the genital area, about 50 times, once a day
- any kind of exercise, or more especially yoga, which improves general body condition *without* creating a muscle-bound condition
- knowledge of male and female anatomy
- masturbation (once or twice a week) to the point of — *but without* — ejaculation
- massage
- Masters and Johnson Sensate Focus
- the Oriental technique of squeezing each testicle once for every year of your life, once a day!

If asked whether I want to feel more alive, more powerful more healthy, relaxed and energetic, I would answer, "Yes." When given the chance to open up more intensity and energy, I often shy away from it; I don't always experience an increase in my feelings of power, energy and awareness as pleasurable. Often I find those feelings *un*pleasant, annoying, even frightening.

I want to learn to tolerate more vitality, more aliveness, in myself without tensing against the feelings in an attempt to tone them down or stop them. The more I can allow intensity, feeling and movement inside myself, the more pleasure I can allow myself to feel.

The breathing and movement exercises in Jack Rosenberg's book, *Total Orgasm,* are all directed at increasing the body's tolerance for intense energy flow. Many of them are from Wilhelm Reich. Some forms of Tantra yoga include other kinds of exercises for helping you learn to allow intense energy to circulate in your body and to allow this while in deep open contact with another person.

During the five years that I was practicing and teaching Hatha yoga, I also studied a form of Hindu Tantra and a branch of Kundalini yoga (which employs fast deep breathing exercises in combination with hatha postures). I am including some of these exercises in this section because I found them to be helpful for getting more deeply in touch with myself and my partner.

There seem to be three forms of Tantric yoga: Hinduist Tantra, Buddhist Tantra, and the Western popular conception of Tantra! The three are entirely different.

The confusion began when Western translators lumped together Hinduist and Buddhist Tantra because their names contain the same word. Neither is a "yoga of sex" as the general Western conception would have it — what is unusual about Tantric yoga as a religious discipline is that it *includes* sex rather than leaving it out or banning it the way most Western disciplines do. Tantra is one of the few world views which does not subscribe to the dualistic (Platonic Orphic-Dionysiac) theory of duality which creates a split between sensuousness and spirituality, and an attitude that spirituality means degradation of the body.

Tantra is religion of wholeness, of acceptance of all manifestations of life without judgements such as good or bad, high or low, important or insignificant. (In this way it is close to some forms of Zen.)

Hinduist Tantra focuses on *sakti* or power. Some of its practices (like the ones included at the end of this chapter) are much like those of Western Bioenergetics and Reichian exercises.

Buddhist Tantra is thought of as the culmination of Indo-Tibetan Buddhism. The *only* informative book of Buddhist Tantra I have seen in English is *The Tantric View of Life* by Herbert Guenther (Shambala, cloth).

There are three basic guidelines to Buddhist Tantric philosophy: (1) Being is made up of two *indivisible* parts, body and mind, (representing sensuousness and spirituality); life is the dance between the two (2) Grounding (through awareness in the body) is the path to reality, or the abolition of all fictions (3) Being is the Means and the Goal; do not try to fixate, to hold on, to evaluate; just let be.

Tai Chi Chuan and other Oriental martial arts evolved from this philosophy; balancing the elements in yourself is thought to liberate the flow of Ki energy.

Fulfillment comes through uniting the parts of ourselves and allowing these aspects to fall into their natural balance. All Tantric exercises include a physical and a mental meditation. There is attention to grounding and to the relation of ground to air — solid to space, hardness and softness, activity and receptivity. The exercise called *Walking With the Ground* which I included in the *Body Awareness* section is a very good example of one of these exercises.

Sexual practices are among the many forms of awareness practices included in Tantra. The sex act (not experienced as relation between subject and object but as communication between two open beings) becomes a search for higher integration and the symbol for the uniting of goddess and god.

When we accept another without judgements or demands, through love, the world is not eliminated or distorted; we see the world as it is — and we experience our oneness with it and with each other.

Non-Looking

Choose a quiet room (or go outdoors) with soft light. Wear nothing or loose fitting clothing. Be sitting opposite your partner but not touching in a comfortable cross-legged position. Let your back be straight but not tense. Relax your hands, palms down, on your knees.

Now look at a spot centered on the bridge of the nose between your partner's eyes. Let your eyes stay with this spot throughout the exercise. If possible do not blink. Allow your breathing to relax, your mind to clear, and your eyes to receive what is in front of them, rather than actively searching out an image. If you feel thoughts beginning to flood your consciousness, allow them to pass  right through without focusing on them. Stay receptively focused on that center spot and allow whatever happens visually or emotionally to be.

220

Your partner should do the same. Do this for twenty minutes. Now share what the experience was like for both of you.

The Palm Circuit

Be sitting opposite your partner, cross-legged, so that your knees are touching. Relax your breathing. Bend your arms and hold them up in front of you, your palms facing outward about chin high. Place your palms against your partner's palms letting them rest together without straining. Look into each other's eyes and stay with this gaze throughout the exercise. Do not try to communicate with each other by facial expressions. Allow your eyes to receive openly and to let yourself come out without trying. You can do this part of the exercise by itself or add the Breath of Fire.

Now begin to quicken the pace of your breathing a bit, puffing out your abdomen as you inhale and contracting it as you exhale, maintaining eye contact. Gradually increase the pace of your breathing until you are breathing as fast as you can through your nose, without sacrificing depth. This is the Breath of Fire.

Stop when the breathing is no longer comfortable. If your arms or back get tired before your breathing, try staying in the position a few moments past the discomfort and the achiness will usually disappear.

Tune in to the feeling of energy inside you, to your partner's energy, and to the current which may seem to be circulating between your bodies through any of your points of contact. Can you relax and allow this energy to flow?

Four-Foot Circuit

Straighten out your legs and move apart so that the two of you can sit facing each other with the soles of your feet touching. Let your back be straight but not rigid. Stretch out both arms, shoulder height, in front of you, palms up. Your partner should also stretch his or her arms out toward you, but palms down and slightly above your hands.

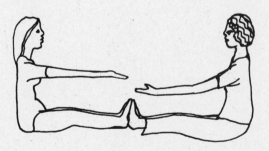

221

Now look deep into each other's eyes. Maintain this position for about five minutes, tuning in to any energy sensations you might feel moving through your legs, arms and torso.

Now try this with the Breath of Fire.

Back to Back

Sit cross-legged, back to back, with your partner. Try to let as much of your spines touch as possible, especially your lower backs. Find a place to rest together where both of you are comfortable and neither feels too leaned-on or leaning. Extend your arms behind you so that you can comfortably rest your palms on your partner's thighs.

Close your eyes. Tune in to your breathing. Pay attention to any energy sensations moving between your hands and your backs, and especially to the breathing at the base of your spines.

Now try this with the Breath of Fire.

Men and This Book

Men and This Book

I see the Women's Consciousness Movement as significant in beginning to discard the current role masks posing for female sexuality – but this is only half of the cultural confusion. The other half, male sexual oppression, is barely being conceived of, much less being dealt with. I am constantly amazed at the lack of perception men I come in contact with have of their own sexual oppression, even intelligent and otherwise sensitive men. Few men recognize the ways in which their given role – including censoring most "soft" emotions, such as tenderness, sadness, crying, vulnerability, openness; having to feel dominant, competitive and on top of a hierarchy to feel Male; and most deeply, the block of possessiveness – robs them of their own power and pleasure and fills them with fears of exposure and inadequacy. Only when men begin to feel anger and loss about their own oppression will new heterosexual relationships be possible. As I see it, a "Human Consciousness Raising Movement" is needed – as well as specifically a female one.

This section includes articles by George Downing and Irving London, who have explored some of these issues in relation to their own internal experience and their external roles. I asked each of them to write an article on how he felt the material in this book relates to himself and to other men. Here is what they said.

If You Are a Man Reading This Book

by George Downing

George Downing is a Gestalt psychotherapist on the staff of Esalen Institute in Big Sur and in San Francisco. He specializes in the use of Gestalt in combination with Reichian and other intensive methods of working with the body. He is the author of *The Massage Book* and of the forthcoming *The Path of the Breath.*

• •

If you are a man reading this book, you probably have a number of questions. Among them might be, "How do I fit into this picture? Have I, as a man, been cut off from my own being in any ways similar to those described by the women speaking in this book? If I have been, is there anything I can do about it?"

The answer, as I see it, is yes. Working with men and women in groups and private practice, as well as my own personal experience, has convinced me that we men suffer as greatly as women from the limitations of our cultural roles and stereotyped emotional patterns. The distortions and hidden conflicts may be different but the price paid, on the inside, is equally high.

If this is true, then what, as a man, can I do? Where do I begin?

Here are two directions that I have found helpful, and have seen other men find helpful.

The first step is to try to make contact emotionally with your own personal loss: realizing in your gut some sense of what the role system imposed on us has cost you personally. Be suspicious of too easy a "sympathy" and "helpfulness" towards the women's movement. Real solidarity with the struggle of women is one thing; playing the male rescuer instead of tuning in to your own anger is another. Accept the need to put in time and to undergo the frustration of exploring what in you wants things to be different.

Comparing notes with other men (with a few friends, or with an organized group) can be a real help. Take a look at the images of masculinity that have been passed down to you from family, schools, the media, wherever; and check out which aspects of these images feel beneficial to you, and which seem in any way destructive. Keep track as you go of how you are reacting emotionally. In the beginning, if you are like most other men, you may find this kind of discussion uncomfortable, even vaguely threatening. If so, try to share these feelings as well with your friends, and see if you can explore on the spot what they may signify about the issues that have given rise to them.

A second suggestion is to begin to confront, explore and develop your awareness of your own body. This may sound less immediately important to you, yet I feel that it is even more critical than the first step. By awareness of the body I mean awareness from within, the depth of your personal, embodied contact with yourself. Why bother with this? Because how much, and in what way we experience embodied self-contact, establishes at our roots how we perceive and act in the world. Because a certain set of styles of living, feeling and organizing the body provides the underlying foundation of man/woman roles as they traditionally have been adopted. At the deepest level if we are bound to roles it is because our bodies bind us. This is the reason why talk, discussion, and conceptual understanding by themselves can take us only part way. Any real transformation must ultimately include transformation of the body.

This is a large subject; I can only point out a few aspects of it here.

Most men in our society tend to be dominated by a need to compete, to perform and to achieve. What is the attitude underlying this need? An extreme orientation towards the future, an exaggerated seeing of the world and patterning of actions in the light of not yet attained goals. What would it mean to change this structure? Above all it would mean coming home to the body itself as the wellspring of our existence in the present moment.

Another common difficulty is allowing yourself full, free expression of emotions. A MAN doesn't show pain, sadness, longing, fear; not "normally;" and above all not among other men. This is not to say that many women do not suffer from the same problem; however, I have seen over and over that the range of feeling which the unwritten rules of our culture permit a man to show openly is even less than that allowed women. Some of the consequences are: partial deadening of your inner life of feelings; periodic sense of unsureness about your own reality and worth; extensive reliance on less nurturing methods of making contact with others, e.g. the sharing of expertise with other men, implicit or explicit "conquest" of women. The path out? The quickest and most direct way is through the body. The more you can bring your body alive, the more clearly and richly you will feel your emotions resonate within. Once your feelings being to acquire substance in this way, to take on flesh, you will discover their own natural flow will be in the direction of increasingly open expressiveness towards the outside world.

Finally, a great many men tend to constrict themselves by limiting and distorting their sexual perceptions of women. Women's justified complaints about being treated as "sex objects" are common knowledge by now; less well understood, however, is that "sexism" is, on the part of men, nothing other than a deep distrust of sexuality. That is, most men project onto women their unconscious discomfort with their own sexual being. The reason is that erotically, as elsewhere, men have been taught to live the body as an instrument rather than as a field of awareness. The consequence is that a body so lived and organized cannot sustain too powerful a build-up of erotic charge. Treating women as objects rather than as sexual equals is a way of deflecting energy, of reducing charge; a way of not getting too dangerously close to the full power and ripeness of sexuality. To change this at the level of the body itself would change a great many things. Men capable of sustaining within themselves a higher charge — of feeling and living, at the deepest levels, the energetic connectedness of the entire body — would be men capable of experiencing a very different life. At the least they would be ready to risk opening themselves, without the barriers created by distorted perception, to the full range of excitement between sexually equal human beings.

You might start consciously changing your relation to your own body by trying out some of the experiments suggested in this book. Pay attention to how different they are in spirit from an "athletic" orientation towards the body. Adapt them to your own needs as a man, and let them give you all the clues you can about directions which you may want to explore further.

Frigidity, Sensitivity and Sexual Roles
by Irving London, M.D.

Dr. London attended Washington University School of Medicine. His post doctoral work was done at the University of Minnesota Hospital and the University of California Hospital in San Francisco. He currently specializes in sleep research and is a sleep consultant to Innerspace, the California company that invented the flotation waterbed.

• •

For the past nine years I have been interested in the widespread problem of frigidity — its causes and effective solutions. This interest stemmed from a course I took as a medical student at Washington University with the now famous Dr. Masters. He gave a series of lectures on human sexual response. I was amazed at the reaction of my classmates. Masters presented a series of slides demonstrating the physical changes of sexual arousal and orgasm. This group of budding young doctors were

228

crouched in their seats as though they were watching dirty movies. I observed their reaction. They blushed and squirmed in their seats; in general the group seemed disquietingly uncomfortable yet fascinated with the content. Students would arrive early to get front row seats. As these lectures progressed I became aware of the general level of sexual ignorance which existed. Watching these reactions, I thought, "These are the authorities people will seek out to talk about their sexual problems!" I was struck by how hung up this "intellectually advanced" group was. I began to reflect on the causes and possible solutions to sexual problems.

American culture stimulates and promulgates sexual frustration. We are taught to regard the sexual act with deep guilt. Women are taught to withhold their genitals, and to use the sexual act manipulatively rather than as a means of communication. Marriage programming with its inherent financial security is still extremely prevalent and sex is the prime lever. This orientation promotes guilt, fear, and frustration while diminishing sensitivity, awareness, sensuality and communication.

Men are programmed to be "strong" and "aggressive." Practically from birth emotional sensitivity is squelched: "big boys don't cry; be strong; stand up straight; stomach in, chest out; take what you want; be a man." What 'be a man' means in the American sense is to be emotionally sterile. What 'be a man' means is don't feel anything. What 'be a man' means is to be sexually inadequate.

Machismo and aggressiveness are in direct contradiction to sensitivity and intimacy. "Taking a woman" is supposed to fulfill this masculine urge. Perhaps this explains why 90% of all men ejaculate within the first two minutes of intercourse! It's not surprising that frigidity is extremely common. Sex as a means of communication is sorely lacking.

When doing frigidity counseling working for Masters and Johnson, I was struck by a recurring story. The man of the house would come home, have a couple of drinks, eat dinner, plop down in front of the television, drift off into a semi-stuperous state, and be helped to bed by his wife. Revived to a half-awake condition by this activity, he finds the stamina to roll over on top of his beloved and following a few furtive swipes, plunges home for a two minutes stint as he falls asleep. She, dejected, depressed, frustrated and guilt-ridden, lies in bed asking herself, "What's wrong with me? Why can't I climax?" Maybe they come for help.

In America sexual inhibitions and male-female roles interfere with full sexual response, enjoyment and orgastic release. Men in our society have been so completely programmed into not expressing feelings that intercourse often does not provide either transference of feeling, nourishment, or energy. Many men seem to ejaculate without having orgasm. If you have ever seen a pornographic movie you may have noticed that the male participants are stoically silent. I have experienced group sexual encounters and was amazed at the lack of sexual noises in the men. Sensitivity was also totally lacking. The men seemed like robots performing a programmed function with little or no emotional content.

I went through a period of my life with similar emotionless encounters. I was obsessed with sleeping with many women despite superficial feelings and empty experiences. My ego was salved by knowing I was sexually desirable. Gradually things changed. I began to tune in to my partner and empathize more with her. Sex became a deep tender form of communication. The more I opened myself and let my partner in, the more moving the experience became. My orgasms became fuller, more meaningful, and much more powerful. By tuning in more and more acutely, I was actually able to experience the emotional sensations of orgasm without ejaculating. Orgasms became a release for my entire self — body and mind. Much to my surprise I found this brought me closer to my lover. Instead of thinking I was a "sissy" she felt warm and close. She felt physically and emotionally full.

In my sexual counseling I often talked with couples about sensitivity and roles. It is risky for a man to open up and let another see him as he really is — a frail being with many fears, emotions and desires. The male role with its aggressive strong front is very thoroughly ingrained. In my counseling, I would try to soften this rigid armor. Many new techniques available today can help couples overcome society's structuring. Trust and risk taking games can be useful. Reichian therapy, Polarity therapy and massage produce extremely gratifying results. Sensitivity training, sensory awareness and role playing can also contribute to an emotional rebuilding. Sexual techniques must be taught and inhibitions worked through. Men must be offered the chance to be vulnerable, open, trusting and gentle, without feeling these to be negative "feminine" traits. I think the time is near when we will see widespread use of these techniques in sexual clinics and a gradual restructuring of male-female role relationships, with resulting diminution of sexual tension and a heightening of deep human sexual communication.

Childbirth, Children ... and You

Childbirth, Children ... and You

This section contains chapters on some of the female cycles connected with childbirth and families.

So much has been written on family life that you can find excellent whole books on any one of the different aspects I am dealing with here in a few pages. I also recommend reading some good medical books so you are thoroughly familiar with the physical changes you'll be going through during pregnancy and childbirth.

I am concerned here with two aspects of the childbirth cycle: how to care for your own body and how to explore new attitudes about families.

I consider the phases of childbirth to belong in the large category of altered states of consciousness. By this I mean that because your body is chemically changing during these times, your emotional and sensual experiences are different from your perceptions during most of your life. Menstruation, pregnancy and childbirth are also periods of extreme change during which you can learn what it means to "go with your changes" and to "live at one with your body." Tuning in to your natural rhythms during these physical changes can carry over and alter how you perceive and live your body life after childbirth.

Menstruation

Do you remember your early knowledge of menstruation? Do you remember what happened and what you felt the time you got your first period?

I don't remember what medical information my mother told me beforehand, except that she told me something and the girls in my class at school told me more. I do remember that one day sometime during my twelfth year I went in the bathroom and discovered some blood on my underpants. I knew what this was and I called my mother. She came, looked and said, "Good, now you can have children when you grow up!" I found that a reasonable response. It gave me a sense of purpose and some interesting things to contemplate as I put on my pads every month.

I've always been grateful for the areas of my young life which my mother handled so naturally. I found her response a lot more fitting than that of my year-older sister when told, who, feeling her age, responded with "Well, it's about time!"

After this brief initial recognition, my menstrual period became a fact I was to be "discreet" about, to accept as part of my private life as a "young lady," but never to mention in the company of strangers or men. Some of my girlfriends had more negative experiences. Their mothers taught them that once a month their bodies secreted a substance which was dirty and smelly which was called "the curse." To me this attitude is uninformed and detrimental to the child. It is part of the mythology that women are "unclean." (Somehow the genital emissions of the male are "cleaner" than those of the female!) It also hints at a negative attitude toward all the processes connected with childbirth, sexuality, and the female body.

Female Rites of Passage

I have heard about tribal customs in other cultures where menstruation is considered a girl's rite of passage into adulthood equal in import to the rites of passage held for young boys. A friend told me about a family she knew who adapted this idea into their own family rituals. When one of their daughters started to menstruate, it was cause for celebration and she was congratulated! She told the members of her family the news in the order that she wanted. That evening's dinner was held in her honor. She was made to feel positive about her body and that "becoming an adult" marked the beginning of enriching experiences instead of the onset of a lot of troubles and repression. Her sense of privacy was honored by the family's checking in with her before they shared the news with anyone else.

234

There are many exercises you can do to release any cramping or lower back pains you may have during your menstrual period. One of the most effective for me is a Shiatsu (Japanese massage) pressure point technique. It requires two people. Try it on a friend and then have her do it to you.

Your friend should lie down on her stomach on a rug or beach towel on the floor. (If you do this on a soft bed, you can't press deeply enough.) Let her arms relax at her sides. Straddle your partner's thighs kneeling so that you can comfortably reach her lower back. Locate the sacrum by pressing with your fingertips around the lower back area to feel the outline of this arrowhead bone, which is wide at the lower

back and pointed at the beginning of the crease of the buttocks. When you have found the two upper outside edges of the bone, slide your thumbs in toward each other so that they end up resting on either side of the spine. Position your thumbs there. Now rise up on your knees so that you can lean the weight of your whole body onto your thumbs. Begin with slight pressure and *gradually* increase the pressure (by allowing more of your body weight to press down on your thumbs) until you are pressing and leaning on your two thumbs as hard as you possibly can. Hold this pressure to the count of ten, and then just as gradually release it.

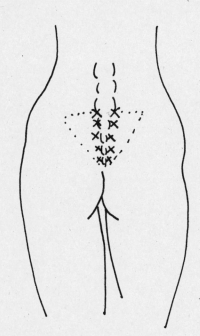

Repeat this pressure cycle down either side of the spine the length of the sacrum ending at the tip, moving down a thumb print at a time.

Each person has different tention in the area around the sacrum. Go more slowly and lightly on someone who is tight and sore in that area. You will probably find — if you move gradually — that most people like as much pressure here as you can possibly exert. If this is hard on your thumbs, pace yourself and if you do this enough your thumb strength will increase so that it is quite comfortable to do. You can also use your knuckles.

The Cobra

If you need to release some lower back cramping by yourself, any gently arching of your back is often helpful. These two yoga postures feel particularly good to me.

Lie on a mat on the floor face down, eyes closed, legs straight. Bend your arms at your sides so that your palms are beside your chest, fingers pointing up toward your head. (Keep your ankles together throughout.) Exhale fully.

Open your eyes and look up toward the ceiling *without* moving your head. Begin inhaling. Now arch your neck and raise your head up and back so that you are looking at the ceiling. Now begin raising your spine off the floor, as though vertebra by vertebra, from your neck to your sacrum. Do this slowly, inhaling as you go, without using your arm muscles at all. Think of yourself as a snake slowly unwinding and rising. You will reach a point where you can't raise up any longer without using your arms. Do so now and continue to arch and stretch until your arms are straight, your head back.

Now begin the descent by reversing the process. Start exhaling and lowering your spine and chest to the floor. On the last seconds of your exhalation, clench your teeth and hiss like a snake. This enables you to exhale more fully. Your head and neck come down last. Close your eyes and rest awhile. Repeat the cobra several times.

The Bow

Lie face down, arms at your sides. Exhale. As you begin inhaling, bend your knees bringing your feet up over your buttocks. Grasp your ankles with your hands. Arch your back, neck and legs as much as possible by pulling up on your feet with

your arms while pulling down on your arms with your feet. Release gradually as you exhale. You can do this with your legs together or apart. You can also rock back and forth on your stomach!

Opening Your Hip Joints

This is one of Dr. Randolph Stone's exercises designed to clear the sinus passages by releasing tension in the pelvis. (You may be wondering about how the two go together. According to Polarity Therapy theory, the pelvis is a polarity for the head and neck. Next time you have clogged sinuses, try this for three to five minutes, and you will find out: your sinuses will drain and clear!) I am including this exercise here because it is an especially good release for tension in the hip joints, lower back and pelvic area.

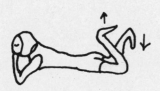

Lie on your stomach, legs about six inches apart, both hands under your chin. Bend your legs at the knees. Begin crossing your feet and calves in front and behind each other kicking a bit so that you can feel the pull inside your hip joints. Do this several minutes.

Reflexology for Female Organs

The Reflexology point for the lower back is at the base of your arch on both feet near the heel. Sit in a chair with one leg crossed and your foot in your lap so that you can get at the sole. Press on the lower back area with your thumbs.

The Reflexology pressure points for the genitals and female organs are along the ankle. Press on the inside of your foot on a spot about half way between your ankle bone and the bottom of your heel for affecting the uterus. Press on a similar spot on the outside of your foot for affecting the ovaries. Squeeze and pinch either side of your Achilles tendon about three inches up from your heel to also affect the uterus.

Abortion

Happily abortions in the United States are becoming cheaper and safer. As the atmosphere of Gothic social disapproval clears away, we are left to face our deepest internal responses to the experiences of having a child within us which we decide not to bear.

Along with the relief at avoiding an unwanted pregnancy, there is a companionate sense of loss. These sad feeling are usually not dealth with sufficiently. As in any other situation where deep feelings are not acknowledged or dealt with adequately, they stay with us at an unconscious level, fester, and may surface in a displaced situation (such as exceptional grief at the death of a baby in a movie or sometimes as negative and avoidance attitudes toward children in general).

Goodbye

One way to explore your feelings about your unborn child and your inexperienced motherhood is through a Gestalt technique of talking to the child as though it were there. Even if you are not consciously aware of any sad feelings about the loss, try this experiment to explore for any buried feelings of loss.

Sit down with another chair or pillow opposit you. Breathe slowly and deeply several times in your abdomen. Close your eyes and try to open yourself to any feelings you might have about your unborn child. "I love you, but I don't want you now. I want to travel (keep my job....be with another man....whatever) now."

Now talk about any feelings you might have of wanting the child, although you feel this is not the right time. "I would like to hold you. I would like to rock you. (Pick up the pillow and cradle it.) I would like to feel you growing inside of me. I would like to see who you are and watch you grow. I feel sad and lonely when I think about losing you."

Explore any other feelings you might have thoroughly.

Now say goodbye to the child. "Goodbye, baby. Goodbye, baby." Repeat your goodbyes to the child over and over again, talking to the pillow which you have put down now. Stay with goodbye until you feel you have really experienced your sadness and loss. If you feel like crying, try to let yourself.

When you have connected with your sadness and feel somewhat resolved, tell the baby that now you are ready to go on. "Now I am ready to move on. I want to leave you now. I want to...."

Deep and significant emotions are only dealt with gradually and not all in one sitting. You may want to do this exercise again over a period of time when unexpected feelings of sadness connected with the event come up. I do a variation of this Goodbye exercise because even though I have never been pregnant, I am aware that I am continually choosing not to have children now. I feel mixed about that. When I acknowledge my sadness I am brought more fully into the present.

Pregnancy and Childbirth

The attitude that the body functions of menstruation are painful, bothersome and unattractive seems to be true of many people's attitudes toward the rest of the childbirth cycle. The intensity of the fear and disgust increases until we reach the moment of birth at which time, in most hospitals, the woman is drugged or anesthetized so she cannot feel the "terrible experience" at all. How far from the attitudes — *and experiences* — of people in many cultures (and of many American women who have allowed themselves more natural childbirth) that childbirth is a peak experience of joy and power in their bodies!

How have we come to such a dismal place in relation to pregnancy and childbirth in our culture? How could I change my attitudes and action to reclaim some of the joy and pleasure in the experience? I feel giving birth is often a difficult and unpleasant experience largely because of two factors: first because we are not taught how to care for our bodies so that pregnancy and childbirth are not beyond our physical capacity, and second because of general fear of natural processes of the body. Another factor is that most doctors are men and thus "outsiders" to the woman's experience; they often find the intensity frightening.

I want to begin to listen to the wisdom of my own body and to the experience of women who have had their babies unmedicated either at home with a midwife and doctor or without drugs in a hospital where their partners could be with them.

Two Births (Random House/The Bookworks, paper and cloth) is an especially good photographic and written account of the experience of two San Francisco families who decide to have their babies at home. *Natural Children* (Warner Paperbacks) is another of my favorite books on an alternative medical approach to childbirth. Juliette de Bairacli Levy (a woman who chose to live much of her life with gypsies and now lives in rural Israel) wrote this book to convey her knowledge of herbal and natural food medicine and self-care for women during pregnancy and childbirth.

239

Juliette had her first child while living with Berber Arabs in Tunisia and her second child living with Spanish gypsies in Andulasia. She talks about how much physical exercise and walking gypsy women do and how because of this their bodies are supple and strong — and childbirth is an easy event for them. She lived this way with them during her two pregnancies, and was bathing in the river and walking her dog minutes after giving birth. I may not want to walk my dog after giving birth, but I can learn some possible alternative attitudes and practices from these other cultures to help me alter the ones I find negative in American society. (One of these is considering having a belly dancer dance during your labor contractions according to the original purpose of this dance!)

It's been significant to me to learn that a woman in good general health is biologically probably her *healthiest* during pregnancy. Learning this from an obstetrician in Marin has really changed my attitude toward pregnancy and how I feel my relationship to my doctor should be. I think it's important to start changing the "normal" medical attitude towards pregnancy which regards the mother as a "sick patient." I need to clear up my own misconceptions about being pregnant and "sick" also. I need to tell my doctor that I am a healthy "client" consulting him for preventative advice not treatment for illness.

Stone Pressure Release

This exercise of Dr. Randolph Stone's is designed to help relieve the extra pressure put on your legs during pregnancy.

Stand with your legs wide apart, feet firm. Clasp your hands and cup them under your lower abdomen just above your pubic bone. Inhale, slowly and deeply, so that your abdomen puffs out. On the exhalation, bend your knees and gradually let yourself down into a squat; at the same time be gradually lifting upward on your abdomen with your clasped hands. Release the pressure slowly as you stand up on the inhalation. Do this several times.

Foot Push

This is a Hatha yoga exercise for strengthening the leg and abdominal muscles. Be lying on your back on the floor, arms at your sides. Put the soles of your feet together and bring your knees to your chest. Exhale. As you inhale, strectch your legs forward until your knees are straight — keeping the soles of your feet together. On the exhalation, bring your knees back to your chest.

It's very important to learn to coordinate your movements with your breathing. When you do any exercise, inhale as you stretch out, and exhale as you pull in. The Vaginal Push Ups described earlier in the section Starting With Yourself are very helpful during pregnancy also.

Massage is a delicious and soothing experience for aches and pains during pregnancy and the early stages of labor.

Toward the Conscious Family

Anica Vesel Mander lives in San Francisco with her husband Jerry and their two sons, Yari and Kai. She and I talked about the disadvantages and rewards of being a family in the middle of a revolution in family structures.

Ani: Being Mrs. Jerry Mander is difficult — that is, to me, being Mrs. *Anybody* is difficult because the label conotes taking on someone else's identity. How to relate to a man whose name I bear, who at the moment is supporting me, with whom I live and with whom I'm identified by society? It make me feel competitive with my husband.

At the same time, the resentment imposed on me by the situation which I sometimes take out on him, I can see in perspective; it's not totally his fault. I'm "Mrs." because it's a convention in which we're all caught — and by my choice also.

Me: Did you consider changing your name?

Ani: Yes. I have a special problem of having changed my name a lot. I had a Yugoslav first name which was unpronounceable in this country so I changed that when I came to the U.S. Then the first time I married I changed my last name, which I changed again when I married Jerry! Today to consider going back to my original name after fifteen years doesn't fit; I'm not that person anymore.

Now I use my maiden name, Vesel, which I've always used as my middle name as an articulated part of my name, Anica Vesel Mander. I've told my children that Vesel is also their name so that they have both names too.

Keeping my identity within the wife role is really tricky. When I married Jerry, I was thirty. I had been married before, but then I was living alone, doing my own thing. I got married, and within a day the roles were defined, you know, in terms of who cooks, or whose work comes first. We were both working, but the work priority was never even discussed. It was just taken for granted. I was living in Cambridge working at Boston University and he was living and working here, so we saw each other transcontinentally. When we decided to live together, it never occurred to anyone that he would move there! It was clear that I would move here.

Me: Some place underneath it all you had to take your own career much less seriously.

Ani: I did take it much less seriously. My work was in many areas very fulfilling, but it never was more important than my personal life. It still isn't though; I think that's the right approach.

I wanted children with Jerry and we had children right away. But I also wanted to work. It was for money only in that I wanted the financial independence. Mainly I didn't want to stay home with the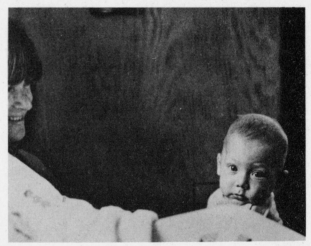
child by myself all day long. I was fortunate because in teaching I worked fairly short hours, so I could do it. I went to work two weeks after my first child was born.

Me: You got a babysitter?

Ani: Yes. It was really very difficult because I was nursing. I would take him to a babysitter, go and teach my courses, come back and nurse him *and* cook dinners, *and* do the diapers. It was a nightmare. I would do it less exhaustively now, because I wouldn't expect of myself to do all the other things which I did at the time because of my role-conditioning. It never occurred to me or to anyone that it wasn't my responsibility to keep the household going, plus everything else. As wife, it was my role!

The Good Mother/Wife

Me: A woman who is in that situation, could try to become more aware of where she's getting caught and strained by her role. She could ask herself, "What do I consider part of the good mother-wife role? Why is it all my responsibility? Where do I need help? Where do I feel guilty even though I need help? And how can I rearrange things so I get the help I need?"

Ani: Often a woman will express her need for help in the form of nagging, which usually doesn't bring the help she wants. It's important to recognize that "nagging" expresses a real feeling. Then she can express her need more directly. Beneath nagging is often a need for nurturing. A woman in this society is asked to do a lot of "mothering." It's helpful for her to recognize *her* need for being mothered. She can ask it of other women, of her own mother if she is lucky, and of her husband. This will cut down on the "bitching," "nagging," "complaining" tendencies. I find that my children give me a lot of mothering also — in the form of warmth, concern, responsiveness.

One problem is that you need to really work it out well with each other, because there is not that much help available from the society. Jerry and I have worked at it for years now, and there's no way to work it out ahead of time. You can't really imagine what it's like to have a child of your own until you have one. So once you have a child you have to re-examine the roles totally.

We did that but it took us five or six years, because every single detail of what goes into living in a household has been conditioned. Jerry was not conditioned to do dishes and diapers and cook, or to even think about it! His mind wasn't prepared to think about buying the milk and toilet paper and the toothpaste. I had to laboriously point out every single one of those things. Very few marriages can withstand it, because it's so much picayune detailed stuff.

Me: It seems critical to find some mutual goals so that you have a feeling of working together. If the husband has the attitude "I want to pay attention to this stuff too because I know these are places where our roles are hurting our marriage," then he can see that there's some benefit for him. He might even like some of the changes!

Ani: Yes. Jerry says, "Doing dishes is wonderful. It relaxes my mind." It's not wonderful to me, because it's not a novelty and it wasn't a choice. But many men whose work is so different from this find a tremendous relief and expansion in the intuitive and physical labor aspect of it.

Also when Kai was born I soon realized I was not much better prepared to take care of an infant than Jerry was, but I thought that as a woman, I *should* know what to do. I had watched my friend Michele with her son and that had been a really useful model for me, but in terms of diapering and dealing with colic and communicating with a baby I was often at a loss. It can be helpful to say to your husband, "I don't know!" Then he can participate in finding out who the child is and what he/she needs. A newborn baby is a stranger to both parents and they all need to get acquainted.

There is also a related kind of relaxation happening to some men who say, "That is great. I'm not the sole person responsible for the money and I'm not the lone head of the family. There are two of us." That can be a great relief. The responsibility for the children and the home used to be all on the woman's shoulders, but it shouldn't really even be on just two people.

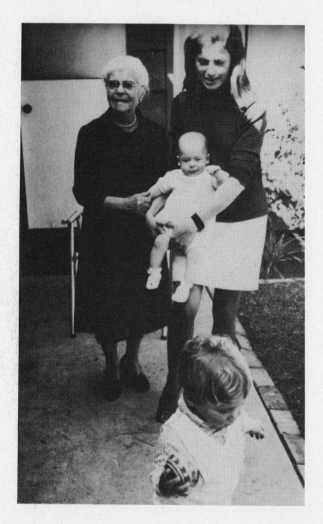

I think that children are members of society and we should all relate to them and look after them, instead of leaving it up to the biological parents alone. It's a very severe problem in this country. It's not so bad in other countries. I do wish men would work it out with each other too because it's very difficult for women to work it out with men.

Me: There's little feeling of community here.

Ani: None at all. You're very isolated bringing up children.

Me: Do you remember a difference in Yugoslavia?

Ani: It was very different. I remember more about Italy than Yugoslavia. I grew up with my grandparents around us because we were all fleeing en masse. It was already an extended family situation. Also if a child is running and falls on the street, an adult who is walking by will automatically pick her up. Here it seems to me the reaction is to look around for the mother because you might get sued. Before you reach out to help somebody, a million thoughts go through your mind about what this act means. That certainly wasn't true in Italy or in Yugoslavia. A child will be crying and people will respond to it, whether yelling at her or embracing her. There's a whole range of responses, but they do respond. They don't pretend that she's not there.

Me: Or that they have no relation to that person.

Ani: ...because it's not their property. You know, children are considered property in this society. That's the oppression of the children. They're people; they ought to have equal rights.

Me: How did you and Jerry arrange sharing the work of having children?

Ani: Between me and Jerry the care of the children was easier to work out than other areas. It's very important because children create most of the problems when they're young, in terms of work, in terms of taking your time away from yourself.

Jerry tuned in to them and had tremendous responses of his own. That automatically brought out a whole number of things in himself where he wanted to be with the children. He wanted to respond to the children, to be involved. That helped enormously, because then we weren't talking about diapers, we were talking about relating to the child.

Me: Do you pay attention to your sex role concepts in relation to the children?

Ani: When I was first pregnant, I really wanted a son. That's sexist conditioning right there! I had it in myself, and I was very glad that he was a son. I soon realized that it was a prejudice which had nothing to do with the realities. I had imagined my baby in a certain way and he didn't turn out the way I had imagined him anyhow. He was an individual, not my preconception of "a boy."

Then during my second pregnancy I wanted a girl! But that soon disappeared with the reality of the child. The child sends all kinds of signals about who he/she is. You have to respond to their signals. You can't impose things on the child; that is very evident right away from a tiny baby. His nursing habits, his crying, everything was his. Just that was very enlightening. I couldn't read books and then do it that way; I had to listen to what this individual was saying.

Me: That seems so important to me. We're generally oriented toward child "rearing," toward molding the child, instead of allowing the person she or he is to develop, instead of listening and learning a lot of what you need to know from them.

Ani: Something that really gets in the way of family communication is the accepted family hierarchy. At the top is the husband. He has power over you, and you have power over the children because they're dependent on you. They're weaker, have no money, and can't drive a car and all that.

Me: Was this awareness a result of your consciousness raising group work?

Ani: Yes. When I started focusing on my oppression (and I'm less oppressed than most women, I am well aware of it) principally I realized that I was a member of a hierarchical situation where certain people had power over me. As part of that hierarchy, I was oppressing other people, including my children.

247

Family Hierarchy

Me: It would seem really important for a mother to sit down and ask herself, "What is the power structure in our family? How can we relate without the power system?"

Ani: You also have to contend with societal trends. I overheard my children playing hospital with their friends. The boys were the doctors, and the girls were the nurses. I just cringed. I went in and said, "Why can't Veva be the doctor and you be the nurse?" But when I take them to Kaiser Hospital, the majority of doctors are male, and all nurses that they've ever seen have been female. So of course they incorporate those roles in their play.

Me: How do you deal with that?

Ani: I talk to them about it. They know about the movement and about the attempts toward change. All I can do is point out the realities. I can't say that it's not that way. It is that way!

Me: At least you give them the choice of another thought.

Ani: There's so much conditioning to combat with either sex. With a female child, you have to fight against the models and not have her succumb. The male child assumes all kinds of leadership and aggression positions. So many little simple things.

When my eldest child, Yari, was about three and a half we went to Woolworth's and he said he wanted a gun. I could have gone through a number of trips, "Well, you don't really want a gun." Or I could have distracted him. Or told him about the evil of guns. But eventually he really wants a gun and I buy him a gun. He has a right to have this toy that all of his friends have. So the socialization is ever present.

Or television — television just fills their minds with sex roles and violence. My attempt and Jerry's attempt is to point it out. They are victims of it to some degree. But they can be conscious of it. Not only that, Yari actually told me, "It's only a toy gun, mother. It can't hurt anybody!"

I'm not very optimistic that it will be all that different, but in the next generation some important things will be different. Their sexuality is being handled differently. That in itself is a big step.

Me: How is that with your kids?

Ani: In their games and in their body play, towards themselves, toward me, towards their father and their friends they are very sexual, or rather sensual. It gives me tremendous joy to encourage it or to let it be, to let it happen, rather than to repress it as those expressions were repressed in me. It gives me tremendous happiness to see them experience it unaffectedly.

248

Our cat had some kittens and Kai, my youngest son was watching her nurse. When the kitten stopped nursing, the nipple was still visible on the cat. He said, "They're just like your breasts." I said, "Yes." He said, "I want to see" and I showed him. He had seen me nude before, but he hadn't examined it. He looked at my breasts and he said, "You mean I drank milk like that?" He knew it, but he couldn't remember it. I said, "Yes." He said, "Let me try." I said, "All right." He put his mouth there and he didn't know how to suck anymore.

Kai was acting quite unaffectedly. From the child's point of view that is not a sexual act at all. It didn't feel sexual to me either, but it was not possible for me to do it without feeling self-conscious. Kai couldn't get into the nursing experience because his instincts weren't there anymore. He just laughed and went on to something else. But I was thinking, "*Now* what am I doing, Dr. Freud?"

I notice an increase in self-consciousness about their sexuality and sex roles as they get older. There's more influence from the outside. They went through a period where they wanted to wear girls' clothes. They borrowed some nightgowns from their friends, and they would wear nightgowns to bed. People would visit and the children would come in their nightgowns, and the guests would say things like, "I thought you had boys!" I'd say, "well, yes, these are boys." Then the older one said, "I don't want to wear nightgowns any more." But actually he does. He just doesn't want to wear them in front of people. They might comment. I wanted to buy him sandals and he'd say, "That's for girls." Their identity has already been imposed on by external symbols like that.

Me: Are you ever aware of using the children to communicate messages between you and Jerry?

Ani: I think Jerry and I are very clear on that point. We deal directly with each other. There's very little using the kids as a buffer or to fight our battles. I do see a lot of that in other families though.

Me: This is a place where a lot of sexual manipulation goes on too.

Ani: Yes. The mother might compete with a daughter she felt was prettier than she, or sexier to her father.

Me: If that goes on, there are usually a lot of subtle messages coming from the father too. The "Daddy's little girl" game. "Come on over and sit on Daddy's lap. Be Daddy's pretty little girl." He may not even be aware that he's using the child to irritate his wife, or that he's acting seductively.

Ani: Some parents today do believe in being sexual with their children.

Me: How do you feel about that?

Ani: That's a very complicated subject. I don't believe in "seducing" children. That implies coercing them into a situation against their wishes. But there is so much love, deep connection, and close physical contact between a mother and her child that sexual feelings and acts are always part of this contact. Most children are naturally attracted sexually to the member of their family. Children repress their sexual feelings about their family when they learn they are taboo. How far to act on these feelings is something each parent has to decide herself. I think that if parents and children are open with each other, if their feelings — good or bad — are allowed to be expressed, then the child will naturally make the choices that suit him or her. A child does not play manipulative games unless she has to. She will not choose something she is not ready for. A small child is not into sex in the adult sense of the word — adults can tune into the child in themselves and thereby respond to his or her sexuality in a natural appropriate way.

Me: I'm also concerned with situations short of actual seduction which are sexually manipulative to the children.

Ani: Yes. Along with the increased sexual openness and relaxation within families comes a lot of acting out on the part of the parents of their own rebellion because we are all so new to this openness.

Me: Yeah, children need privacy as well as group openness. I would need to sort out where I'm working out my own repressions and where I'm doing something which feels comfortable and right for the rest of the family. I could check by asking myself, "Am I getting an inordinate amount of pleasure out of this? Do I look forward to exposing myself? Am I still trying to be "different from my parents?" If

the answers are yes, chances are I'm acting out with the child. I can tell the difference when I feel natural and comfortable about the atmosphere.

Every family has different sexual lines. The most critical factor I can see is that the lines be definite and openly communicated. A good game to play to explore this would be to act the part of your child in the situation and try to get into how he or she feels.

Ani: Or you could simply *ask* the child how he or she feels!

Family Systems

Virginia Satir is the originator of Family Therapy. It was her realization that people who live in families live within a small community with distinct systems, rules, and contracts. Therefore, to single out one family member as "sick" and try to give isolated psychological counseling to this person is useless because their behavior is a response to the family system. As soon as they return to their family, they revert back to their original behavior in order to fit into the system again. It was Virginia Satir's idea that the whole family should come into therapy together. This way, the therapist can see the behavior of the person singled out as "sick" within the context of the family interaction. The therapist then points out the interrelatedness of each person's role in the family, and the whole family becomes aware of how they affect each other. Virginia Satir's book, *Conjoint Family Therapy* (Science and Behavior Books, paper) is an excellent outline of her family therapy and her communication theory.

The following role-playing exercise is from her work. It can be done with family members or simply with friends to bring more awareness and perspective on your roles and relationships. It is best done with three or more people. When I do this I am always surprised at how thoroughly self-perpetuating the systems are — there is no way to really communicate or to mutually resolve conflicts as long as the members stay in their defined roles. It is important to become aware of these roles in order to break the endless loop which often develops in families of power struggles and miscommunication.

Satir divides family roles into five categories: (1) the Rationalizer (the reasonable one, the intellecutalizer, cold, aloof, frequently a man's role, non-feeling) (2) The Blamer (the bitch, the complainer, the paranoid, the martyr) (3) The Irrelevant One (the distractor, often the one labelled as 'crazy,' the schizophrenic child, or simply the bratty attention getter who interrupts all the time, the clown) (4) The Placator (the Mona Lisa smiler, the go-between, the keeper of the peace) (5) The Congruent One (there may be one person in the bunch who's together and not caught in her roles!).

Each person will play all these roles from time to time, but will have one of them as their characteristic family posture. If you recognize your dominant role, choose another for yourself for this exercise; your partners pick their roles (hopefully one of those is your characteristic role so that you can experience how it feels to deal with that personality). Decide who's mommy, who's daddy, and who's the child.

Now sit in a circle together and pick an imaginary family conflict which you will attempt to resolve. It can be as simple as deciding what to do on a holiday or as difficult as your son's recent jail sentence. Begin talking over the situation together *always responding within the character of your role.* Pay attention to how it feels to be this type. How do you experience the other roles? Do you recognize yourself in these caricatures? Can you experience how the roles of the other two people keep you locked into your role? Do you see any way to alter the family pattern within that role system? What happens to the system when one of you drops their role?

Afterward, share with each other how it was to play your role and how you experienced the patterns. Now switch roles and try another system.

The Child in You

Marion Saltman is a wonderful woman who is also a Play Therapist, leading groups now mainly for adults. I went to one of her all-day workshops one sunny Saturday in September.

I walked across a muddy parking area and onto the zig-zag wooden dock which leads to the old houseboat where Marion lives in Sausalito, California. The boat itself is like a huge wooden magic Never-never Land house, filled with plants, costumes and trinkets, with big windows that look out onto the bay. The side windows look down the line of the waterfront where other fantastic boathomes which people have constructed float.

Outside the air was hot and quiet, and the boats creaked. Inside Marion's boat was darker and cooler. Three or four people were sitting on the floor talking. Marion came over to tell me that we were waiting for some more people to arrive. I wanted

to explore the boat. I found there were seven rooms. One was a space for paints and crayons with stand-up drawing counters. One was a bedroom. Another was half-filled by a giant sand-box; the other half was a costume room with old carved mirrors and trunks and racks of clothes. Plus two bathrooms and a loft. The main room was the biggest. At one end was an open kitchen and the rest was covered with rugs and pictures and plants and pillows and playthings, including an adult-sized hanging rocking horse with glass eyes and a hollow head. (If you look inside there is a tiny room of gems and brocade.)

Living Your Past

After awhile about twelve people of different ages assembled in a circle. Marion asked us each to close our eyes and think of a time in our childhood when we were playing. We went around the circle and each person shared their play memory. A woman remembered playing outside and enviously watching her older sister walk a fence which seemed enormous to her. Some people remembered secret hideaways or special fantasies they acted out.

I immediately recalled playing "Vampire," an absorbing fantasy game I played with my friend, Sally. I was about eight years old, and my parents were living in the country in Maryland on land which used to be an old dairy farm. There were what seemed to me endless green hills and pastures and pine forests to play in. There were also some deteriorating shacks in parts of the far woods which were once barns or shops. Sally and I loved to play in a small tool shed with counters and tiny drawers still filled with screws, washers, nails and machine parts of many sizes. Everything was rusted and cobwebbed now, but it was the perfect headquarters for two young vampires.

Sally and I would go there, rummage around in the tools and fixtures which seemed so mysterious and important to us, and tell each other scary stories. Sometimes we would make excursions into the woods and fantasize capturing someone to become another vampire.

The memory was vivid to me. I could see the tool shed and the woods and I could remember how I felt there. In remembering, I knew that the vampire was a personna of great power to me, a role in which I was Lord of All and always got my way and I was quite evil. I contrasted this in my mind to the role I played inside my parents' home—sweet, good and obedient. Clearly the "good girl" was a figure without power and without her own will, always trying to please others.

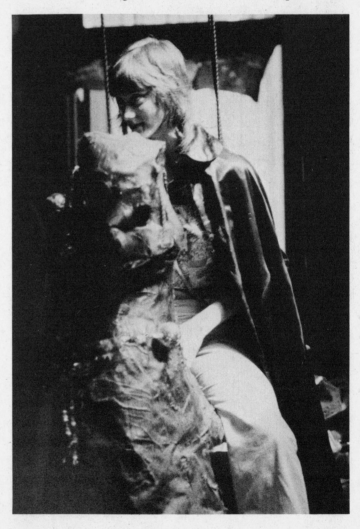

Marion asked us if we saw ways that we continued our old play patterns and roles today. The woman who remembered her sister walking on the fence got in touch with a consistent sense of herself as more fragile and cautious than other people. She could see how she held herself back with this self-image. I realized how strongly I felt that being evil was the only way to be powerful, and that being "nice" meant giving up my personal power. I decided that this didn't fit me anymore and I wanted to integrate those polarities more as an adult.

Marion suggested we could experiment with these play roles in her workshop. She said her home was open to us, and that we had all day to do anything we wanted. People filtered off into different rooms, and I went to find a vampire costume.

I found one — a black satin cape, a red sash and paint for designs and fangs on my face. I tried hard to be evil and manipulative all day. It was so hard not to smile and try to make friends! That's a picture of me in my cape riding the hanging horse.

Some people painted, others played in the sand, made music on the instruments or went off on an excursion in the rowboat. We had brought food and came together for lunch. Late in the afternoon we did some massage in the loft. Afterward we talked about our experiences of the day.

Later Marion and I talked about her perspective on her play groups and the kinds of reactions people have.

"We prohibit play in the strongest of terms. The children shall rise at 5 in the morning summer and winter. The children shall be indulged with nothing that which the world calls play. And these rules shall be observed with the strictest of nicety for he who plays when he is young will play when he is old." — a 19th century church school statement.

"Man is made as God's plaything and this is the best part of him. And, therefore, he should be of another mind than what he is at present and live life accordingly. Life should be lived as play." — Plato, from *The Laws*.

Marion: I see all adults as they might have been at four years old. I can really imagine what they were like in kindergarten. I taught pre-school for many years and kindergarten, and I worked with children up until the last five or six years. I used these same techniques with children. My feeling was, "Why couldn't this be applied to adults?"

In all of us there is a frightened little girl and that person comes out under various conditions. Many of us are not in touch with that. Under certain circumstances you revert back to however you coped with things when you were four years old. Eric Berne's behavior model says that we have a child, adult and parent in each of us. The child is screaming to come out and the parent is constantly pushing it down by saying, "You can't do that, it's not appropriate; you'll get your dress dirty; you'll get your feet dirty." The positive adult that wants to emerge gets squashed in this fight between the negative parent and the negative child. In order for our adult to emerge freely, we have to allow the child in us to be expressed.

Children can do a lot of the things that parents don't give themselves permission to do so the parent gets angry at the child for doing them. That's why a lot of adults can't stand the noise that children make or the smells they make and stuff. They can't let themselves have that kind of freedom so they resent it when children indulge themselves. Play Therapy gives us the opportunity to express and resolve our childhood conflicts so we can then allow our offspring to be children in their own right.

Me: It might be a good idea for parents when they're angry at a child to say, "Am I really annoyed at what she's doing, or am I jealous of her freedom?"

Marion: And then to say, "Maybe I could do that too. Why not?"

Me: How do people react in your play workshops to being given permission to express those parts of themselves?

Marion: People can do whatever they want in my workshops. That releases a lot of energy. Some people find that they're terrified by that, particularly I've seen it happen a lot with women. They say, "Oh, that's too much for me. I can't get into that."

Or they'll say, "These people were playing with the ball and these people were playing with the blocks, and somebody else was doing this and I wandered around and I wanted somebody to play with but I didn't know how to approach anybody. I was afraid. So I got in touch with how shy and frightened I am." Or they'll say, "After wandering around I finally got up courage to ask somebody, 'Could I join you?' " Or, "I finally decided to do some dancing myself." That comes out of this non-structure.

You see, in everything that I've experienced, we're always told how to behave, even in the most loose groups. And pretty soon people learn how to play that game. Whereas in the play thing it's freaky because here is an environment with all these things, and I say, "OK, here's the place. Here's the things. Here're the people. Here you are."

We are educated entirely to follow directions and rules rather than to be innovative, especially in group situations. When I taught school in the L.A. system in kindergarten they had very strict rules, like five year olds couldn't carry more than three blocks! (Probably some kid carried more and it fell on his foot and he went home and cried and the parents came in and blamed this on the school system.) How can one learn one's own inner direction, one's own strengths and weaknesses, always having regulations on the outside directing? How could that child learn what his capacities were? By picking up a whole load of blocks and having a few fall, he could get in touch where his own strength is. If you're told that you can only carry a certain amount no learning takes place.

The same thing goes having the kids all line up to put the blocks away. Instead of "The blocks have to be put away, all right?" If it gets to be a shambles with everybody knocking each other over, pretty soon the group itself will sit down and say, "This isn't working, what can we do?" But have it come from them, instead of from the top authority.

At Tahoe, in a weekend session of ten people, two men got together with blocks and they built an airport. It was a very elaborate airport. They had windsocks and hangers, and it was like two four-year-olds building. It was utterly lovely! One woman there wanted to play with them but they wouldn't let her. They said, "No girls allowed." She kept trying to get in there in all kinds of devious ways. She finally did. She said, "Well, you need some flags; can I make the flags for you?" So she got in through offering a feminine thing.

The exclusiveness of the men was valid in a sense. These two guys had a thing going and they really didn't want anybody else in. But I've seen this happen with  men, and I don't see that happen with women. Women don't say, "We don't want any guys in here." Usually the girls are trying to get into the man play. And lots of times it does happen, freely and openly. I've heard women say, "Wow, I could never be that tomboy when I was a kid, I really had a good time today."

Me: I'd like to talk about any patterns you observe in the women who come to you for Play Therapy. Do they seem to go through stages?

Marion: A lot of women initially act out a fairy princess thing, the "good girl." I'm thinking of a women in her late thirties who was here who was quite heavy, and she just loved putting on a white tule costume I have with all kinds of sequins on it, which is kind of like the Junior Prom dress. She had it on for maybe an hour or so, and suddenly she said, "Shit, I don't want this anymore. I've had this. I'm tired of this. It's not where it's at for me." And she took the whole thing off!

The other striking thing is how women begin to understand their own children's playfulness. I remember a lady who was playing in the sand and she said, "Wow, I'm really enjoying this. Now I know I'm not going to be angry at my children

259

anymore for coming home from school with sand in their shoes and making a mess in the house." Or "When I fingerpaint, I can understand why my child likes to get messy with this, because it just is a groovy thing to do, and I feel good when I do that. So I'm not going to scold my child for doing these things anymore."

Me: Trying out the child's play is something a mother could do on her own. Getting out of the observor-peacekeeper role and into the spirit of it.

Marion: Another interesting pattern women seem to get into is that of playing disapproving mother to their husbands. It's not only the children they are jealous of. In a play session at Forest Hospital in Chicago we worked with parents of adolescents who came in from the outside. We did sessions with them, sessions with their parents, and then we put the two together. During one session, three women were very upset because their husbands were having a good time! They said, "Look at him. He should be home fixing the fence or something." They had to be the mother keeping things clean and administering. They couldn't get out of that role and be playful.

Me: I catch myself getting into a negative mother role, taking over a lot of responsibility planning, doing all kinds of work alone that I don't need to do. But I take it all on — and then I feel resentment against my man when he's enjoying himself!

Marion: The play experience is particularly geared toward helping a person get in touch with their own child within. Hopefully this way they can relax and learn to express their natural selves.

Me: Do you think of the child as the person without any roles?

Marion: Right. A two-year-old is a natural being. He's right out there, not in any fixed role. I was reading just recently where in a school, they had the six-year-old girls bake cakes, and the boys were going to judge which was the best cake by tasting it. You're judged on your worth by the taste of your cake. Those things are put in the consciousness of children so early!

I am beginning to research the relation between sexuality and play. I want to develop play therapy which deals with play between men and women and how they can get it on together and get rid of their isolating sex roles.

Me: How do you start people getting in touch with their early patterns?

Marion: I start a session with some talk about play and then I do a guided fantasy. I encourage people to close their eyes and take a little trip on a magic carpet back into their own childhoods. Want to try that right now?

Let yourself go wherever you happen to land. Just be there; be aware of the smells and how you feel, what you're wearing, what's going on in that situation. Instead of just observing it, try to put yourself in that place and let yourself experience it. Be aware of what was really happening there, the smells, touch, feelings.

Me: I'm playing in my backyard.

Marion: What's happening?

Me: I'm with my sister. I must be six or maybe younger because we're living in Kentucky. She and I had a place we played which was under a lot of bushes. We were small enough to get under and it made a kind of cave. And there was a lot of mud. We used to go under there and there was a little table and we'd make mud pies and play and have a meal, a mud pie meal at this table. It was nice to be outside and it was really nice to be in the mud and sort of mess around.

Marion: How did you feel there?

Me: I liked being secluded. It was away from other people, adults. And it was our cave and other people were too big to get in.

Marion: How neat!

Me: But I remember a feeling of loneliness too. There was sort of a double feeling. People couldn't get in but it was too bad I wanted to keep them out. It was too bad that they were enemies.

Marion: It was the two of you in a safe place against a cruel world? Can you get in touch with whether you sometimes do that now?

Me: I think of my house that way! I think of my house as a refuge. It has a lot of trees around it and I think of it as a refuge from the rest of the world.

I think that's a quality about your house here that's really attractive to me. You have built your own world that really speaks to me; it's related to my fantasy.

Marion: That comes from where I was as a child. I was an only child and much of my existence was creating my own scenes and playing in them. I always had this thing laid on me of "Oh, Marion, you don't understand reality. Why don't you grow up?" I had this trip so heavy on me, I can't tell you! I still get it, and both my daughters are in their twenties. A few years ago a Freudian analyst said to me, "Umph. You not only have fantasies, you live them." I said, "Yes! I live 'em and I love it! The more I can live, the better I love it!"

Playing Out Your Own Mythology

Marion: I believe that every one of us has our own personal myth that's related to some story or some fairy tale. It can be important to get in touch with what your favorite fairy story was and what it means.

My favorite one is Peter Pan. I didn't understand what that was all about until just this year when I realized that the reason I do what I do is that I am playing out my own myth. I see Peter as play; he's also the bridge between the land of the Darlings and the land of the Lost Boys. It's very important to keep that bridge open. When we get to the stage of being twelve or thirteen, when you start your period, and it's time to put all childish things away and now you are a woman, many things are no longer appropriate. You shouldn't sit on the floor with your legs up in the air playing jacks. You've got to wear a top with your bathing suit; and you've got to begin to be aware of your body as a woman in a negative way.

Me: That tells a child you have fun when you're a kid but when you grow up it's terrible and you have to toe the line and this is the end — the end of your fun.

Marion: Yes, and from now on you must be serious and you must worry and you must take care and think about security.

Me: My reaction to that is, "I don't want to grow up!"

Marion: Yes. Kids look at this and say, "Who needs that?" There's Mother slaving over a stove and Daddy's reading the paper and nobody's getting it on and who wants that kind of a grim scene? At that point we can come to a place of not wanting to mature in a healthy way, not allowing our positive adult.

Me: There is no positive image of an adult.

Marion: Exactly. So we grow up absurd.

Me: Miserable, nostalgic and serious.

Marion: That's related to many people's concept of the dichotomy between work and play. Most of us are brought up to think that you can play one specific

262

time and then you work. They're very separate. They should never meet. And most of us when we're playing wish we were working and when we're working, we wish we could be playing. We feel guilty either way. So we take our books to the beach, you know. I think this is a particularly important thing with women in the home because they feel if they are there they have to be working all the time.

Me: You have to go outside to play.

Marion: Right. It's sinful to play; I should be doing the wash or scrubbing the floors and so forth. To just put on some music or put some finger paint on the kitchen table and enjoy that with your family can be a wonderful thing. After play sessions, women often say to me, "Now I realize I can be more playful with my children. It's okay. I don't have to always stay in the mothering role."

It's often the same with professional people. At a hospital, we had one man come in, a psychiatrist, and he couldn't sit down on the mats with the people. He had to sit on a chair, ten feet away, in order to continue his image of the therapist. The same thing happens with parents. They feel if they get down on the floor one-to-one with their kids that they will lose their ability to discipline or to mind the store, so to speak.

Me: The hierarchy is gone.

Marion: Ideally, there is no hierarchy. It's people to people, person to person.

Me: A woman could experiment with that in her home by really playing with her kids outside her role and by examining the family hierarchy.

Marion: And playing by herself. The central point is to try to get it on for yourself. Not as something I do for my children because I need to play with my children.

It's important also to clarify your idea of what a child is. There is a difference between childish and child-like. People get confused. They ask me, "Am I supposed to play like a child?" People have fantasies of what children are. The classical thing is the idea of a kid with a lollipop talking baby talk. That's playing at being a child, and that is very much discouraged. That's not where it's at.

The point is that you are what you are right now, and your child is still there. Maybe you've lost tough with that child, but as Jung says, that's where my energy is, that's where my creativity is, because it's the child who says, "Hey, let's get it on. Wow, what's going to happen? How else can I do it? This is fun!" And it's the positive parent who says, "Sure, go ahead and see what you can do with that. You want an extra dollar? Can I help you?" The adult is the road map, gets you from here to there. The adult is non-emotional and allows the child and parent to live. When those three are in harmony then you're just floating along real nice.

Me: So you see your play therapy not as trying to bring the child part out to get rid of it but as trying to allow it to happen?

Marion: The idea is integration, integration of the parts of yourself.

A lot of today's toys come from that distorted image of what a child is and what she likes to play with. Many of the toys children have now are really degrading. Hopi Indian children are not given phony toys. A boy is given a bow and arrow and he learns to use it and as he learns to use it in a more adult way, he has an initiation to do it. It isn't work; it isn't a meaningless toy. In every play group where I've said, "Go back to your childhood; what is your fondest memory?" no one has ever once mentioned a toy. I've worked with literally hundreds of people.

The toys I have here and use in my work are what I call adult toys: musical instruments, paints, clothes, games. It has very little to do with the toy itself. It's a change in attitude about your activity.

Me: What kinds of games do people play together here?

Marion: A lot of men when they play or dress up want to wear women's costumes. Men have the same role restrictions laid on them that women do. "Boys don't do this, that and the other thing." If you take the human being in Jung's term of having an anima and an animus, the boy has not had an opportunity to express his anima, so here he's given a chance. "I can wear robes; I can wear feathers; I can allow my anima to express itself." Men have an equally bad trip in that they're afraid to express their feminine side for fear of being called homosexual.

People also often play out rituals. Funerals, weddings, executions, various myths. It's spontaneous. All of a sudden people decide we'll do this thing and they get it together and go through it and it might last two minutes and it's over with. That's the beauty, you see. It's not planned.

Children are so in the here and now that if, for instance, they get angry at each other, you've heard kids say, "I don't want to play with you again. Get out of my house. I don't want to see you again and stuff."

Me: I won't be your friend.

Marion: Right. And two minutes later, a half an hour later, the next day, they have their arms around each other! It's fun — until the mother comes in and says, "What? How could you possibly talk to him when he did that to you yesterday?" Sometimes that kind of rigidity goes on in people's lives for lifetimes.

Through play a lot of people realize they can just live a little on the lighter side. They don't have to take everything so heavy. And that's a lovely thing.

Me: I'm interested in how you feel about the Montessori technique of child education.

Marion: One aspect of Montessori, which is common to many child psychologies, is that they talk about the child's play being the child's work. This is so in a sense because the child is working on her mastery of the environment, but often if the tone is too serious, it takes all the "play" out of it.

Like Gestalt or anything else, it's who is doing it that counts, and where and how they're doing it. Some of the Los Angeles Montessori Schools were, I felt, really terrible. They were usually in Beverly Hills type, upper white middle class communities where they had carpets on the floor and the children were encouraged to be small adults. They learned to set the table just right and they had a beauty shop set up where you called to make an appointment!

Me: Oh, no.

Marion: But I think probably the Montessori schools around here are very free and expressive. The Montessori idea of learning through tactile experience and so forth is great. It depends on what people do with it.

Me: It seems to me that sexuality is closely tied in with playfulness. How do you see play development affecting sexual development?

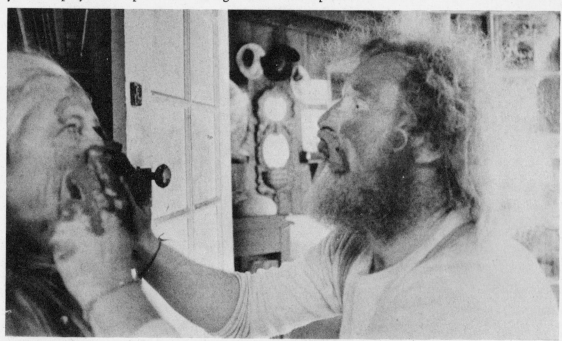

Marion: All children are very sensual, and they want to touch and smell and explore and get into gooky things. Parents and society implicitly let them know that there's something wrong with that. "You should stay clean. Don't touch. Don't put it in your mouth because it will poison you. Don't point. Don't show your panties." And on and on.

I want to give some workshops in sensuality, starting with feeling things, like fur, sticky things, mud if we ever had it available, to get people in touch in themselves with their own sensuousness in terms of just tactile things. Not with one another in the beginning, but exploring their own enjoyment.

Me: Yeah, anything is yummy!

Marion: Right. Looks nice to me: may be a pile of shit, but it's all right, you know. Then the society says, "Oh, no. Certain things are yucky." Over a period of time, the child censors herself. "I have all these gooey feelings and these sensuous feelings and feelings of wanting body pleasure and masturbation or whatever, but I'm getting the message from parents and teachers that I'm not supposed to have anything to do with that." I think that the child then begins to feel that "Because I have these thoughts, and because I like these things, and because I do these things when nobody's around, that means that there's something wrong with me. I'm not clean; I'm not good; I'm not okay." I really feel that this has a tremendous bearing on how people experience themselves.

Me: It has to because we all have those qualities in our bodies even though we're not "supposed" to. We have sticky secretions, and smells, and so much effort is put into getting rid of anything that we naturally produce with all the soaps and deodorants and perfume sprays. It sets up the choice, "Do I do this by myself and have fun, or do I give up myself in order to connect?"

The limitations that sets up are many. Expecially with sex. Sex is gooey and smelly and messy, which is completely antithetical to any kind of good girl/good boy trip. What must happen is that the person comes to the conclusion, "Not only am I bad, but the person I'm with is bad too, because he's gooey!"

Marion: Yeah. "If I let myself be gooey, then I won't be liked by him because he'll think I'm not a nice girl. I keep myself pretty and neat and clean all the time so he'll love me. He won't know how messy I am. I'm really a slob." When all the time he's a slob, too!

Me: There's an underlying feeling with a couple that they don't really like each other in a natural state. That puts a masquerade trip on them which takes a lot of effort to keep up.

Marion: The energy and effort that goes into that is so ridiculous, because you see that this whole trip is anti-life; it's anti-human; it is not loving. If you feel really loving you have no trouble being playful. When you love that baby it is so easy to hold. When you love the cat, it's so easy to be playful with it. When we're truly loving each other then we're naturally playful because that which is natural is playful.

Naturalness, playfulness and lovingness are all the same. So what we're really dealing with in the play thing is *loving*. That starts with being able to say, "There are no heavy expectations, I dig you, I'm me, and you're you, and let's just do our thing together."

Western culture is involved in so much violence and we call it love. I'm going to spank you or make you feel miserable because I love you. I'm going to make you wear a shirt and tie and say the right things and do the right things because I love you.

Instead, I want to teach from the positive. Playfulness is an attitude and an environment in the home which allows a child to express herself and grow without pressure to be a certain way. It involves total acceptance of where one is right now.

Play is a matter of attitude rather than a particular activity. If you're washing dishes and you play with the soap and play with the whole thing, well, it's a lot of fun to do. Whereas if it's a grim task that has a lot of rules and regulations and has to be done now, then play stops.

I feel that we're all playing all the time but we don't know it. We're playing house. We're playing writer. Whatever we're doing. Varda, the artist who lived in this boat before I came here, was a master of this. He actually had his work and play together. Which is what I feel is the nicest thing that can happen. And it's beginning to happen more and more to a lot of people, particularly young people. If raising plants gets me on that's what I am going to do. And it becomes a playful thing.

I've done a lot of research on this, and I've found that most of the books that are written on play are written by theologians, who understand, you see, the higher basis of play as being the ultimate that Plato talks about — that man is God's plaything and all the universe is play. The wind in the trees, the water and everything else is a very playful kind of thing on another level. Play in terms of education. Play in terms of various therapy techniques. There are many different levels.

When I ask people why they come to my workshops, most of the time they will say, "I feel something's missing; maybe this will do something." I feel what they're really struggling for is to find their own naturalness, their own freedom, to drop some of this rigid role playing that gets started so early. That's what they really want. I do these groups because I believe that change and growth can take place with pleasure as well as pain. Pleasure can bring tremendous discoveries.

Back to Yourself

Back to Yourself

I find that I need to alternate periods of outward orientation and opening up to other people with phases of clearing these away in order to tune in to my inner life. Alternating this way keeps me balanced. I can tell when I need to change when I feel the need for more outside contact or some fresh input, or when I feel so overwhelmed and crowded by outer stimuli that I have neglected my inner life and need to withdraw temporarily to be alone. I move back and forth between these two orientations not only over long time periods, but also within the space of one day.

Deep fantasy and meditation are two different techniques which I find useful for bringing myself back in touch with my internal world. Deep fantasy can be done effectively sporadically; meditation must be done regularly (each day, even just for a few minutes) to be fully experienced. Healing can be an aspect of both experiences.

Deep Fantasy

Deep fantasy can be used for exploring your body internally for new "discoveries" or can be used as a healing process when you have a specific emotional or physical pain. Like Gestalt, deep fantasy is most easily done with an outside person acting as your guide, but you can learn to do it by yourself.

The basic idea is to imagine that you can shrink yourself down into a tiny person; this tiny you can walk around until it decides where it wants to go, and then can enter your body to explore and perhaps do some internal maintenance. It is  critical *not* to pre-plan a story; simply try to let the events occur. They will.

Lie down in a quiet warm room on your back. Relax your breathing. If you have a spedific ache or pain you want to work on, locate it and then choose the nearest natural body opening as your "entrance way." Imagine that you can shrink yourself to about a half-inch size or smaller. Talk out loud, and describe how this little person looks and is dressed.

The journey in and out is just as important as the events at your destination. Try not to hurry or miss any steps. As your proceed, talk out loud explicitly about what you are doing and how it feels to you. If you have a pain in your shoulder you want to reach, you could enter through your mouth. Look around. Look at the settings and describe them. "I am walking up to the mouth. I am crawling over the lips. As I let myself down inside, the surface becomes slippery. It's dark in here. I'm walking towards the back of the mouth on the teeth. They feel sharp and bumpy. It's hard to get to my throat."

When you reach the back of the mouth, you'll need to decide how to get down the throat (and later into the shoulder). "There's a deep hole here like a well. There's no way to get down except jump, but I don't know where I'll land." You can decide to go on or turn back and try another way. "I think I'll just jump." Describe your descent, what you see, how you feel. Almost always a surprise landing takes place; if not, pick something to catch onto to stop yourself, or whatever, when you feel you've fallen far enough.

When you land, decide how you're going to get to your sore shoulder muscle. You can swim through an artery or dig through a wall! When you reach the sore muscle, look around. Describe what you see. Try to figure out some way you could perhaps massage the muscles by walking on it or squeezing it. Imagine you are doing this and describe the the process outloud as you go.

When you are done, begin your journey out of the body any way you want. When you're out again, imagine you can blow yourself up to your normal size and merge with your large body again. Take a moment to check in to how the previously sore muscle feels now. Often it will feel greatly relaxed!

One of the possibilities of this exercise is that some place or event may interest you on the way to your destination; if so, go with it. Perhaps you'll want to keep falling down your throat into your stomach to explore there. Or when you reach your sore muscle, you may find another person or animal "inhabiting" it. Talk to them and see if they "answer." Treat the fantasy the way you would a dream which you were Gestalting in which each object and character is a symbolic aspect of yourself, offering to communicate. Use the fantasy journey to become more aware of your patterns. How do I deal with decision-making? How do I deal with the unknown and fear? How do I deal with obstacles? (Do I go around them, through them, or make a deal?)

This kind of fantasy, though it may sound superficial, can actually be one of the most powerful techniques for opening up deep and usually unconscious body feelings. Practice it a few times into different parts of your body and with different aims (an old wound, an emotionally charged area) and sometimes without a specific destination, but simply to explore and go with what happens. You can also try doing this kind of internal fantasy exploration with a mate. What would it be like for you if your partner "came too" imagining they were also journeying to massage your sore muscle and talking along with you? Pay attention to the dialogue between you and to what you can learn about your patterns by how you work out completing a task together.

Meditation

Meditation is another means of opening up to consciousness deep parts of yourself on which you do not normally focus. While deep fantasy requires concentration on a specific "movie," meditation requires you to eliminate any visual pictures or any thoughts which may cross your mind. The easiest way to do this is to concentrate on your breathing. Sit down, comfortably erect. Stay focused on your breath rhythm and count up to ten (counting each inhalation and exhalation as one unit). As thoughts come in, let them "pass through" instead of holding onto them. Let your attention be on your breathing. After awhile the mental static which usually jumbles us during the day will clear away, and the state of meditation takes place.

Many people think of meditation as a mental exercise. Ideally it is not; it is a way to open yourself to the deepest happenings in your body, and to allow these events to become part of your everyday consciousness. When I stick with it, just a few minutes each morning and a few minutes each evening changes the quality of my day.

There are many types and techniques of meditation to choose from. My favorite book on the topic is *Zen Mind, Beginner's Mind* (Weatherhill, cloth) by Shunryo Suzuki. Another helpful book is *Concentration and Meditation* by Christmas Humphreys (Shambala, paper).

Healing

I don't consider healing anything unusual or mysterious. My experience is that it is quite ordinary, that is, everyone has healing powers, but we either do not use them, do not know how to tap them, or don't label some of the things we do and feel as "healing" because it is not generally recognized in our culture as possible or even desirable. (What would the AMA say?!)

Most healers I know consider regular meditation the way to mobilize the intuitive spirit in yourself and to open yourself to your unused inner powers. *This is because the key to unblocking energy in someone else is being able to unblock your own.* This is true of any of the "therapies" outlined in this book. The techniques can be learned by anyone; the depth and power with which they are used is dependent on the development and balance of the person transmitting them. What I have found most "therapeutic" is simple close contact with clear centered individuals.

276

Meditation is one of the most powerful means I know of clearing your own channels. It is also one of the most simple. I have attended several groups given by healers and each prescribed a simple daily ten minute meditation as the doorway to opening your healing powers. (The meditation described earlier is fine. I also recommend Tai Chi Chuan which can be a moving meditation.)

I went to some meetings held by Betty Bethards, a healer who lives in Novato, California. She led us through a short meditation. She talked about how our healing powers are inside us and we simply need to stop, be quiet, and open ourselves to these messages.

She also said that each person has a slightly different inner gift and that this is what you are opening yourself to through meditation. For some people healing is their form; others can be teaching, writing, leadership or spiritual development. The first stage in the process is to get in touch with your individual power through a form of meditation; the second step is to learn to focus and direct the energy. The form may change as you change and some other activity becomes more appropriate to your growth.

Your Hands

Any of the centering exercises described in the section *Body Awareness Exercises For Yourself* is a good preparation for self-healing or tuning in to a friend. This exercise is for experimenting with channeling energy through your hands.

Be sitting either on the floor or on a chair with your feet on the ground (legs uncrossed) and spine comfortably erect. Relax your hands in your lap, palms up. Let your breathing settle low in your abdomen until you can feel your belly move in and out as you exhale and inhale. Try to clear away your thoughts and allow any tense muscles to relax.

Now imagine that as you inhale, your breath moves down your torso into your belly; as you exhale it moves up through your torso into your arms. What would it feel like if you could do this? Imagine what it would feel like if your exhalation could move down through the center of your arms as your circulation does.

Each time you exhale your breath moves farther down the inside of your arms until it reaches your hands. Imagine that you exhale you can send your breath through your arms, into your hands and out through a spot in the center of your palms about the size of a coin. Can you feel the breath moving out through this spot? (A frequent variation is for a person to feel the energy moving out through her fingers.)

Now keeping your arms relaxed raise your hands off your lap, holding them close but not touching, facing palms. Stay with exhaling out your palms. Pay attention to the space between your two palms. Do you feel anything happening between them?

Move your hands slowly apart; pay attention to the space between your two hands as you do. Does the sensation change with distance? Now move them toward each other and see how that feels.

Now let your hands move as they want to. Try not to think of things to do but to let the motion come from your hands themselves. How would they like to move now? At what distance apart and in what position are they most comfortable? Uncomfortable? Play. Let your hands experiment with different movements and positions, tuning in to any sensations you might feel between them as they move.

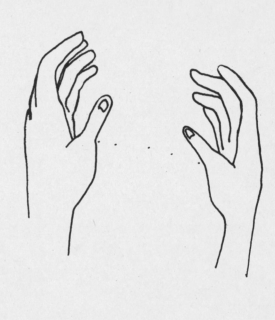

Now let your hands rest in your lap again. Tune in to anything you may be feeling in your arms, torso or other parts of your body as a result of this exercise.

Slowly open your eyes. Can you stay with these new feelings in your hands and arms even when your eyes are open?

This exercise gives you a chance to feel some of the sensations of channeling your energy in your body. Just as you could probably feel something (heat, vibration, magnetism, streaming, relaxation) in your arms and hands from this exercise, someone else could receive this energy into their body by making contact with you when you are relaxed, open and focused. In a simple way this is the mobilization and exchange of healing energy. Physical and emotional tension block it. Relaxation, vitality and centering increase it.

You can channel this healing energy throughout your body. It seems to be particularly strong through your arms and hands. To experiment simply place your right hand (palms down) on any spot on a friend's body which is tense or sore. Place your left palm on any other part of their body. (One especially good position is to have your hands opposite each other — that is your right hand, say, for stomach pain, on the stomach and your left hand *opposite* it on the back.) Close your eyes and relax your body. Center yourself and begin "exhaling" out your palms. You can also try imagining that the tension is moving from your right hand toward your left and dissipating. After five minutes or so, slowly take your hands away and ask your friend if any of the soreness or tension has gone.

Self-Healing

Meditation and centering are two basic forms of self-healing because they are means of rearranging unbalanced energy (un-health) and balancing (health) the flow throughout your body. Another approach is to use images. If you have an ear infection or a liver problem, for example, you could find a picture of a healthy ear or liver in a medical book and spend ten minutes a day visualizing your ear or liver to look just like these healthy ones. (You can also do this visual healing with someone else's ear or liver.)

The basic idea is that the organ is "sick" because you have withdrawn the life energy from that part by tension. By focusing your attention on the neglected parts and allowing life energy, spirit, and joy to move through them again, you can heal.

Getting Older,... and Dying

In the United States, most women are considered "old" at about thirty-five, that is, useless, unattractive, and unwanted. This attitude toward getting older is nearly unique to our culture. What purpose do these ideas serve in our culture? Are there any "old people" myths and prejudices which mainly affect women? What are my own stereotypes about old age, aging, death, and change? Do these stereotypes fit any old people I know? Do I know of old people who do not fit these stereotypes?

Consider the phrases older man and older woman. "Older man" usually has very positive connotations: grey temples, wise, mature and worldly, sophisticated, mellow. Who is he "older" than? He's older than her — therefore, he's a good, sobering, educational, kindly influence on younger her.

What about the "older woman?" Who is she "older" than? Him! Therefore, she's obviously taking advantage of his innocence, playing mother, corrupting him, or too hung up to get a man her age. This double standard seems to also apply to the phrases mature and experienced men and women. Experience is desirable in a man. In a woman, it can mean she's "used up" and "second hand." Going by these stereotypes, the ideal match is between a younger woman and an older man, who knows more than she and can guide her.

I'm examining my own "old age" stereotypes and finding some intense fears and prejudices. I'm looking around for new, more vital models of "older people" — political activists, writers, sages, artists, actors and actresses — who seem to get better at what they do with experience and maturity. I'm looking to other cultures. The Chinese, for example, traditionally revere their aged people as seers who have acquired wisdom and perspective from living which young people cannot have. Their old people are honored, and listened to.

Because I feel that each age has its place on the spectrum for me, I regard my friends of different ages accordingly. A person in her teens today knows things and sees the world as I never can from my perspective. A woman in her 40's could share things with me she knows from living that I cannot possibly know until I live through those years for myself. Each period is a unique phase. One of the sad things to me about our dismissal of old people today is that young children miss out on the positive non-judgmental parent figure that grandparents can provide to balance the disciplining function of the parents. I'm also interested in how my link fits into the chain of the development of our culture, and in how my heritage has effected me.

The current cultural attitude toward aging also puts me in a fearful and untenable relation to death. In one of the greatest books I've ever read, *Journey to Ixtlan* by Carlos Castaneda (Simon and Schuster, cloth) the Indian Don Juan talks to Castaneda about his death.

He says that he is wasting one of his greatest powers by his hopeless and fearful attitude; our death is imminent always and gives our living intensity and perspective if we confront instead of avoiding it. Don Juan also says that it is only those who do not live fully who fear death.

280

In our culture, these fearful attitudes toward death are reflected in some common notions about our bodies. Many people think that if we do less and feel less, and if we can somehow arrange the future before it happens, then we can change the fact of our death. We may even live longer.

Paradoxically this course, instead of prolonging life, by keeping our bodies rigid, trying to stop time, and focusing mentally and emotionally on the future, quickly brings death into the present. When I set myself in this frame of mind, I miss the vitality of my present; I remain in a conceptual state once-removed from reality, instead of allowing myself to experience things as they are. If I can let myself move, flow, open up and evolve, rather than trying to stop time at one "young" age, then death could be another phase on the continuum.

Start the Day

I remember reading a dance exercise in Laura Huxley's book, *You Are Not the Target* (Farrar, Straus & Giroux, paper) which I particularly like. The basic idea is to start your day by dancing nude.

Close your door. Be in a room you like. Choose some music to play which pleases you. Take off all your clothes. And dance!

Dance for yourself. Dance to the music or out of it. Try not to think about what your movements look like from the outside. This is a chance to allow your inner rhythms and expressions to be. Every now and then stand still and allow any feeling or sensation inside of you to build and spread and move out into your limbs to become a motion. Try to open yourself and let any movements which your body, you, want to make.

Forget your appointments. Forget your obligations. Forget any other people or thoughts. Forget anything you've learned. Forget anything you've read in this book.

Dance!

What I Left Out, and Where to Go

Race, Communes, Politics ...
and The Growth Movement?

I define "therapy" as anything which helps and which is aimed at counteracting the holes in my training and upbringing. I define "politics" as the struggle for power *within* the current social hierarchy. Each age and each culture develops its appropriate therapy for the ills of that age and culture. It is connected to and often in conflict with politics because the goals of most politics are usually antithetical to the goals of good therapy.

The current growth movement population primarily consists of white long-hairs, students and professionals. People of other racial and ethnic groups express (and realistically I think) the attitude, "We don't trust you because you can't possibly know what our life is really like. We want to work separately on getting our own identity together, and not on getting along with you." The Feminist Movement is beginning to bridge that gap somewhat because women of all races and groups are discriminated against on the grounds of their sex, and are beginning to unite to change that custom. It is becoming clearer that a society which oppresses some people with its hierarchy really prevents everyone from having the freedom from roles to be themselves.

I have been involved in different groups in the past and will be in different places in the future, but for now, because my working world includes a relatively narrow range of people, it is my loss because I grow less and more slowly in these other social areas of consciousness.

I did not deal separately with communes or group living because I have found that a group of ten or twenty does not operate with much different emotional dynamics than a group of two. Any material useful for relating to one partner can be applied to relationships within a larger group. The biggest difference, as I see it, is that child-care is less of a strain on a couple within a group, and "parenting" is less of a strain on the children because they have a choice of more adults to relate to.

How It Feels to Make This Book

This whole project has taken three months longer than I thought it would, from last May — when someone close to me said, "Why don't you do a book on women psychologists in the Bay Area?" — until now, late January, 1973. During those nine months, I have been consumed emotionally and mentally with putting the book together: interviewing women, arranging for photographs, doing art work, writing, rewriting, exploring areas of feminism new to me, and dealing with my own conflicts about revealing personal stories about myself in my writing.

The book has grown a lot larger than I'd planned to the extent that I quit all my regular activities (teaching, seeing private Polarity clients, my own therapy, keeping up with my friends, and traveling) to make time to work. I'm looking forward to doing some of these things again. I also feel that because of immersing myself in the subject of feminism and my own female identity I won't be approaching any of these areas quite the same again. I need some "empty" space now to let new parts of me surface.

Why did I write this book? I wanted to explore Feminism more deeply; the Bay Area, as the center of the phenomenon, the Human Potential Movement, has collected many fine female therapists and psychological innovators; I could earn some money from royalties; I thought I had something to contribute. I'd been thinking for quite awhile that there were many good books out on ideas, and none I knew of on working with yourself as your body, on changing feelings as well as ideas.

Frannie Clark took the photo on page 5. Maury Cooper took the photos on pages 256 through 269. Jack Edelson took the photo on page 246. Randy Kielich took Shelly's photo on the next page. Jerry Mander took the photographs of his family on pages 242 through 252. John Pearson took the photos on pages 25, 287, and 290. Walter Proskauer took Magda's photo on page 26. Mara Sabinson took Marion's photo on page 255. All other photographs are by Shelly Dunnegan who put in a major amount of care, love and skill; here is a photo of her.

Pamela Martell, Marsha Metcalf, Barbara Corso and Toby Silvey typed most of the original manuscript. Nan Greenberg and Pat Rosenberg proofread it. Dorothy Pitts and Vera Allen (Vera Allen Composition) typeset it. Random House will distribute and publicize it.

Don Gerrard (The Bookworks) edited the book with me and helped hold me together by giving me a great deal of himself. Jean Porter, Don's assistant, helped hold him together. That's the three of us in the photo.

You are the next link in the circle. Welcome!

Places

For information about any of the Gestalt therapists mentioned in this book, or for information about their training program, write to: ·

> The Gestalt Institute of San Francisco
> 1719 Union Street
> San Francisco, California 94123

For information about Feminism, write to:

> Alyssum: A Center for Feminist Consciousness
> 1719 Union Street
> San Francisco, California 94123
> 415 — 421-3128

> San Francisco Women's Centers, Inc.
> A women's skills and organizations information center.
> 1026 Masonic Avenue
> San Francisco, California

Up Haste
This is an excellent bookstore of women's literature.
You can write to them for information about their books at:

> 2506-B Haste Street
> Berkeley, California 94704

The Women's History Library address is:

> Women's History Library
> 2325 Oak Street
> Berkeley, California 94708

Send $1.00 plus a large, stamped, self-addressed envelope for:
a list of their publications, the library's history, and micro
filming information.